The Way the Floorboards Creak

A Collection of Plays

by

Tucker Atwood

© 2024 by Tucker Atwood. All rights reserved. All wrongs denied.

Contact me at atwood.tucker@gmail.com if you're interested in producing any of these plays. You want me to beg? I'll beg.

ISBN: 979-8-8693-4237-9

ABOUT THIS PLAY COLLECTION

The plays included here were all produced – or at least read on a stage (yes, my bar is low here) between 2022 and 2024. The process of transforming ideas into fully realized productions proved to be quite long. In fact, it was impossible without a significant amount of time and energy – apparently just opening a window and tossing scripts at pedestrians doesn't work the way it used to. At some point I realized all the half-ideas I had scattered through my notebooks would have to wait while the full-ideas took center stage.

So, I stopped writing and shifted my attention to getting these plays on Broadway. Or, no, sorry – at a couple of community theaters I act at in Maine. In the spring of 2022 I received my first full-length production when *Dance Again* was produced by the Belfast Maskers, a theater group in Belfast, where I currently reside. The next fall, I was given permission to self-produce a full-length, *Waiting in the Wings*, at Lakewood Theater in Madison, where I have spent my youthful summers growing as a theater maker. A week after *Waiting in the Wings* closed at Lakewood, *A Dolphin Disguise* opened as part of a One Act Festival back in Belfast. A couple of months later, in conjunction with the Maskers, I held a staged reading of *Nobletiger*, which was followed by another One Act Festival in Belfast that included *Triassic Park*. I once again self-produced a full-length, *The Potluck Farce*, at Lakewood in the fall of 2024.

When people ask me how many plays I've written, I tell them that's a difficult question, because some are at different levels than others. For now, I've drawn the line at: any play I would gladly produce without needing to read back through the script and make significant changes. If those are my standards, then these are all the plays I've written. Lately my break from writing has been demanding to be unbroken, but I think whatever I write next will feel like a different era of writing, so it's a good time to package up *this* era into one little collection and send these plays out into the world together. With their combined strength, they will surely be more successful in getting the attention of pedestrians when chucked out the window. Enjoy.

Thank you to everyone who was involved with these plays. Without you, it would've been just an empty stage up there, and the reviews probably would've been terrible.

TABLE OF CONTENTS

FULL-LENGTH PLAYS

Waiting in the Wings..7

The Potluck Farce..83

Dance Again..155

Nobletiger...217

ONE ACT PLAYS

A Dolphin Disguise..291

Triassic Park...309

Waiting in the Wings

A Play in Two Acts

by

Tucker Atwood

WAITING IN THE WINGS premiered as a self-produced production at Lakewood Theater in Madison, Maine in September 2023. It was produced and directed by Tucker Atwood, the stage manager was Carolyn Snowman, the lighting design was by Jake Junkins, the set design was by Tucker Atwood and Allison Turlo, and the costume design was aided by Susan Quinn. The cast was as follows:

MARY..Bianca Stoutamyer
OWEN..Jonas Maines
BETTY...Kaylee Pomelow Book
HERB...Arturo Meneses
JESS...Payton Snowden
VINNY..Jared Lennon

SHORT SYNOPSIS

Four years ago, a star actor at a small summer theater passed away unexpectedly, leaving a possible love interest and a friend/mentee grieving and wishing they'd had one last conversation with him. When a new director who claims to speak to the dead arrives with her niece as a stage manager, she vows to help them establish contact with their lost friend. Meanwhile, the dead actor and a long-forgotten usher roam around as ghosts, critiquing the plays, pulling pranks, and discussing life and death. During a seance conducted by the new director, an unexpected connection is established between their two worlds – but with it, comes further complications.

CHARACTERS

MARY — 20s. Reserved and polite. She still hasn't recovered from the death of her best friend four years ago. She was a talented actress but hasn't acted since the tragedy. She works in the box office.

VINNY — 20s. A bit of a goofball; everybody's friend. He has been acting for a while and still has improvements to make, but he's driven to succeed. Also paints the sets, shirtless.

BETTY — 40s to 60s. A free-love hippy type. She believes she can communicate with the dead. She was recently hired to direct.

JESS — 20s. Betty's niece, taken in and raised by Betty when her parents died young. She's been brought along to stage manage for the season.

OWEN — 20s. The actor who passed away four years ago. A great actor, but through natural skill more than dedication. Alternates between pulling pranks and getting angrily philosophical with Herb.

HERB — 40s to 60s. An usher who passed away fifty years ago. Probably nobody alive even knows who he was anymore, but he's at peace with his death and acts as Owen's unofficial "death mentor."

PROPERTY LIST

Piles of random props and furniture. Items should appear to be from a wide assortment of past plays. Have fun with it.
A painted sign (words specified in script)
Painting supplies
A half-painted chair
Two mediocre paintings
A cauldron
A pitcher of water
Cups
Candles/tea lights
Box of crackers
A book
Sound/lightboard
2 water bottles

COSTUME NOTES

Since the play takes place over the course of a summer, costumes will change between most scenes. They don't need to be huge changes, but some indication that time has passed should be shown. There are also instances where specific costumes are implied – i.e. when Vinny is actively in a performance, Jess and Mary are working backstage, or everyone is wearing pajamas for the seance. Jess and Mary have a couple quick changes between scenes, but this can be accomplished by wearing layers – throwing a black sweater over a previous costume, wearing black pants underneath pajamas, etc.

Owen and Herb are entirely in grayscale. Their clothes from when they were alive have lost any color they might have once had.

SET REQUIREMENTS

The play takes place backstage at a summer theater over the course of a full season. It should be quite messy – old props and furniture all over, like a fire hazard collage. A couch sits near center stage, with chairs scattered around. There is a stage door, which leads to the audience; a back door, which leads outside; a hallway leading to dressing rooms and bathrooms; and an entrance to the stage, which itself is unseen. Since the play covers an entire season, the entrance to the stage should not be specific to any one show. Perhaps there is just a series of masking flats, behind which a more specific set is implied.

LIGHTING AND SOUND NOTES

During performances, Jess or Mary will be at a stage manager's desk, making sound effects heard by the "other" audience – so, to the real audience, these sound effects should sound muffled.

There are full backstage lights, but during performances these should be turned off, with lower lights supplementing the scene. There are also moments where only a ghost light is on; the "lower lights" from other scenes can be used here to allow actors to see where they are.

MISCELLANEOUS NOTE

With the play taking place at a theater, there are opportunities to add in references or information about the theater where it is performed. This is intended to make things feel more personal to the actors and audience. Where the script says *"[show],"* these can be references to other plays that have been or will be performed at your theater, for example, earlier or later in the season. Alongside any references to *"[show],"* there are some phrases also put in brackets that may be altered to fit with the personalization. Other places in the script which reference the theater, such as Mary's opening bit about the seating or Ms. Martin's cat being spotted at the snack bar, may be slightly altered to better describe your theater; however, please keep the original intention of the line similar.

ACT I

Scene 1

Lights up. We are backstage at a summer theater. VINNY, shirtless, with paint carelessly splattered on his hands and torso, is almost finished painting a sign that says "Auditions Here – Appointment Not Required – Walk-ins Begged For!" He paints in silence for a few seconds, then suddenly breaks out into song. He sings loud and off-key, then shakes his head in frustration and stops. He tries the same tune several times, at different keys, none of which quite sound good, getting more frustrated each time. Suddenly, the stage door opens and VINNY cuts off his song abruptly. MARY leads in BETTY, giving her a tour of the theater.

MARY. ...about 650 or so, but we never fill that many. There's a good hundred, hundred and fifty maybe, up in the balcony we never sell. Remind me not to bring you up there.
To VINNY, referencing his lack of shirt.
Really?

VINNY. I told you, I've ruined too many shirts already.
Noticing BETTY.
Oh, shoot. You're doing the <u>full</u> tour.

MARY. Yes. I told you that's what we'd be doing.

VINNY. I thought you meant, like, the lobby and the box office.

MARY. Backstage is pretty important to new directors, too, don't you think? I'm sorry, Mrs. Withrow, I didn't think –

BETTY. Oh, my dear, don't you worry. I certainly don't mind getting the "full tour." I want to experience it all!

VINNY. Well, just you wait for your first closing night! We've got a tradition where we go down to the lake with a couple bottles of wine and see how long it takes for somebody to take off their –

MARY. How about an introduction first?

VINNY. Sorry. Hi Mrs. Withrow, I'm Vinny.
He wipes his hand on himself and goes for a handshake.

BETTY. Please, call me Betty. And sorry, but, no thank you.
She shoos his hand away. He smiles and waves instead.

I take it you're involved with the stage crew?
VINNY. Just painting. Lost too many tools and set plans to cut it on stage crew. But I love painting, so I'm completely okay with that demotion. I'm an actor too, by the way.
BETTY. Wonderful! Will I see you at auditions?
VINNY. Yes, ma'am! Oh, I had a question about singing at auditions.
BETTY. Yes?
VINNY. *(Beat.)* Do we have to?
BETTY. *(Laughing.)* Well, if you don't want to be in a musical, of course not.
VINNY. Right, right, but see – I like the talking parts of musicals. And I can follow a dance step or two. But singing – singing isn't really my strong suit.
BETTY. Hm. I'm sorry, love, but I'd really like to hear everybody who wants to be in the musicals sing.
VINNY. *(Defeated, but not discouraged.)* Right. That makes sense.
BETTY. You do, however, look the part for the lead in *[show]*. That's the [comedy in June]. Maybe that's a good fit for you.
VINNY. You think so?
BETTY. Can't hurt to audition for it and see how it goes. How are you at monologues?
VINNY. *(Beat.)* Maybe I'll just do the painting this year…
    He goes back to painting the sign.
MARY. So, do you have any questions so far?
BETTY. *(Regarding VINNY.)* Is he any good?
MARY. Oh, uh – I meant, any questions about the theater.
BETTY. Actors are an important part of the theater, aren't they?
VINNY. The most important!
BETTY. After <u>directors</u>, love.
VINNY. Sure.
BETTY. *(Back to MARY.)* Well? How is he?
MARY. Yeah, he's good. Very good.
BETTY. You're not just saying that because he's your friend?
MARY. No, no. Honest. He can act. Singing, no, monologues, eh – he can fake his way through one, if needed, but I wouldn't count on it. But yeah, he's got character down, great comedic timing… Could work on picking up his cues…

VINNY. *(Long beat.)* Thanks, Mary.
    Stepping back to show BETTY the sign.
Yeah, I'm as good an actor as I am a painter!
BETTY. *(Hiding a grimace.)* Well, there's a role for everybody!
    VINNY smiles, unaware of the insult. BETTY turns to MARY.
What about you? You must be an actress, aren't you?
MARY. Me? Oh, I – used to be. Yeah, it's fun. But I haven't for a few years now.
BETTY. Why's that?
MARY. Just – really busy with the box office. We get calls like every day. And we've got this new ticket printer this year, which I'm sure is going to take some serious getting used to.
BETTY. A ticket printer? That's what's keeping you?
MARY. *(Beat.)* The tickets are a completely different size this year.
BETTY. Hm. That's too bad. You look perfect for the lead in *[show]*. That's the [farce we're doing in July].
MARY. I saw that character, yes.
BETTY. So you read the audition notice?
MARY. I skimmed it.
BETTY. Even though you weren't auditioning?
MARY. It – it was just a "Let's see" type of thing.
BETTY. And?
MARY. And what?
BETTY. Didn't see anything you liked?
MARY. Not this year, no.
    Beat. BETTY is trying to "read" MARY.
BETTY. This theater has some history, doesn't it?
MARY. Oh, yes. Over a hundred years old and going strong. The next play will be, let's see – number 1287, I think? Back in its heyday, there were all kinds of Broadway stars that spent their summers here. We've got a list and a bunch of pictures in the loft above the box office, if you're interested.
BETTY. Oh, how enchanting! My, I can just about feel the memories floating through the air, can't you?
MARY. Yeah, it's pretty cool. For sure.
BETTY. There's nothing quite as magical as a theater, is there? A stage can completely transport you to other time periods, other ways

of being. A play can change the course of your life, grab you by the shoulders, shake you, force you to experience any emotion it feels like. And best of all, it can connect you to other humans in utterly inexplicable ways. Isn't that right?
MARY. *(Feeling a bit uncomfortable.)* That's right.
BETTY. You know, there was this summer theater in the town where I grew up that my parents would take me and my sister to. I remember we'd get all dolled up in our best Sunday dresses and wait outside the stage door for the actors to come out. And even if they didn't, we'd take photos in front of the headshots. I'd always make sure I stood next to the cutest of the actors.
 Laughing.
She always hated that.
 Beat.
You must have some wonderful memories here, don't you, love?
MARY. I do, yeah.
 Beat. MARY smiles awkwardly. BETTY smiles knowingly.
BETTY. Something's shaken up inside you, Mary. I can see it. I'm quite gifted at reading people. I sense things – about anyone, anywhere, even when I don't want to. It's not something I choose. These waves of spiritual energy just consume me, show me an extra layer of color in our world. It's a blessing and a curse.
MARY. That's nice. Maybe we should check out the furniture loft...
BETTY. My gift has provided lost, desperate people with strength, conviction, hope. I've walked up to strangers on the street and cured them of their every worry. I dive deep into the pool of spirituality, much deeper than most others are comfortable doing. I can make connections between worlds. I'm like a highway of spirits.
 Noticing MARY is drawing further inward.
Granted, my gift is not always well-received. Some folks prefer not to explore that side of life. They're content with nothing more than a surface-level understanding of the world. They ridicule me, lash out at me, banish me from their book clubs... I'm used to being censored. But still, I offer my services to anybody who needs it.
 She looks expectantly at MARY, who says nothing. VINNY doesn't realize she isn't talking to both of them.
VINNY. You mean, like, seeing the future? Could you help me win

the lottery? I've been developing this system, but it's not finished yet. I feel like visions of the future would help me out a ton.
BETTY. No, love. I'm talking about communicating between the living and the dead.
VINNY. Oh. I see.
   A look at MARY.
Maybe we should get started with auditions...
BETTY. *(To MARY, with sincerity.)* You've lost somebody, haven't you, Mary?
   MARY is silent. She quietly expresses hundreds of emotions in five seconds. Trying to get something out:
MARY. That's none of your –
   That's all she can muster. She hurries out the stage door. BETTY is surprised and turns to VINNY for an explanation. He sighs and stops painting.
VINNY. He was an actor here. Great dude. The three of us were in a bunch of shows together. One day he went out for a swim and didn't come back. It'll be four years next month.
BETTY. Oh, my. How tragic. I could tell there were years of pain and sorrow inside her. Don't tell me; they were lovers?
VINNY. "Lovers"? No, I don't think so. I mean, you could tell they both adored each other, but they always swore they were just good friends. I always thought it would happen, but it never did.
BETTY. Oh, the poor soul. Mary lost the love of her life before she could tell him how she really felt.
VINNY. Again, I think they were just close friends.
BETTY. Oh, you're so naïve. They were meant for each other.
VINNY. Maybe.
   Trying to change the subject.
So, should I have <u>prepared</u> a monologue?
BETTY. Oh, come on, love, we're discussing life and death here.
VINNY. Well, it's just – I <u>can</u> do monologues, but I usually need a lot of practice. And I know some directors make you prepare them before auditions, but I didn't see anything on the notice...
BETTY. Don't you worry. I'll have you cast within two minutes. In fact – I've gotten a good look at you now. I could cast you already.
VINNY. What?! You mean – I've been auditioning right now?!

BETTY. In a way, yes.
    VINNY tries to counter, but BETTY changes the subject back.
You know, I bet I can bring Mary some closure this summer.
VINNY. Really, I don't think she wants you to –
BETTY. *(Not really listening to him.)* Yes, I can connect her to this lost friend, I'm sure of it. I've been doing it ever since I was a little girl. My grandpappy used to sit on the swingsets with my sister and I on warm summer afternoons. When he passed, the tradition never broke. He still joined us on the swings – often, he'd be waiting there for us, actually. My family all said it was how we processed his death – but no, he was there.
VINNY. You saw him there?
BETTY. Well, my gift wasn't fully developed yet. I saw him, in a sense, by how the swings moved. It was the same way they had moved when he used to sit in them.
VINNY. Y'know, wind can do that too.
BETTY. Are you doubting me?
VINNY. No no, of course not. Sorry.
BETTY. I could hear him, too. He sent me signs, messages in the air, sort of like a whistling…
    She realizes what it sounds like.
No, it was not the wind! It was –
VINNY. Your grandfather, yes. I believe you.
BETTY. Yes. And ever since, I've had my profound connection to the dead. My body can sense when spirits are around.
VINNY. Yeah? What's that like?
BETTY. I get this tingling chill down my spine whenever they enter the room. And though I can only see them under certain conditions, I can always sense their presence. I know when they're around.
    *From "onstage," OWEN and HERB enter. They are ghosts, unseen, and though BETTY has made claims to the contrary, she can **not** sense their presence. OWEN plays with various props, careful not to let the living see them move; HERB only plays along when OWEN makes him. Right now, HERB is in the middle of testing OWEN's theatrical knowledge.*
HERB. What about "Everyone likes a kidder, but nobody lends him money." What's that one from?

OWEN. Oh hey, this must be the new director.
VINNY. Can you see all of them, or just the ones you know?
BETTY. All of them. My gift doesn't discriminate!
HERB. She could also be here for auditions.
OWEN. You think a new actress would just waltz backstage and Vinny wouldn't kick her out?
VINNY. What about… Robin Williams?
BETTY. Oh – well, I don't know how I'd possibly find <u>his</u> ghost.
HERB. You're right. If she was an actress, Vinny would be kissing her by now.
OWEN. Nah, she's too old for Vinny.
VINNY. Couldn't you ask around?
BETTY. That's not really how the afterlife works, I'm afraid.
HERB. Anyway, it was *Death of a Salesman*. Of course, you know who wrote it, don't you?
OWEN. *Death of an Audience* is more like it. Let's let them talk for a second. I can't hear myself think.
HERB. Fine. But don't you start –

> *OWEN steals and hides VINNY's paint can, making sure VINNY and BETTY don't notice.*

– And you've started.
VINNY. What's the point in talking to the dead if you can't talk to Robin Williams?
BETTY. I don't think you understand. I wouldn't know where to look for Robin Williams. He could be anywhere!
VINNY. Or, oh, how about Marilyn Monroe? I've always wanted to see how she compares to some of the more modern ladies.
BETTY. Again, I think contacting someone like Marilyn Monroe would require more connections than what I'm capable of. Is there anybody else, more local, you want me to connect you to?
VINNY. Like who?
BETTY. I don't know – any family members who've passed?
VINNY. There's my great-grandmother, I guess.
BETTY. Okay. Do you want me to try to find her?
VINNY. *(Thinking about it.)* Nah, that's okay.

> *Noticing his paint is gone.*

Hey, did you move my paint?

BETTY. No, I've been right here, love.
VINNY. Damn it. This happens all the time.
BETTY. *(Sarcastic.)* Things get lost around here? I don't believe it.
VINNY. I know, I know, it's a mess. I forgot to clean up at the end of last season. But don't worry, at crunch time, the work gets done. I take it more seriously.
> *He looks around for the paint. OWEN is cracking himself up.*

What the hell, though – It's like it disappeared into thin air…
BETTY. *(Finding an old paint can elsewhere.)* Is this it?
VINNY. Let's see. No, that's – Hey, wait, this is the [red] for the trim in *[show]* last year. I lost it and we ended up with mismatched trim.
OWEN. That was hilarious.
HERB. You mean hideous.
BETTY. I'm not surprised things go missing. An old, historic theater – There's bound to be spirits hanging about.
VINNY. Wouldn't you sense them?
BETTY. Absolutely. If there were spirits around me, I would know.
> *OWEN takes this as a challenge and stands very close to her, imitating her current stance. She doesn't notice a thing.*

I have a feeling they sense it, though, so they stay away from me.
> *OWEN copies BETTY's every movement as she moves to check out the sign.*

This is good. We'll find the paint later. Just get this out to the lobby.
VINNY. Sure. I wanted to add more pizzazz, but – it's fine. It'll do.
> *He picks up the sign, careful not to touch the wet paint, and carries it toward the stage door.*

BETTY. Need a hand?
VINNY. No, I've got it. Could you just get the door?
BETTY. *(Opening the door for him.)* Of course. Here, love. Oh, by the way, if a young lady with a clipboard drops by, send her my way. She's my stage manager. And niece.
VINNY. It isn't theater without a little nepotism.
BETTY. There's no arguing that!
VINNY. So, do ghosts die too, or do they stick around forever? Are there, like, prehistoric cavemen floating around everywhere too?
BETTY. Well, that's – hmm, I've never been asked that before…
> *They exit. OWEN messes around with the props some more.*

HERB. I've told you, you really shouldn't be doing things like this.
OWEN. Oh come on, he's never suspected a thing.
HERB. Just be careful. You don't want to –
OWEN. I know, I know. Thanks for looking out for me, Mom.
HERB sits among the mess, like he's at home.
HERB. Did you spend any time there this winter? Over at your parents' place?
OWEN. A little. Just to say hi. Y'know, they've still got my shrine up. Still got that awful graduation pic, bam, right center stage.
HERB. The one where you're – how do you put it?
OWEN. Hungover as balls.
HERB. That's it. Such a way with words.
OWEN. Still waiting for Dad to finally say "Alright, I'm turning his room into a man cave."
HERB. Would your mother let that happen?
OWEN. Doubt it. She's pretty sentimental. Hell, my toothbrush is still in the same exact spot it was the day I died.
HERB. Why don't you move it?
OWEN. You kidding? Around here, nobody notices when things get shifted around. But if I move anything at home, Mom would freak. And she'd blame Dad, and he'd have to live with Uncle Jerry for a couple weeks. Actually, he probably wouldn't mind that. They always say how they don't spend enough time together. Hm. Maybe I'll steal the toothbrush after all.
HERB. No, leave it be.
OWEN. I will, I will. So, what about you? How was your winter?
HERB. *(Very content with it.)* Same as always.
OWEN. Didn't leave the grounds again?
HERB. Like I say every year: what's the point?
OWEN. The point?! Bro, we can go wherever the hell we want.
HERB is about to correct him.
With limitations, whatever, yes. You know what I mean. You realize how much everything's changed since you cooped yourself up here?
HERB. Changed for the worse, from what I've heard.
OWEN. Not everywhere. There's some cool shit out there. And not just the living world. Have you heard of that huge ghost orgy they've got going on, way out in, like, the middle of the woods in Nebraska?

HERB. Nebraska, yes. You've mentioned it.
OWEN. Just an example. The world is turning, things are happening, and here you are, wasting away in stone-cold solitude all winter at a desolate theater you never even acted at.
HERB. Oh, so we're back to the "You're just an usher" conversation.
OWEN. That wasn't my point.
HERB. I have every right to be here, just as any actor does.
OWEN. That's debatable, but not the debate I'm picking...
HERB. And if it's so desolate here, why do you keep coming back?
OWEN. I come back for the summers! When it's not desolate.
HERB. And when you leave, what's on your mind the whole time?
OWEN. What?
HERB. You heard me. When you're not here. When you're out in your vacation lands, doing your sightseeing and orgy parties, what place do you always have in the back of your mind?
OWEN. Come on, it's not always – I mean, I'm glad to be back, I've missed it, but – oh, stop being right about everything! It's annoying.
HERB. Sorry. Can't help it. My duty as your death mentor.
OWEN. That's not a real thing.
HERB. Fine, then you're on your own.
OWEN. No, no –

HERB smiles. OWEN returns it. A moment of sweetness.

Man, I missed you, bro.
HERB. I missed you too. Welcome back.
OWEN. "Bro." Come on, say it. "I missed you, bro."
HERB. I'll say it when you tell me who wrote *Death of a Salesman*.
OWEN. *(Beat.)* Shakespeare, right?
HERB. You didn't do any of the reading I assigned to you.
OWEN. Those old plays are – well, old. They've got nothing to do with the modern world.
HERB. Shakespeare is old, I'll give you that. Arthur Miller is not.
OWEN. Ah, right. He was my second pick.

The stage door opens and VINNY returns, looking around for the paint can.

VINNY. Where the hell... It was right here...

As he searches, JESS enters from the back door. She is holding a clipboard and audition forms. Throughout this

21

scene, when JESS gets close to the ghosts, a noticeable "chill" runs down her spine.

JESS. Hi.

VINNY. Huh?

Amidst his searching, he turns to face her, but OWEN kicks a piece of furniture in front of him and he trips.

Son of a bitch.

JESS. Sorry! Are you alright?

VINNY. I'm fine – it jumped out in front of me, did you see that?

JESS. I did! Yes, it's quite agile.

She's laughing at him, so he has no choice but to laugh at himself. They are immediately enamored with each other. They both start to say something, then laugh awkwardly. The awkwardness continues throughout the following.

Sorry, go on.

VINNY. I was just saying, I'm Vinny. Hello.

JESS. And I was just saying, there's a cranky woman out back who says her cat's loose in the theater. Oh, and I'm Jess.

VINNY. Hello, Jess.

He goes to shake her hand, but pulls back.

Sorry, I'm splattered with paint.

JESS. That's fine, I'll touch you later. Your hand, I mean. I'll shake your hand once you've cleaned it.

VINNY. Right. Anyway, don't pay any mind to Ms. Martin. Her cats always find their way back to her. I'm sure it'll be fine. A couple summers ago, we found an entire litter under a couch in the prop loft. Ms. Martin didn't even know she was pregnant!

JESS. That's funny.

VINNY. The cat, I mean. The mother cat. Ms. Martin didn't have the litter herself.

JESS. Yes, I knew what you meant.

VINNY. I have a cousin who's pregnant. Not that that has anything to do with anything. Um, I like your shirt.

JESS. Thanks. I like your... chest. Where the, uh, shirt usually is.

VINNY. Oh! Yeah, I'm not usually – I paint the sets here, see, and I've ruined a bunch of shirts, so I figure it's not worth it anymore. Plus, I've been working out. Which is also irrelevant. I'm sorry.

JESS. No, that's okay. You've done some, uh, good working out. From what I can tell. From your, um…
She motions toward his torso. VINNY gets self-conscious.
VINNY. I'm gonna go clean up before auditions start.
JESS. Oh! Right. That's also why I'm here. I'm stage managing.
VINNY. *(Under his breath.)* Oh, hell yeah.
JESS. Sorry?
VINNY. I said, yeah! Yeah, I heard, about you and how you're doing the stage managing for us. Your aunt is the director, right?
JESS. Yes, the old hippy, that's her.
VINNY. She seems nice. She's in the lobby, if you're looking for her.
JESS. I am.
VINNY. Okay.
JESS. Great, so I'll just… Go find her, then. Are you – are you auditioning? For the auditions?
VINNY. Yeah, I am.
JESS. *(Letting him know she heard him before.)* Hell yeah.
VINNY. So, I'll see you out there?
JESS. Yup! I'll see you at the –
As she exits, she forgets to open the door and runs into it.
VINNY. You okay?!
JESS. Yup! Fine!
VINNY. It's one of those doors that, uh, opens.
JESS. I see. Bye!
Embarrassed, she runs out. VINNY waves.
VINNY. Not if I see you first!
Under his breath.
Idiot! "Not if I see you first"? Idiot, idiot, idiot…
He exits to the dressing rooms to get cleaned up. OWEN and HERB, who have watched the whole thing, smile knowingly.
OWEN. So, they're gonna bang.
HERB. No doubt about it. All I ask is, they keep it off the stage.
OWEN. Good for Vinny, too. He deserves a looker for once.
HERB. What about that funny actress last year? In *[show]*?
OWEN. Oh, Herb. My guy. Come on, she was a 4 at best.
HERB. She had real talent, though.
OWEN. Talent's nothing if you don't have the looks. If an audience

sees you and feels more comfortable with their partners, you ain't gonna cut it. Why else do you think she's not coming back this year?
HERB. Because you broke them up!
OWEN. For Vinny's own good! Now he gets to sleep with this Jess chick! And the saddest part of it all – he'll never even know how much I helped him.
HERB. The saddest part was, she still had to play romantic partners with Vinny in the season finale.
OWEN. It's theater. Everyone understands the business side of it.
HERB. Poor girl was near bawling every time she came offstage.
OWEN. Oh, I'm sure she's moved on by now.
HERB. Y'know, back in my day, she would've been a real knockout – or as you would say, an 8.
OWEN. Yeah and back in your day, it would've taken like an hour to get her clothes off, what with the layers and corsets and hoops or whatever, and by that time the interest would be gone.
HERB. …How old do you think I am?
OWEN. And could you quit it with the "back in my day"? I've told you, it's cliché and overused, to the point where people make fun of people from back in your day by saying "back in my day." Really, I'm saving you humiliation.
HERB. Who's going to humiliate me? You're the only one I talk to.
OWEN. There's your answer, bro. Anyway, who cares, I'm just amped up 'cause of auditions and I'm ready to be entertained! C'mon, let's see who gives the worst read this year.
HERB. My money's on Lorraine.
OWEN. That's a good bet. Why does she keep coming back? It's so embarrassing, it's sad, really –

> *He notices MARY has re-entered quietly. He is momentarily frozen as she approaches, focused on her every movement. She is deep in thought and a little sad, but not on the verge of tears. HERB recognizes the moment.*

HERB. I'll save you a seat, my friend.

> *HERB pats OWEN on the shoulder and exits to the stage.*

OWEN. Thanks. I'll be right there.

> *MARY takes a seat nearby, listening intently to the beginning of auditions. OWEN just looks at her for a while, studying*

her. He hasn't seen her since last season, so he has catching up to do. VINNY re-enters, cleaner and with a shirt on, in a rush to auditions.
VINNY. Have they started?
MARY. Just barely. I think you'll still make the cut.
VINNY. Gonna come check it out? Not to audition, of course, but y'know... just to watch?
　MARY smiles painfully.
MARY. Not this year. Break a leg, though.
VINNY. Thanks. I swear to God, if I have to monologue...
　He exits. OWEN sits next to MARY, listening to auditions together.
OWEN. Oh, Mary... You've been backstage too long. It isn't you.
　Beat. Sigh.
Maybe next year, then.
　Lights down, slowly.

Scene 2

Lights remain low. It is just before intermission of the first opening night of the season. JESS and MARY are working backstage – JESS as stage manager, MARY as a helper, teaching JESS the ropes. Their voices are hushed.

JESS. God, they're dead tonight. It's not always like this, is it?
MARY. No, but once in a while. Sucks for opening night. Makes you wonder if the show is any good.
JESS. …It is good, right?
MARY. *(Not quite convincing.)* I think so?
JESS. It's a bit of a thinker. Not as many laughs.
MARY. There should be a couple, though. It's not *Les Mis*, people.
JESS. Oh! Was that a laugh?
MARY. No, just a sneeze.
   Referencing the soundboard.
Sound cue.
JESS. Thanks.
   She presses a button and makes a sound effect.
MARY. So, I couldn't help but notice. You and Vinny, huh?
JESS. Oh, no, we're – just friends.
MARY. Right. And I'm "just friends" with the ticket printer.
JESS. What do you mean?
MARY. Every time I try to print a ticket, it fucks me.
   Beat.
But anyway, we were talking about you and Vinny.
JESS. No we weren't.
MARY. Come on…
JESS. Listen, our cue's coming up.
MARY. Yeah, yeah. Where do you want me?
JESS. Curtain. I'll get the lights.
MARY. Got it.
   MARY moves offstage to lower the curtain while JESS brings the stage lights down, then turns the backstage lights on, illuminating our view. MARY re-enters.
Shit. I counted at least three people asleep.
JESS. Yikes. How long should we go, twenty?

MARY. I'd say fifteen. I'll check with Charlie and get updates on the line for the women's room. We'll adjust accordingly.
JESS. Okay. FIFTEEN, EVERYONE!
>*She exits to the dressing rooms.*

VINNY. *(Entering quickly, with a half-painted chair.)* Thank you, fifteen! God, I'm such an idiot.
>*He puts the chair down and runs off to retrieve some paint. He's back in no time.*

MARY. What's wrong?
VINNY. *(Ripping his shirt off.)* I never finished painting this stupid chair. We were cutting it close there at the end of the build.
MARY. Yeah, I could tell by the nail gun and paint tray that were onstage for the first scene.
VINNY. Do you think anybody noticed when I tossed them offstage?
MARY. They probably heard the gigantic crash, yeah.
VINNY. Damn it.
MARY. Lorraine's here. Right in the front row.
VINNY. I know. I could feel her staring directly into my soul.
MARY. Think she's pissed she didn't get cast in anything?
VINNY. I mean, she's gotta know how bad she is, right?
MARY. Some people are blissfully unaware they're bad actors.
VINNY. True.
>*Beat.*

Wait, what do you mean by that?
>*MARY smiles. BETTY enters from the stage with a painting.*

BETTY. What was I thinking? This is <u>so</u> wrong! Mary, love, could you find me something better than this?
MARY. Betty, that painting is the least of our worries.
BETTY. Everything revolves around the painting! It's supposed to <u>pull</u> them in, but I'm feeling them being pushed away. The energy in the room, it's flowing the wrong direction, can't you feel it?
MARY. We do have the heat on. Maybe that's what you're feeling? It won't be an issue next month.
BETTY. Oh, just bring me to the portrait room, I'll pick one with better energy.
>*As she passes by VINNY.*

And that chair!

VINNY. I'm taking care of it!
BETTY. With <u>that</u> color?!
> *To herself.*

No, Betty, no. Let it go. Trust the process.
MARY. *(As they exit.)* Won't they notice it's a different painting? What if they think that makes it part of the plot?
BETTY. What's wrong with a little red herring? You know, my ex-husband was a fisherman, which is important because...
> *And they're gone.*

VINNY. Okay, done!
> *As he starts to leave to put away the paint, JESS re-enters. Both turn their attention to each other.*

JESS. Vinny!
VINNY. Jess!
JESS. Hey, you're doing great out there. Don't listen to the crickets, you're killing it.
VINNY. Thanks. I'm just happy I don't have any monologues.
JESS. I'd rather you trip over a monologue than watch Greg mumble through every scene.
VINNY. Typical opening night wackiness. Greg gets easily distracted by things like, y'know, props we're using for the first time. He'll be better tomorrow. Oh, and you're doing great too. With the lights, and the sounds, and the... cute sweater.
JESS. This? It's just the only black I could find this morning.
VINNY. Well, yeah, it's really... it's –
> *They can't hold back anymore; they kiss for a few beats, then fall behind the couch as OWEN and HERB enter from the stage, chatting about the play.*

HERB. ...I do, however, appreciate the overarching themes of the play. Mortality, acceptance, the effects of time. It's nothing that'll provide laughs, but it's honorable.
OWEN. Honorable. Hah! Do you hear yourself? Nobody goes to the theater to see an "honorable" show, they go to see –
> *He catches a glimpse of JESS and VINNY behind the couch and squeals in delight.*

Aha! I knew it!
HERB. Oh, merciful Heavens. Look at them.

OWEN. *(Putting his arm around HERB.)* Don't you miss it, Herb? Physical contact?
HERB. ...You know we can still physically contact each other? You're touching me right now.
OWEN. *(Removing his arm.)* Whoa, Herb, buddy – I think you're a charming fella, but let's not ruin a good thing.
HERB. I meant – Oh, hush, you know what I meant.
Still watching them, then turning away.
Goodness, I never did anything quite <u>that</u> animated in my life.
OWEN. Well, times are changing. No shame in it anymore, bro. As religious guilt makes its exit, sexual freedom makes its entrance!
HERB. No need to drag religion into it.
OWEN. Exactly. You got it.
HERB. That's not – No, we're not having this conversation again.
OWEN. Why not? Because I'm right?
HERB. Just because we're not in "Heaven" doesn't mean it's not out there somewhere!
OWEN. But if you were such a good person, shouldn't you be there?
HERB. I will be, in the <u>next</u> afterlife!
OWEN. Where's your proof of that?
HERB. Mary and Betty are coming back. We should alert these two.
OWEN. Ooo, and now he's intervening with the living...
HERB. "Truth or illusion, George, you don't know the difference." "No, but we must carry on as though we did." What's that from?
OWEN. C'mon, you know I don't believe in homework...

HERB drops a prop, careful not to let JESS and VINNY see. They both hear it and leap up just in time for MARY and BETTY to return with a new painting. They adjust their clothing and fix each other's hair.

MARY. I'm sorry, but I'm just not comfortable with – Oh, what's going on here?
JESS. Uh, Vinny's costume –
She realizes VINNY is still shirtless, not wearing his costume.
I mean, hair – I was helping with his hair.
BETTY. Oh, sweetie, it looks so much worse. Here, let me – Jess, dear, why are you wearing stage makeup?
JESS. Well, because... I always do, in case I have to step in.

BETTY. Please, if anyone's an understudy, it's Mary.
MARY. What? You've never even seen me act.
BETTY. I see it in your eyes. It radiates from you, like a spotlight. I'm telling you, if you'd just let me help you –
MARY. Again, why?! Why are you so <u>obsessed</u> with Owen?! I don't need "closure," and especially not from you!
HERB. *(Beat. To OWEN.)* Hey, they're talking about you.
OWEN. I got that. What's this "closure" she's talking about?
VINNY. What's this "closure" you're talking about?
OWEN. Thanks, Vinny.
MARY. She thinks she can contact Owen and hold some sort of spirit party to bring him back.
BETTY. It's called a seance, dear, and it really works! You'll get to tell each other the things you never could before! You'll feel so much better, I guarantee it. And who knows, maybe it'll get you onstage again. Isn't that what you want?
MARY. You don't know what I want! How would you?! You don't know me, and you didn't know Owen! You think you're special with your "spiritual gift" and ability to "read people" and you're just <u>wrong</u>, about all of it! You're wrong! I'm not going to – I'm – I'm sorry, I'm not meaning to get all – Let me put your painting up.

She takes the painting from BETTY.

I'm sorry.

She exits, hurt and ashamed and sad.

BETTY. Wow, that poor girl <u>really</u> needs my help.
JESS. She does not, Aunt Betty. You can't cure everyone. Didn't you learn that from the Old Gatland Church fire?
BETTY. Yes, we <u>all</u> learned some valuable lessons that day…
JESS. Just, let her go about things her way. It's not your place.
BETTY. I understand, dear, but look at her – it's been four years, hasn't it? And has she gotten any better?
VINNY. *(Realizing he's the only one who can answer.)* Oh! Well, I think she's gotten better, yeah. That first summer, man, it was <u>rough</u>. She couldn't be distracted by a ticket printer that year.
HERB. That was a rough summer for you, too.
OWEN. I was a newly dead, give me a break.
JESS. See? She's made progress. At her own pace.

BETTY. Oh, who am I kidding, you're right. Gosh, now I feel so terrible at my insistence. Let me go talk to her...
> *VINNY and JESS stop her.*

JESS. No, that's the opposite of what we're telling you to do.
VINNY. Give her some space.
JESS. Maybe go check on the audience, see how they like the show?
BETTY. Please, even I can't bring <u>them</u> back from the dead. But sure, yes, I'll go try to feel out their vibes. Sometimes it's the quietest audiences that love the plays the most. If Mary comes back, tell her I'm sorry, okay?
JESS. If? She's definitely coming back.
VINNY. Yeah, she's just on stage. I see her now.
BETTY. *(Looking onstage.)* Such a strong woman. Not a single tear.
> *Beat.*

That painting is wrong, too. Shit.
> *She exits to the audience.*

OWEN. Well... I wonder what these two think about this "seance" –
> *VINNY and JESS have gone back behind the couch.*

Never mind.
HERB. So, Mary doesn't want to talk to you.
OWEN. Is that what you got from this? No, Betty's full of shit and Mary knows it. Everyone knows it, including Betty herself. I bet she's just trying to make a quick buck.
HERB. She seems genuine to me.
OWEN. You'll meet all kinds of "genuine" people in this business.
HERB. And I didn't hear her mention anything about money.
OWEN. You're not saying she can actually talk to us, are you?
HERB. It's been done before, I've heard. Back in my – I mean, back when I was alive, seances were quite common. And who knows? Maybe they actually worked.
OWEN. "Back in your day," they believed everything. I bet when you saw your first airplane, you thought God Himself was the pilot.
HERB. I died fifty years ago. How long do you think airplanes have been around?
OWEN. Ah, I'm just making fun of you.
HERB. I know what's going on here. You have a glimmer of hope it might work. Heck, I do too. I have some curiosity.

OWEN. Are you crazy? This is just one of those old tales people used to tell before fact-checking and video evidence existed, back when anyone could say anything and people believed them. "I can talk to the dead!" "I can part the sea!" "I can turn water into wine!"
HERB. A couple unnecessary cracks at religion, there.
OWEN. So what? Stop pretending all that bullshit is true.
HERB. How do you know it's not?
OWEN. How do you know it is?!
HERB. I only know what I believe.
OWEN. Look around you! Where is your God? Where are the pearly gates? Where's my childhood dog I was promised I'd meet again?
HERB. You never know what's beyond this stage.
OWEN. Sure. Yeah. Maybe Stage Two is Heaven. Or maybe it's nothing, or reincarnation, or maybe everything is just invisible layers of consciousness pulled back one at a time. Who knows what's real, or truthful? Does anybody know anything for sure? Maybe I really am dead and this is what the afterlife is. In which case, I haven't seen any "God" to speak of. There was that guy haunting the liquor store downtown who claimed to be God, but I wasn't buying it. But maybe this isn't real, you know? Maybe this is me hallucinating an eternal extra lifetime in the microseconds before I die. Maybe you're the one hallucinating, and I'm just some sentient vision. Maybe it's all an alien's fever dream and once they wake up we'll have never existed in the first place. The thing is, any of these are real possibilities, so why is your two-thousand-year-old fairy tale the default?
HERB. I think we've gotten off-topic.
OWEN. Whatever. All I'm saying is – if anybody can communicate with us, we'd know about it, right? With technology today, videos and media and whatnot – some evidence would exist. But there's nothing.
HERB. That doesn't mean it's impossible. Why not believe?
OWEN. Because – why get our hopes up, y'know? Anyway, it's not my decision, it's Mary's. Why are we even fighting about it?
HERB. I'm not fighting.
OWEN. Neither am I!

He realizes he's still yelling.

I mean, neither am I. I don't care. We're getting too serious. Let's get back to our hijinks.

By now, VINNY has gotten up and is checking on the chair he painted. As JESS comes up behind him to kiss him some more, he turns and starts to sit. OWEN pulls the chair, causing VINNY to fall on his ass and JESS to fall on top of him. OWEN laughs and MARY returns.

MARY. Alright, Charlie says the ladies' room is clear, so – Oh.

JESS. Right, I was just calling places!

To VINNY, inches away from his face.

Places, Vinny.

VINNY. Thank you, places.

They stand up quickly, brushing their clothes, fixing hair, etc.

MARY. Sorry if I interrupted.

JESS. Interrupted what? PLACES, EVERYONE!

She exits briefly to notify the rest of the cast.

VINNY. I should get this chair back onstage.

He starts to exit to the stage.

MARY. Vinny!

VINNY. Yeah?

MARY. Shirt?

VINNY. Right.

He finds his shirt and puts it back on, careful not to get paint on it. MARY smiles briefly and settles back at the soundboard with a deep breath. BETTY pokes her head in.

BETTY. They're all seated, let's go!

MARY. Yup, just a second.

BETTY. Oh, sorry, I thought you were Jess. By the way, one of the patrons said they saw Ms. Martin's cat over at the snack bar. We should look into that.

MARY. Will do. She's been going crazy looking for that damn cat.

BETTY. That cat does not like her, and she can't take the hint!

They both laugh.

Hey, and I know I can be crazy too. I'm forward, too forward, and I make a habit of thinking I know what's best for everyone. But of course, I don't. I'm sorry, dear. I was just trying to help.

MARY. Thanks. I know you were. It's okay.

BETTY. I suppose it's the director in me. Gotta have creative control over everything, don't I?

She slightly adjusts a prop to her liking. Very sweetly:
Which reminds me, if you see Greg, can you tell him if he doesn't project his second-act monologue, I'm going to rip his throat out?
MARY. *(Laughing.)* You got it.
BETTY. Thank you, dear.
> *She exits. JESS re-enters and takes a seat next to MARY.*

JESS. Everybody at places?
MARY. *(Exiting to raise the curtain.)* Looks like it.
JESS. Okay – house lights... music... And curtain...
MARY. *(Barely offstage.)* Curtain's up!
JESS. And lights up. Okay.
> *The second act begins. JESS and MARY are silent, paying attention to the play. OWEN and HERB are still around: HERB watching the play, OWEN watching MARY.*

HERB. Are we sticking back here for Act Two, or returning to our seats? Or – we could go onstage, best seats in the house!
OWEN. No, let's do that tomorrow when they know their blocking a little more.
HERB. Fine, fine. So, then...?
OWEN. I'll catch up. Go ahead.
HERB. I'm always just the seat-saver. Boy, am I glad all my friends are dead. Won't see me getting caught up with the living, no sir...
> *He exits. OWEN takes a seat near MARY. JESS feels that chill down her spine.*

MARY. You chilly?
JESS. No. Maybe. I don't know.
MARY. I'd have thought you'd be all heated up. Y'know, from that "places" call with Vinny.
JESS. Oh, no, that was just –
> *She doesn't see the point in hiding it anymore.*

We were just making out.
MARY. No shit.
JESS. You knew??
MARY. Yes, and I knew during dress rehearsal, and last week, and the week before that.
JESS. I thought we were being sneaky.
MARY. Love will blind you.

JESS. I wouldn't say <u>love</u>...
MARY. Fine. <u>Lust</u> will blind you.
JESS. I guess so.
    They smile. Beat.
By the way, I'm sorry about Aunt Betty. She gets all...
MARY. Forward. She just apologized too. It's fine.
JESS. I was going to say crazy. But yes, forward too. She thinks she can just magically cure everybody. This one time, a kid fell out of a tree and broke his leg. She was the first on the scene, and y'know what she did? She fed him this special <u>potion</u> to "cast out his demons." Didn't do anything to his leg. When he got to the hospital, he needed his leg fixed <u>and</u> his stomach pumped. We had to move not long after. Everyone in town was calling her an incompetent witch. Imagine that. Not only does everyone think you're a witch, they also think you're bad at it.
MARY. Did you say "we"? Did you live with her?
JESS. Oh, yeah, most of my life. My parents died when I was young. She always wanted kids but couldn't, so... To her, it all worked out very well.
MARY. Sorry about your parents. That's awful.
JESS. Thanks. I barely remember them. And now any memories I have, I'm not sure... if they're real...
MARY. What do you mean? Oh – sound!
JESS. Thanks.
    She makes a sound effect, then continues.
Well, when I was younger, Aunt Betty was under the impression that I "inherited her powers." She – I'm not sure how to describe it, or what was real or not, but – I saw them. My parents. After they were dead. And it freaked me out – I couldn't sleep, I didn't eat... I told Aunt Betty I never wanted it to happen again. And she listened. She never tried to conjure anything up, at least not with me around.
MARY. Do you think it was really them?
JESS. No. I mean – I <u>really</u> don't think so. I'm sure it was some trick with lights, or actors she hired, or something. To be honest, I've avoided the memory my whole life.
MARY. I see. Even now that you're older.
JESS. It's just not something I'm interested in exploring. Not for me.

MARY. That's understandable.
> *Beat. OWEN is next to MARY, trying to break through to her.*

You know, this "seance" idea your aunt has...
OWEN. It's crazy, Mary. It'll never work, it's a scam –
MARY. I'm... a little curious about it.
OWEN. – But there's no harm in giving it a shot.
JESS. You mean, you actually want to try it?
MARY. Maybe. Is that bad?
JESS. No, I get it.
MARY. It's just – What if, you know? What if I <u>do</u> get a last conversation? To know he's still – something... To tell him how much he meant to me, to everyone. I mean, I'm sure he knew, but there were some things – things we never got around to discussing...
JESS. I can be there with you. If you want.
MARY. But you said you have no interest in it.
JESS. Not for me. But – I know how Aunt Betty can be. Don't you want a third party around? We can leave whenever you want.
MARY. Yeah, that'd be nice. Thanks – oh, sound, sound, sound!
JESS. Oh, shit!
> *She makes a sound effect.*

Oh man, that was embarrassing. Think anyone noticed?
MARY. Well, they're chuckling, so maybe it was for the best.
JESS. Let's just focus on the show.
MARY. Good idea.
> *Beat. HERB pokes his head in.*

HERB. Owen, did you see that?? Somebody just messed up! I love it when that happens!
OWEN. Yeah, hilarious.
HERB. You're so much more fun when your girlfriend's not around.
OWEN. She's not my girlfriend.
HERB. *(Mocking him.)* "She's not my girlfriend."
> *OWEN shoos him away.*

OWEN. Get out of here. Kick the back of Lorraine's chair for me.
HERB. I can't <u>believe</u> that woman keeps coming back...
> *HERB exits, laughing to himself. OWEN sits next to MARY, both with the tiniest bit of hope. Lights down.*

Scene 3

Ghost light up. OWEN and HERB are sleeping. All is still for a few moments, except maybe some snoring. We hear voices in the distance, then the door opens and someone turns the full lights on. JESS and BETTY enter and begin preparing a seance. OWEN and HERB wake up abruptly.

OWEN. What the…?
HERB. Agh! Turn that off, Owen!
OWEN. Me? You know we can't do lights.
HERB. Then what's – Who is – ?
OWEN. It's Betty and Jess.
HERB. What do they want?
OWEN. I dunno, want me to ask?
HERB. Smart alec.

They both start yawning, stretching, etc. Over the following, BETTY and JESS bring a table center stage and place four chairs around it. OWEN follows them around; whenever he gets near JESS, she gets that chill down her spine. BETTY mimics this, but at random times.

BETTY. No, dear, not that chair.
JESS. What's wrong with it?
BETTY. It is <u>radiating</u> bad energy.
JESS. Right.

She's too tired to argue, so she gets a different chair.

So, remember, don't <u>force</u> her into anything, alright? She's on the edge about this already.
BETTY. Yes, I know. I am here only as a guide, a translator, an ambassador of spirits.
JESS. I didn't realize you had a title. Apologies, Mrs. Ambassador.
BETTY. I'll be respectful of Mary's boundaries. You know what, I probably don't even need a handful of her hair.
JESS. Great. She'll be so relieved.
BETTY. But if you do have some, just one or two strands…?
JESS. *(Beat.)* What? No, I don't have any of her hair.
BETTY. Well, I guess I hoped you'd have the instinct. But you don't, of course. And that's fine.

JESS. Good.
BETTY. It just means so much to me that you're here, love.
JESS. I'm here for Mary.
BETTY. And me. A little bit.
JESS. Nope.
BETTY. Just the slightest amount? A smidgeon of interest in the family tradition? You know, your mother once told me –
JESS. Aunt Betty. No. Not right now.
BETTY. Alright, love. I understand. Come, now, back to the car...
> *JESS and BETTY exit to gather more seance items.*

HERB. Well. I guess tonight's the night.
OWEN. She did say the next full moon. Like the moon has anything to do with us. Isn't that funny?
> *OWEN takes a seat at the table.*

HERB. What're you doing?
OWEN. What, we don't get seats at the table?
HERB. I'm guessing these two are for Mary and Vinny.
OWEN. You think Vinny's coming too?
HERB. He said so at the *[show]* closing night. Don't you eavesdrop?
OWEN. Oh. I figured these would be Betty, Jess, Mary, and me.
HERB. And I'm chopped liver?
OWEN. To them, yeah. They don't know who you are.
HERB. Oh. Right.
> *He takes a seat next to OWEN.*

Still think it won't work?
OWEN. Not gonna get my hopes up otherwise.
HERB. Ah, but they're already up. You can't hide it.
OWEN. Do I <u>hope</u> it works? Of course. I'd give anything to have a last conversation with her. Do I <u>think</u> it'll work, though? Completely different question. Betty thinks she can do the impossible, just by setting up a silly little table under a full moon? Come on.
HERB. Guess we'll see.
> *Beat.*

"I don't want realism, I want magic!" What's that from?
OWEN. No, I'm not awake enough for this.
HERB. Come on, we just read this one last week.
OWEN. <u>You</u> read it.

HERB. "Yes, yes, magic! I try to give that to people. I misrepresent things to them. I don't tell the truth, I tell what ought to be the truth. And if that's sinful, then let me be damned for it!"
OWEN. That play Virginia Woolf wrote?
HERB. You're a scene behind. Wait – do you think Virginia Woolf wrote the play *Who's Afraid of Virginia Woolf*?
OWEN. I told you, I'm not awake…
HERB. Oh, but there is a good clue here. This other playwright's first name is also a state…
OWEN. Dakota Fanning.
HERB. Good Lord.
OWEN. Orlando Bloom.
HERB. That's not a state.
OWEN. Cuba Gooding Jr.
HERB. Okay, that's enough. You're embarrassing me. It's Tennessee Williams, *A Streetcar Named Desire*.
OWEN. Great. Another useless piece of information for me to forget.
HERB. How do you call yourself a thespian if you don't know any of the great American plays? Aren't you interested in the rich history of the theater?
OWEN. "Back in my day…"
HERB. No! This isn't another "Back in my day." Yes, I do believe the peak of theater was back in my day, but that's not what I'm talking about. The stage is a sacred place, with a sacred history. If folks these days only knew what it was like…
OWEN. Magical, I know. Says the lifelong usher.
HERB. Just because I didn't act doesn't mean I don't appreciate what theater represents! There used to be culture, enlightenment…
OWEN. Alright! Fine, I'll read your plays. I don't appreciate my theatrical ancestors, blah blah blah. Just, let me wake up first?
HERB. Sure.
OWEN. I'll learn all about those classics of yours. Don't worry.
 Changing the subject.
God, look at how cheesy this is. All we need is a circle of candles and a cauldron of rotten stew.
 BETTY and JESS enter, carrying candles and a cauldron.
I spoke too soon.

BETTY. Right in the center, there, dear. Perfect. I'll situate these candles around it, if you could find some matches.
JESS. You didn't bring any?
BETTY. I sense their presence. They're already here.
JESS. Where were you last week when I lost my car keys?
BETTY. And a pitcher of water, too, we don't want a repeat of the Old Gatland Church Fire.
JESS. Why not? Think of the insurance…
BETTY. You've got quite the sense of humor, love.
JESS. You mean honesty.
> *She exits. As BETTY arranges the candles, OWEN tests her "connections" by jumping out and waving at her, etc.*

HERB. Would you knock that off?
OWEN. Look, Herb, she's not even flinching. She says she senses when we're around. It's bullshit.
> *He twerks beside her, barely avoiding touching her. She continues setting the candles and starts humming happily.*

HERB. It's not a great start, I'll give you that.
OWEN. This is gonna suck. And look, they didn't even bring any snacks! How can you make people watch you talk to the air in the middle of the night, and not have the decency to bring a veggie dip, or crackers and cheese?
HERB. Vol-au-vents.
OWEN. What?
HERB. That's what I would've brought. Vol-au-vents.
OWEN. You're shitting me. That's not a real word.
HERB. They're little cylindrical pastries, and I miss them dearly.
OWEN. Oh, like Zebra Cakes? Or Ring Dings?
HERB. …Every day I'm more grateful to be dead.
> *JESS enters with matches, a pitcher of water, and cups. She lights the candles over the following.*

JESS. Here. I got cups too.
BETTY. Thank you, dear. Now, time for my elixir!
> *She dips a cup into the cauldron.*

JESS. You're not gonna wait for them to get here?
BETTY. It takes a few minutes to kick in. But don't worry, the effects last for a full hour.

JESS. Right. And what is it again?
BETTY. *(Taking a swig.)* The All-Seeing Elixir. It allows me to open my eyes further to the heavens, to let in and experience all forms of life, come and gone.
JESS. I meant, like, what is it? What's in it?
BETTY. It's a secret, my dear!
>   *She giggles and bops JESS on the nose playfully.*

But it's mostly toad juice. You want some?
JESS. Toad… juice?! What?!
BETTY. *(Filling another cup.)* I'll have some ready, just in case.
JESS. Sorry, but – by "toad juice," you mean…
>   *Before any other questions can be asked, VINNY and MARY enter. They are wearing pajamas, yawning, a little nervous.*

BETTY. Hello, loves! You made it!
MARY. Hi Betty. Hey, Jess.
VINNY. Lovely moonlight we're having, isn't it?
BETTY. It sure is.
JESS. Yeah, let's go skinny dipping.
BETTY. Hush now, Jess. Okay, let's all take a seat here around the table. Order doesn't matter –
>   *VINNY is about to sit; she bats him away.*

But that's my seat. I called it.
VINNY. Sorry.
>   *He instead pulls out OWEN's chair, who reluctantly stands up. HERB also stands to let MARY sit in his chair. MARY is trying her best to stay positive.*

MARY. You know, I like being here in the middle of the night. It's so peaceful and serene. I should come in after hours more often.
VINNY. Just make sure it's not being used.
MARY. Who uses the theater after hours?
VINNY. Well, sometimes Jess and I sneak in and –
JESS. Vinny…
VINNY. *(A look to BETTY.)* And we – we pray.
BETTY. Oh, come on, dear, you can lie better than that.
VINNY. Nope, that's the best I can do.
BETTY. Water, anybody?
ALL. *(Ad lib.)* Sure, thank you, etc.

BETTY pours out cups of water, passing them around.
VINNY. Holy, my seat is <u>cold</u>! Feel this.
JESS. Don't mind if I do.
> *She reaches under VINNY to check the seat, grabbing his butt in the process. She's joking around, but she gets another involuntary chill down her spine.*

VINNY. You okay?
JESS. Yeah. It is very cold, you're right.
VINNY. Wanna help me heat it up?
BETTY. Alright, you two, that's enough. Let's begin.
> *To MARY.*

As long as you're ready?
MARY. I am.
> *BETTY takes her hand lovingly.*

VINNY. Do we all hold hands, or just you two?
BETTY. I will give the instructions, dear.
> *VINNY holds JESS's hand anyway. As BETTY gives her directions, the others follow along.*

Now. Everyone close your eyes. Take three deep breaths: in, out, in, out, in, out. Find a space within yourself where there is true, total silence. Free yourself of unnecessary thoughts. Three more deep breaths: in, out, in, Vinny close your eyes or so help me God, out, in, out. Good. Now, I will begin to guide our party into the otherworld. Do not interrupt. This will take immense focus and precision.
> *Everyone remains very still as BETTY takes a deep breath in, lets it out, then yells very loudly, jolting everyone out of their serenity, including OWEN and HERB.*

Oh, knowing eternal ones, I approach you tonight with peaceful intentions! I seek a connection between our world and your own! I seek a spirit, one who gave every ounce of his life to this theater! I ask you to cast him forth and to allow communication between his soul and ours! All-knowing heavens, I ask you to send me Owen...
> *Briefly breaking the rhythm of things. To MARY:*

Last name?
MARY. Hm?
BETTY. What's Owen's last name?
MARY. Oh. Rogers. Owen Henry Rogers.

BETTY. Send me Owen Henry Rogers, oh eternal ones!
> *She waits. Everyone waits, including HERB and OWEN.*

HERB. Well, go on.
OWEN. Oh, right.
> *Nervous, but hopeful, he crosses to BETTY. Before he says anything to her, he asks HERB:*

How do I look?
HERB. Well, I wouldn't have worn that, but...
> *OWEN waves HERB's sarcasm aside and turns to BETTY.*

OWEN. H – Hello? I'm here.
> *Beat.*

Can you hear me?
BETTY. Hello? Owen, are you in this room right now?
OWEN. Yes, I'm right here. Can you –?
BETTY. He's here, Mary, he's here.
MARY. Oh?
OWEN. Wait, can she actually – Betty, can you actually hear –?
BETTY. Owen, your friend Mary is here. She is the reason I have called you forth tonight.
OWEN. Hi, Mary. Can you – ?
BETTY. He says he loves you, Mary.
OWEN. What? No, I – Not yet –
MARY. Really? Are you sure?
OWEN. Yes, Mary, I do, but first –
BETTY. Positive. Owen, Mary wishes to finally say what she never had the chance to say before.
OWEN. Before we move on, I just want to make sure you can –
BETTY. Go ahead, Mary, he's waiting.
OWEN. No! I said, before we move on –
MARY. Owen, I know we had a... complicated history. I – I guess I'll start with "I miss you."
> *She pauses, waiting for confirmation.*

OWEN. I miss you, too. Every day.
MARY. Should I go on?
BETTY. Of course.
MARY. Has he said anything yet?
BETTY. No. Still waiting.

OWEN. She's lying! I miss you too, Mary, I do!
BETTY. Go on, dear, he's being patient.
> *The following lines overlap slightly, the ending of each blending into the beginning of the next.*

OWEN. I am not! You don't know me, and you don't know Mary! How dare you! You fraud!
MARY. Four summers ago, when you passed, it felt like, like I had been sailing through life with this marvelous sailboat, and one day, without warning it just – flipped.
OWEN. Mary, she can't hear me, she's a fake! I'll do jumping jacks and she won't mention it! Look! Push-ups! Mary, don't fall for it!
MARY. And I know it's been long enough, but I still feel like I'm just floating, without direction, in this unending sea of despair and hopelessness –
OWEN. She's just after your money, Mary, she doesn't care about us, she's taking advantage of you!
HERB. She's never mentioned money, Owen. Let's calm down.
MARY. I don't live anymore. I wake up, I walk around, I eat, I smile at the right people, but it's like – it's like I'm dead, too. And I can't stand it. I just want to be alive again –
OWEN. Mary... Mary, please –
> *Feeling helpless, OWEN loses his cool and begins throwing props. MARY stops talking abruptly and everyone gasps and screams, including BETTY. OWEN yells and rampages around the room. HERB tries to stop him, but can't. Finally, OWEN runs straight at BETTY and pushes her down.*

JESS. Aunt Betty!
VINNY. What the hell!
MARY. What is happening?!
> *JESS runs to check on BETTY. VINNY also jumps to action, trying to protect everyone, though he doesn't know what he's protecting them from. OWEN has stopped. He is breathing heavily, but also realizes he's just done something very bad.*

HERB. Owen! What have you done?!
OWEN. Shit. I didn't – I wasn't –
> *Suddenly, he starts getting pulled by invisible forces. They're dragging him offstage, and though he's not in pain, he is*

clearly weaker than these forces. He panics and screams.
OWEN. Herb! What's happening?! Mary! Mary, I'm sorry!
HERB. I've got you! Hold on!
He tries to pull OWEN back, but gets dragged along instead.
OWEN. Don't let them take me, Herb!
HERB. I'm right here, I won't let you go...
They are both dragged offstage by the invisible forces.
JESS. Aunt Betty, are you okay?!
BETTY. I – I think so –
VINNY. Come and get me, spirits! Come at me!
MARY. What was that?! Somebody tell me!
JESS. Everyone, calm down!
All is quiet.
Okay, Aunt Betty, please explain what just happened.
BETTY just stares, wide-eyed and confused.
Are you serious? You don't know either?
BETTY. Well, that's never happened before...
MARY. I am about to freak the hell out.
BETTY. No! No, dear – it's alright. Owen is just – so excited to see you, he got – overwhelmed, I suppose. Isn't that right, Owen?
No answer, obviously.
He says yes, that's it.
VINNY. He's still here? Owen, buddy, not cool! Come at me!
JESS. Vinny, stop it.
BETTY. I know what it looked like, but he's – still learning how to express himself, is all. These boundaries between our world and theirs – they're blurry, undefined. I've never seen anything like this, but you know what that means? It means his love for you, Mary – his longing, his passion – is so strong, he makes otherworldly things happen. Isn't that special? Mary?
MARY. *(Beat.)* I'm gonna go.
BETTY. Are you sure, dear? He's still here. He says – he says he loves you, will always love you, until the end of time.
MARY. He doesn't believe in the end of time.
BETTY. It's an expression.
MARY. I know. But it's not something he would – Just, thank you, Betty. I appreciate what you've done. But I need to go now.

JESS. You're completely valid, Mary. Let's go.
MARY. No, it's okay, Jess. I'm going for a walk. And I want to be alone. I need to be alone.
She opens the door and turns to face them.
Thanks for coming, everybody.
She smiles half-heartedly and exits. Beat.
VINNY. You're not hurt, Betty?
BETTY. I'm fine, dear. Thank you.
VINNY. The Owen I know, he wouldn't do that.
BETTY. He's processing his death. It's okay. We should forgive him.
VINNY. You sure he's still here?
BETTY. *(Not entirely convincing.)* Of course.
VINNY. Can I talk to him?
JESS. Vinny, we should just get to bed –
VINNY. If Mary gets to talk to him, so do I. He's my friend too.
JESS. What if he gets violent again?
BETTY. I think he's calmed down. Let's – let's try again. Yes, Vinny, go ahead and start talking. I'll let you know what he says.
VINNY. Thanks.
He clears his throat. VINNY starts this monologue very nervously, but gets more confident as he goes on.
Okay, uh... Dear Owen – Wait, that's not how you start a conversation. I'm gonna start over. Hey dude, Vinny here. We forgive you for your tantrum. And – I'm sad about you dying. And being dead. Damn, I'm not good at this. Uh... Hey, d'you remember, one of my first years here, we both got cast in *[show]*, you were the lead and I was some featured role. And you had this huge monologue, with all kinds of clever wording and talking to yourself – guess that's what a monologue is – and you just blew it out of the water. Every show, I'd stand there just offstage, watching you <u>kill</u> it, man, thinking, "That's it. I want to do <u>that</u>." Then I'd get distracted, miss my entrance, bumble my lines, and trip over my own feet... But I still think about that. About the kind of actor you were, the actor I wanna be. And – I think I'm getting there. We just closed *[show]*, and there was one scene, I could never get it right – until I thought "How would Owen do it?" And, at the risk of sounding weird, there were moments during rehearsals where I'd – I'd <u>feel</u> you around me. I would say a line, or

make a face, and think, "Oh wow, that was Owen." I guess, all I wanna say is, I know I've still got improvements to make, but I'm making them. I'm getting better. And I owe it to you. So thanks, dude. I'm better because of you.
>*Beat.*

Still can't nail a monologue to save my life, though.
JESS. That was really well said, Vinny.
VINNY. Thanks.
>*To BETTY.*

Did he say anything back?
BETTY. Oh, yes, he says – that's a wonderful sentiment, and he's so very proud of you. Proud of the actor, and person, you've become.
VINNY. Aw, shucks. You're just saying that.
BETTY. Jess, love, do you have anything to add?
JESS. I didn't know the guy.
BETTY. Right. In that case, shall we call it an evening?
JESS. Yes. I'm exhausted.
BETTY. Okay. I'm gonna use the ladies' room real quick. Could you two get things cleaned up?
JESS. What do I look like, a stage manager?
>*She laughs at herself.*

Yes. Run along.
BETTY. Thanks, love.
>*She exits to the dressing rooms. JESS and VINNY start cleaning everything up. In this process, VINNY unknowingly swaps a cup of the elixir with a cup of water.*

VINNY. Wait – she didn't really "end the call" there. Is he still here?
JESS. You think he was here at all?
VINNY. Oh. You don't?
JESS. I don't know. Something weird happened, obviously, but I'm still skeptical. I think Mary was too.
VINNY. Hm. Guess I'm just gullible. And man, am I hungry! I wasn't gonna say anything, but I kinda expected some snacks.
JESS. Snacks? It's the middle of the night.
VINNY. Exactly.
>*He crosses to a pile of props and reveals a box of crackers from seemingly nowhere.*

But don't worry, I've always got my secret stash.

JESS. Where did those come from?

VINNY. I've got emergency snacks all over, for situations like these.

JESS. Just crackers, huh? Wish I had some cheese.

VINNY. You do not want cheese that's been sitting around back here.
With a look of horror at a past memory.
Trust me.

JESS. Glad you've learned your lesson.
She bites off a cracker and exits with some seance items.

VINNY. So, my long speech to Owen – I coulda just been rambling to the wind there.

JESS. *(Off.)* Maybe. Maybe not. But remember, I've got a weird relationship with all of this, so don't take my word –
She chokes a little on cracker and starts coughing offstage.

VINNY. You alright? Want some water?

JESS. *(Entering, coughing.)* Yes, please. Gimme.
VINNY grabs the nearest cup and gives it to JESS. She takes a drink before she realizes:
Ugh. What is – Is that the elixir?

VINNY. Oh, shoot. Sorry.

JESS. Y'know, it actually doesn't taste that bad. Water, though, gimme some water.

VINNY. Right.
This time, he makes sure to grab a cup with water.
You gonna be okay? With the elixir, I mean?

JESS. I'm fine. Aunt Betty drinks it, no reason I can't.

VINNY. Guess you'll see if it really works, huh?

JESS. *(Joking.)* Yeah, there's ghosts all over the place! Ahh!
BETTY returns, quite excited.

BETTY. Cats! Fighting outside!

JESS. We should not get in the middle of that.

VINNY. Ms. Martin's cat! I'm on it! Where are they?!

JESS. No, Vinny – they're cats, they'll figure it out.
But BETTY is leading VINNY out the back door, explaining the noises in great detail. JESS, sarcastically:
Sure, I've got it from here!
She checks that the doors are locked, turns the ghost light on,

and the full lights out, humming the song VINNY sings at the beginning of the play. HERB enters, distraught, without OWEN, and sits near the ghost light. To himself:
HERB. Oh, they're still here.
JESS stops humming. She looks toward the ghost light and barely sees HERB.
JESS. Vinny, let's go.
HERB looks around for VINNY.
Vinny? I'm leaving. Come on.
HERB. *(Turning around.)* Hm? Where is he?
JESS lets out a small yell.
JESS. Who are you?! What are you doing here?!
HERB. Someone else here?
JESS. YOU! I'M TALKING TO YOU!
HERB. What's going on? What is she upset about?
JESS. WHO ARE YOU?! I – I'LL HURT YOU!
HERB. *(It suddenly hits him.)* Me? Are you talking to me?
JESS. YES! YOU! WHAT ARE YOU DOING HERE?!
HERB. Oh, dear Heavens…
He steps closer to her, revealing himself.
Did you die?
JESS. What?! No, I didn't die! What are you talking about?!
HERB. You're not dead?
JESS. No! Why?
HERB. …Because I am.
JESS. You… you're…
JESS, shaking, walks up to him and slowly reaches out a hand. She just barely touches his arm, making sure he's real.
HERB. So I guess the toad juice works after all, huh?
JESS screams and faints. Lights down.

ACT II

Scene 1

Ghost light up. JESS is alone, unconscious. She has yet to recover from her fainting. HERB is not around. VINNY starts pounding at the back door.
VINNY. *(Off.)* Jess? You still in there? The cats got away! Jess?
Beat.
Are you mad at me?
JESS wakes up and looks around, confused. She wonders if seeing HERB was a weird dream. VINNY continues calling to her until she goes to the door.
JESS. Is Aunt Betty out there?
VINNY. *(Off.)* No. Are you alright?
JESS. Come in.
She lets VINNY in and closes the door.
VINNY. Jeez, I thought you'd left without telling me. You wouldn't do that, though, right? You okay?
JESS. Yeah, I – had a weird… moment, I guess.
VINNY. Yeah? Here, sit down, take a breath. You look white as a – as a – oh, come on, I'm setting you up. White as a…
JESS. Ghost, yes. Vinny – I saw him.
VINNY. Saw who? Trevor? Your ex? I told you, I'm not comfortable with –
JESS. No, no. Owen. I saw Owen.
VINNY. Oh. When he was here earlier? Why didn't you tell Betty?
JESS. No, not earlier. Just now. Or – however long you were out there with the cats.
VINNY. Now? Is he still here?
JESS. *(Looking around.)* No, I guess not. I don't –
HERB steps out from the darkness, cautiously. JESS freezes.
VINNY. You okay?
She points at HERB.
Is – is he here? He's right there?
JESS. *(Barely audible.)* Yup.
A long pause.

50

VINNY. Owen, buddy! How are ya?
>   *Beat.*

What'd he say?
JESS. Nothing. Ex – Excuse me, are you…?
HERB. I'm not Owen. Sorry I made you think so.
>   *JESS starts to faint again; VINNY catches her.*

VINNY. What? What'd he say? Did he hear my speech earlier?
JESS. He's not Owen.
VINNY. Oh. Then – wait – what? Who is he?
JESS. Who are you?
HERB. My name is Herbert. You can call me Herb. I was an usher at this theater. I died about fifty years ago.
JESS. Oh.
VINNY. What?! Who is he?
JESS. His name's Herb, he used to usher here. He's been dead for fifty years.
VINNY. Whoa. Cool. But you gotta tell him we're looking for someone else.
HERB. I can hear everything he's saying. He doesn't need to tell you to tell me things.
JESS. He can hear you. You can talk to him directly.
VINNY. Oh, okay. So, right, when he says things, you can just relay them to me. Like a translator. Oh! What if I drink the elixir too??
>   *He grabs a cup of the elixir and gulps it all down.*

JESS. Sure, try it out. So, Herb – Can you explain what's going on?
VINNY. Hey, you're right, this tastes pretty good.
HERB. Well, I'm dead, and you're alive, and we're speaking. I've never done it before, but I guess it's possible. This is what your aunt –
VINNY. What'd he say?
JESS. Shh. You interrupted him.
VINNY. Oh. Sorry.
HERB. This is what your aunt wanted earlier. Except, I suppose, it turns out <u>you're</u> the, uh, dead-talker, not her.
JESS. But it's not possible. None of this is possible.
VINNY. What? What'd he say that time?
JESS. Look, Vinny – I'm not gonna repeat everything he says, okay? I'll fill you in later.

VINNY. Right. That's fine. I'll just wait for the elixir to kick in.

JESS. So, Herb, you were here earlier?

HERB. I'm here all the time.

JESS. All the time?

HERB. Yes. This is my home.

JESS. All the time…

HERB. (*Beat.*) Oh, I give you privacy when you and Vinny sneak in to have... relations.

JESS. Oh, God…

HERB. I swear, I never watch. I'm not interested in – Let's move on from that part of the conversation, shall we?

JESS. Yes, please.

HERB. I know Owen. I know him very well, actually. He's lived here with me every summer since he passed. Nice kid.

JESS. Where is he, then?

HERB. Well, he's – he's in some trouble.

JESS. For what?

HERB. That little fit he threw earlier.

JESS. That – that really <u>was</u> him??

HERB. Yes, it was.

JESS. Aunt Betty was actually talking to him?

HERB. No. She was faking it. She can't see or hear us. Which is why this – this is unexpected.

JESS. You're telling me. So what kind of trouble is he in?

HERB. Well, there are very strict rules against what he did. Moving objects while the living can see, making physical contact with the living, causing harm to the living – that's the big one.

JESS. Yeah – he pushed Aunt Betty down.

HERB. He was frustrated. You've seen how Mary misses him. He misses her just as much.

JESS. So when Betty was pretending to hear him, but couldn't…

HERB. Yes, that angered him.

VINNY. I don't think my elixir is working.

JESS. Shh. Okay, so – these rules, what happens if you break them?

HERB. Well, he could go to prison.

JESS. Ghost prison?

HERB. We just call it prison, but yes. There's that. But the laws he

broke, the physical contact and harm... It might not be prison.
JESS. What would it be?
HERB. I'm not saying this is likely, but it's not exactly unlikely either. I'm no expert on ghost law, but...
JESS. What? What would they do?
HERB. They could banish him. Banish him permanently.
JESS. Banish him? To where?
HERB. Banish him from this – this realm. This life.
JESS. Oh. Like a – death after death?
HERB. Yes.
JESS. So, where does he – what happens when –
HERB. I don't know. Nobody knows. Whatever's next.
JESS. I see.
HERB. Now, as I said – who knows what they'll decide. Right now he's just in a holding cell. He'll be there until his trial.
JESS. Damn. Trials, laws, banishments... The afterlife sounds like a real downer.
HERB. It's not that bad, if you behave. But Owen isn't the type to walk the straight and narrow.
JESS. When is his trial?
HERB. End of August, I think they said. I'll be testifying. I'll do what I can to get him off the hook, trust me.
JESS. And in the meantime?
HERB. He'll be held there.
JESS. Is there any way to get him here, even just once? For Mary?
HERB. I'll try my best.
JESS. Thanks. So I guess – We'll be in regular contact, then.
HERB. If you want, sure. I'll enjoy the company.
JESS. I'll have to get more elixir from Aunt Betty. Don't know how I'm gonna do that.
VINNY. Tell her you like the taste. I do.
JESS. It's weird that it was good, right?
VINNY. Yeah. So, uh, mind getting me caught up?
JESS. Well, apparently there are ghost laws, and Owen broke a few tonight. His trial's at the end of August. Until then, he's in a holding cell, waiting for his sentencing.
VINNY. Like a purgatory.

HERB. Nice metaphor.

JESS. Herb says nice metaphor.

VINNY. Thanks. So, what are they gonna do to him?

JESS. Well, he could get banished. From the afterlife.

VINNY. And where does he go then?

JESS. Nobody knows.

VINNY. Oh. Kinda like... oh.

JESS. Yeah. Either way, we want to help Mary talk to him before – if, that happens.

VINNY. Wow. That's – I'm having a hard time wrapping my head around this. Where do I begin...

> *He pauses, then barrages HERB with questions.*

Can you walk through walls? Can you see through walls? Do you know all the other dead people? How many of you are here right now? Did you see the movie *Ghostbusters*? What about the female reboot? Can you see into the future? Do they make more *Ghostbuster* movies? Do we get three wishes? Do you ever say "Oooooooo" down a dark hallway? Have you met any famous people? Like Robin Williams? Or Marilyn Monroe? Or how about –

> *Sometime over the above, after attempting to answer but unintentionally being talked over, HERB has walked away, shaking his head.*

JESS. Vinny, he's not here anymore.

VINNY. What? Where is he?

JESS. He just walked away. I don't know.

VINNY. Bring him back! I have so many questions!

JESS. You didn't let him answer any of them.

VINNY. How would I have known he was answering? You should've told me he was going to.

JESS. You just kept going, bam, bam, bam –

HERB. *(Off.)* Both of you, turn around and close your eyes!

JESS. What? Why?

HERB. You'll see. Just for a moment.

VINNY. Why what?

JESS. He told us to turn around and close our eyes.

VINNY. Why?

JESS. I don't know.

VINNY. Does he have a gun?!
HERB. No, of course not!
JESS. No.
VINNY. Is he naked?!
HERB. Heavens, no!
JESS. No. Just do what he says. I'm too tired to be arguing with ghosts and boyfriends.
VINNY. But – Wait, boyfriend? I thought you weren't looking for anything serious.
JESS. I wasn't, but you – No, not the time for this conversation.
VINNY. *(Elated.)* You want to be boyfriend-girlfriend! Yes!
JESS. Just close your eyes and turn around... boyfriend.
VINNY. Sure thing, girlfriend!
JESS. *(To HERB.)* Okay, do your worst!
> *HERB enters with a book. He places it down somewhere in view, careful not to let VINNY or JESS see him do it.*
HERB. Okay, you can look again.
> *They turn around.*
VINNY. Well, is he naked, holding a gun?
JESS. No, he's the same.
VINNY. What's this?
> *He picks up the book and starts flipping through.*
HERB. That contains the answers to many of your questions.
JESS. Answers to your questions.
VINNY. How'd he type this so fast? It's like a thousand pages long! Can he pause time?
HERB. No, I didn't write it just now. It was written by someone who was alive, but obviously had help from our side of things, because it's all correct. I don't know who wrote it – it just sort of appeared, some years ago. Wish I could've had it when I first died, would've saved me time figuring things out. When Owen died, this was the first thing I gave him. Mostly because he bombarded me with questions like Vinny just did. I had to shut him up somehow. I've never shared it with the living, so this is a special occasion. Knock yourself out.
JESS. He says it's a bunch of true stuff about ghosts. Written by a living person, somehow. FAQ type of thing.
VINNY. Wow. This is incredible. Can I borrow this, Herb?

HERB. As long as nobody dies and needs my assistance anytime soon, it's yours.
JESS. He says yes.
VINNY. Sweet! Thanks! Oh, man, this is so cool...
> *He starts flipping through, losing himself in the book.*

JESS. Why did you have us turn around and close our eyes?
HERB. I can't let you see me move anything. It's against the law for us to interfere with you.
JESS. Right.
> *Beat.*

Wait, isn't <u>this</u> "interfering"? Are you breaking the law right now?
HERB. Well, <u>you</u> initiated this.
JESS. That's it? That's all it takes?
HERB. Yes. You can contact us, we can't contact you. It's all explained in the book. Since you established our communication, we can talk as much as we like.
JESS. That seems strange. Kind of arbitrary and senseless.
HERB. Well, we've got the same lawmakers you used to have. Are you surprised?
JESS. No, I guess not.
VINNY. *(From the book.)* Aw, no walking through walls. That sucks.
HERB. Sure does, kid. Some folks give up on the afterlife as soon as they figure that out.
JESS. For good reason.
VINNY. What's he saying?
JESS. You're right. Not walking through walls sucks.
> *She double takes to HERB.*

Oh, no.
VINNY. What?
JESS. You're starting to fade, Herb. I think the elixir is wearing off.
VINNY. Why don't you just drink more?
JESS. We should get to bed. It's like two in the morning, and we've got rehearsal at nine.
VINNY. Oh, shit. Forgot about that. Let's just call in sick.
JESS. I'm the stage manager. I'm the one you call in sick <u>to</u>.
VINNY. *(Beat, then a fake cough.)* I think I'm starting to come down with something.

JESS. You're hilarious. Herb, let's call it a night. You're only half there. That's so weird...
HERB. It's been nice to talk to someone other than Owen for once. Thank you.
JESS. Are there no other ghosts around here, then?
HERB. There are others who stop by. But one benefit to being dead is, you can go wherever you want. So most of them go where they never did when they were alive. Tropical paradises and romantic cities... Some folks treat death like a vacation, and all the power to 'em. But me – I couldn't stay away from this dusty old theater my whole life, and I can't escape it in death either. It's where I belong. I want nothing more than to sit out in that audience, or that stage, or this booby-trap maze of a backstage, and watch every passing season till the end of time. "And past that," as Owen would say. He doesn't believe in an end of time. Gosh, I hope I get to keep him.

Beat.

You can't hear me anymore, can you?

Long beat.

VINNY. Boy, he must be on a long one.
JESS. No, I don't see him anymore. I was just letting him finish his story without being rude.
VINNY. Ah. Well, now that he's gone – what'd he look like??
JESS. I'm sure he's still here, I just can't see him.
VINNY. Oh, right.
JESS. Herb, if you're still here, sorry if we interrupted. We'll be back. Probably with a hundred more questions.
HERB. Goodnight, kiddos.

As he's walking off.

Oh, I forgot! We can't do lights, so turn off that ghost light! We all hate it! Hello?! Ah, darn it.

He shakes his head in disappointment and exits.

VINNY. Well. Time for some shut-eye?
JESS. Yes, please. Feels like I've died and come halfway back to life.

They once again make sure the doors are locked, check the dressing rooms, etc.

VINNY. So we're dating now, huh? Officially?
JESS. Yup. You finally wore me down.

VINNY. That's what I'm best at!

JESS. Thanks for being here, Vin. I would've convinced myself I was going crazy without you.

VINNY. You're welcome. Hey, for all I know, maybe you are crazy. It's not like I saw him.

JESS. Yeah, that makes me feel better.

VINNY. Maybe you were hallucinating!… Wait, you didn't find my emergency mushroom stash up in the furniture loft, did you?

JESS. Your – what? No.

VINNY. Good. Good.

They're about to leave. Referencing the ghost light:
Aren't you gonna shut that off?

JESS. The ghost light? No, it's on for them.

They exit. Lights down.

Scene 2

Low backstage lights up. MARY and JESS are both working at their respective places: JESS at the soundboard, MARY at the curtain. There is immense tension in the air.

MARY. Come on, Greg, come on...
JESS. Should I give him his line?!
MARY. No, he's got this.
JESS. Doesn't look like it.
MARY. Trust me. It'll look like a dramatic pause – Ah! There we go!
JESS. Finally! Lights... Curtain down...
  MARY lowers the curtain.
Sound, and... Curtain up!
  MARY raises the curtain. We hear applause as the actors take their bows. Eventually, MARY lowers the curtain.
...And that's a wrap!
  She turns the full backstage lights on.
MARY. Well, it was better than last night.
JESS. If we consider this another dress rehearsal, it's a huge success.
MARY. Sure is. Fourth successful dress rehearsal in a row!
JESS. Tomorrow we've got to remind Vinny about when he thinks he exits stage left but doesn't. He was so helpless.
MARY. He figured it out eventually.
JESS. Think anybody noticed when we pushed him back on?
MARY. Oh yeah. Definitely.
VINNY. *(Entering, in costume.)* Babe, I'm so sorry. I completely spaced on that exit stage left.
JESS. It's fine, nobody noticed!
MARY. I certainly didn't!
VINNY. And Greg's pause there at the end, jeez –
JESS. What pause?
VINNY. You didn't notice? I feel like it was noticeable.
MARY. No, of course not!
VINNY. I almost swooped in and saved him.
MARY. *(Glancing offstage.)* Oh God. Is that what Greg's hair looked like the whole time?
VINNY. Uh, I dunno, I don't really pay attention to hair.

JESS. You should, though.
MARY. And his fly is down!
> *Chasing Greg offstage into the dressing rooms.*

Greg! Get back here!
JESS. Thank you, Mary!
> *To VINNY, a bit quieter.*

I'm so nervous.
VINNY. How'd the trial go?
JESS. I don't know, I had some elixir before the show but Herb hasn't shown up yet. I think I'll need more, but I'm almost out.
VINNY. I'm telling you, just ask Aunt Betty for more.
JESS. But she'll just yammer on about the family tradition and "I told you so"...
VINNY. So just hit her with the, "I know you're faking it."
JESS. But it'll break her heart.
VINNY. Or, tell her it's for me. Tell her I drink it for the taste. Which really isn't too far off. It's tasty.
JESS. *(Beat.)* This is the longest we've been alone together without making out.
VINNY. What is wrong with us?
> *They start making out, falling behind the couch again.*

BETTY. *(Entering.)* Remind me again why I settled for summer theater? Why am I dealing with actors who don't know their....
JESS. *(Raising her head above the couch.)* Line?
VINNY. *(Also raising his head.)* Sorry, was that me?
BETTY. Oh, silly kids. You don't have to hide from me.
VINNY. I think we just like to, at this point.
> *He and JESS get up and adjust their clothing accordingly.*

So, Aunt Betty, what'd you think?
BETTY. Well, there's – still some improvements to make.
VINNY. Improvements, sure. Like what?
BETTY. You're doing fine, sweetie. But, well, Greg for example – he just needs to be... better. Just so much better.
JESS. Maybe <u>that</u> type of direction is why you're in summer theater.
BETTY. What a sweet comment, dear. Oh, by the way, I found this water bottle back here earlier. It's yours, right? I must have mistaken it for mine, my elixir was in it! But don't worry, I dumped it out.

JESS. What? Wait – No!
VINNY. Jess, does that mean…?
JESS. It means! – That! –
    She searches for an excuse.
That I have something to confess, Aunt Betty.
BETTY. Oh?
VINNY. She <u>loves</u> the taste of it!
JESS. Vinny? Let me?
VINNY. It's delicious! I think so too! I put it in my coffee!
JESS. Aunt Betty, don't listen to – You what??
VINNY. But it's got nothing to do with seeing dead people. She's not interested, and never will be.
JESS. Can't you let me do this?
VINNY. Didn't you say I should stand up for you more?
JESS. Yes, when someone cuts us in line for popcorn at the movies. Not now. But thank you, I appreciate you.
BETTY. Is that true, dear? Is that where my elixir's been going?
JESS. Yes, but it's because – I can see them, Aunt Betty.
BETTY. See who?
JESS. The dead.
    BETTY registers this. She is shocked at first, then ecstatic.
BETTY. Oh! Oh, I'm so happy! You're doing it! It's your calling! I knew it, all your life, haven't I always said – ?
JESS. Aunt Betty…
BETTY. Yes, dear?!
JESS. You can't. I know you can't.
BETTY. I can't…?
JESS. You can't see them. I know.
BETTY. What – no, I –
    Another, more genuine, moment of realization.
Holy shit, you actually can.
JESS. Yes.
BETTY. You can see them…
JESS. I didn't believe it for the longest time. Then, a few weeks ago, I accidentally had some of your elixir, and I… I saw a ghost that night. I honestly did. And I've been sneaking the elixir ever since, to stay in contact with him.

BETTY. *(Emotional, coming to terms with herself.)* Oh, my… Jessie, dear, I know this is no excuse, but – your mother, she could too. She had the gift, ever since we were kids. And I was so jealous, Jessie, I – I always claimed to see Grampa, but it was her, she was the one…
    She flops onto the couch and breaks into tears.
I've been living a lie – Oh, Jessie, I'm so sorry. I didn't mean to!
    She falls onto JESS's lap, over-the-top crying. JESS is taken aback, but she comforts her. VINNY feels out of place.
JESS. Hey Vin, could you go get some tissues?
    VINNY gives a thumbs-up and exits quickly.
Hey, Aunt Betty – it's okay. Really. It's not the end of the world. You have the best of intentions. You haven't done any harm! In fact, I bet you really have saved a few souls.
BETTY. You think so?
JESS. Of course. Sure, some of 'em got ticked off, or banned you from their book clubs, but mostly you help people. You do.
    She takes BETTY and forces eye contact.
You're a great person, Aunt Betty. You've done nothing wrong.
BETTY. What about the Old Gatland Church Fire?
JESS. Okay, maybe one thing. But nobody's perfect.
BETTY. *(Sniffling.)* What's it like? Are they solid, or see-through? Can they walk through walls? Do they –
JESS. I'm not doing this again. I'll give you a book at tomorrow's rehearsal. Vinny just finished it.
BETTY. Can he see them too??
JESS. God, no. But he's been there with me. For me.
    MARY enters but sees the tender moment, so she stays back.
BETTY. So – how many times have you seen them?
JESS. Off and on, the past few weeks. Middle of the night meetings.
BETTY. Meetings with – the young man? Owen?
    MARY's interest is piqued, but she stays hidden.
JESS. Well, no. It's been – complicated.
BETTY. Oh, ghost drama! How exciting.
JESS. We've been seeing this old usher named Herb. Old, as in, he died fifty years ago. Apparently he lives here and watches the plays.
BETTY. Oh, how magical. I can feel him – I know, I know, I can't see him, but honestly – I feel him here. His presence is in the air –

JESS. Aunt Betty? I'm explaining what's going on.
BETTY. Right. Sorry. So, Herb, does he know Owen?
JESS. Yeah. From the sounds of things, they've become good friends the past few years. It's a little weird, but actually pretty wholesome. The problem is, when we had our seance, when all the props got thrown around and you got pushed over...
BETTY. Yes! That was freaky!
JESS. Well, that was Owen. And apparently he broke some laws –
BETTY. They have laws?
JESS. I know, right?! But that's the awful part. He's on trial for it. He could be banished from their – their realm. Like a death-after-death penalty. And they're announcing the verdict tonight.
BETTY. Tonight? Oh my.
JESS. Yeah. So, long story short, I needed the elixir that was in my water bottle. I really needed it.
BETTY. Oh, that's fine. I've got plenty in my car.
JESS. Your car! Of course! Okay, then everything's fine!
BETTY. *(Excited to be involved.)* Yes! Okay! I can still be helpful!

VINNY enters with a box of tissues.

VINNY. Sorry, apparently we've got every prop in the universe except a box of tissues. I found this one at Ms. Martin's place. Don't worry, I got out before the guard cats saw me.

He realizes BETTY's no longer crying.

Damn, I missed my opportunity. You okay, Aunt Betty?
BETTY. I'm fine, love. My world's been turned upside-down and I'm a lifelong fraud, but yes, fine. I'll go get that elixir, be right back!

As she exits, VINNY notices MARY.

VINNY. Hey, Mary!
MARY. *(Approaching them cautiously.)* Hi.
JESS. Oh, shoot – Mary! Um, what did you hear?
MARY. Well, I'm trying to decide whether I'm dreaming or you're playing some sick joke on me.
JESS. Mary, we would never do that. Here, sit. Come here.

MARY sits. At the same time, HERB enters, out of breath, unseen by everyone, including JESS.

HERB. Jess! Can you hear me right now?!
MARY. You can – you can see them? Honestly?

JESS. Yes. I never believed it before, but – yes.

HERB. Jess! Please! Drink your potion!

JESS. I can see them, and hear them, as if they're right here in the room with me.

HERB. Oh, now you're just mocking me! Fine, I'll wait.

He takes a seat to catch his breath.

MARY. And, what you said about, Owen… He's in trouble?

JESS. Yes, but we're hopeful. He's got a good record, and Herb was testifying for him, so – we'll see.

VINNY. We'll get him back, Mary. We will.

MARY. How are <u>you</u> in on this?

VINNY. *(A look at JESS, then MARY.)* You don't know about us?

MARY. What?

VINNY. Jess and I are dating.

MARY. I know that! I mean – Do you see the ghosts, Vinny?

VINNY. Oh! No. I don't have "the gift." I've been there, though.

MARY. And – no offense, Jess, but – Vinny, you believe her?

VINNY. It's pretty believable, Mary. It sounds like this Herb guy knows Owen well. The Owen we knew.

MARY. I see.

VINNY. He's still out there, Mary! Isn't that exciting?

MARY. Yes, it certainly would be.

JESS. I'll prove it to you, Mary. Somehow.

BETTY enters with the elixir and four cups.

BETTY. Sorry, everything was topsy-turvy, looks like the cats got into my car again.

VINNY. No, that was me. I was looking for tissues and I know you cry a lot in your car.

BETTY. How embarrassing. Okay, Jess, here you go. Drink up and tell us the news. And I'll have some too, just in case.

VINNY. Oo, me too. It's yummy. Great in smoothies. Try it, Mary!

MARY. …Okay, sure. I'm not getting my hopes up, though.

Everyone drinks their elixir. VINNY finds something nearby to paint and instinctively starts taking off his shirt.

What are you doing?

VINNY. Well, I probably won't be able to see Herb. So I figure, while I'm here, might as well get caught up on work.

64

BETTY. That's a good lad.
JESS. I guess it might be a late night, huh?
 Calling to Greg, offstage:
Oh, goodnight Greg! Jeez, he was still here?
MARY. I kind of assumed everyone was gone.
JESS. Me too. I'm such a bad stage manager. Is everyone else gone?
BETTY. Nobody's out front. Except for, what's her name, Lorrie? That poor girl who can't act to save her life.
MARY. Lorraine. Ignore her long enough, she'll leave.
VINNY. I can't believe she keeps coming to the shows.
MARY. It's so awkward.
VINNY. She brought me flowers last week...
HERB. And they were half-dead!
 JESS's ears perk up... and so do MARY's.
JESS. Oh!
MARY. What was that?
VINNY. I said, "She brought me flowers last week."
MARY. Not you.
JESS. Shh – Herb, are you here?
HERB. Ah! Finally. Good evening, Jess.
JESS. Yes, there you are! Okay, Herb, so –
 MARY suddenly screams and points at HERB.
MARY. No! You're all playing a joke on me!
JESS. Mary, we would never – Wait, can you...?
MARY. Why are you doing this to me?! Stop!
HERB. Mary, can you see me too?
MARY. No, I'm dreaming – You're not a ghost. You're – you're an actor, they've hired you...
VINNY. Mary, you know we wouldn't do that. Can you see him too?
MARY. Are – are you serious? Vinny, you can't see him?
VINNY. All I see is the four of us.
MARY. *(Taking VINNY by the shoulders.)* Vinny, I swear to God, I know where you live, I will burn down your house if you lie to me. Do you see that man, right there?
VINNY. I honestly don't, Mary.
MARY. But this isn't – This can't be...
BETTY. Okay, now I'm disappointed. <u>Both</u> of you can see ghosts??

MARY. He's right there – He's – wearing an argyle sweater, and one of those – those caps Owen always liked.
HERB. Really? He's always making fun of this.
MARY. This isn't real!
JESS. It is. Herb, Mary. Mary, this is Herb. Owen's friend.
HERB. I know you, Mary. You've been here since you were, what, six? I've seen all your performances. And this summer, I've heard all your creative curses for the ticket printer.
MARY. Oh? Like what?
HERB. I – I feel wrong saying most of them. But last week, I believe you said it was a "slut that refused to put out"?
MARY. Holy… Okay, so you're either a ghost, or a spy…
BETTY. What did he say?
JESS. We'll give you the recap at some point.
BETTY. Oh. I understand.
VINNY. They do the same to me.
JESS. So, Herb –
MARY. Where is he?
> *Beat.*

Where is Owen?
HERB. Well, there's good news and bad news. Mostly bad news, I'm afraid. He won't be around much longer.
MARY. *(On the verge of tears.)* But he just came back.
> *JESS takes her hand. VINNY and BETTY instinctively reach out to comfort her.*

HERB. So that's the bad news. The good news is, he's been granted one day, to say a final goodbye.
MARY. Goodbye…
HERB. September 18th. He'll be free for the day. You can be here, Mary. You can see him again.
MARY. I – need a glass of water…
> *VINNY dashes away to get some water. While he's gone:*

When – when he's gone… Where…?
HERB. Where does he go? Nobody knows. That's the great mystery, isn't it? Some of us think one thing, some think another. We bicker and fight. Me, I like to think there's a Heaven somewhere, a place of eternal happiness, whatever it may be. But, nobody really knows.

Maybe everything is just… invisible layers of consciousness, pulled back one at a time.

MARY. That sounds like something Owen would say.

HERB. It is.

MARY. *(Beat.)* You really know him.

HERB. I do. I know Owen very well. His talent. His passion for good, modern plays – his distaste for the true American classics… I know his tendency to always play with props, and do silly pranks. His mother's shrine dedicated to him, his father's quiet longing to see his son again. His desire to see you succeed in life.

VINNY returns with a glass of water and gives it to MARY.

MARY. Me? He talks about me?

HERB. Of course. Sometimes, I can't shut him up. Lately, though, he doesn't talk as much. He just… sits next to you – and hopes, I guess.

MARY smiles a little.

VINNY. Does he talk about me, too?

JESS. Not now, Vinny.

VINNY. Sorry. Should've known.

He "zips his lips" and goes back to painting.

HERB. He does talk about Vinny, too. But it's mostly notes.

MARY. *(Laughing, lightening up.)* He could use those.

HERB. I know. But for the sake of his confidence, tell him I think he's the greatest actor ever born. Go on. He'll love it.

MARY. Okay.

To VINNY.

Herb says you're the greatest actor ever born.

VINNY. What?! Me?! No! Me! I couldn't –

To JESS.

Did he really?

JESS. He sure did.

VINNY. Wow! That means so much. Thank you, sir. Thank you!

HERB. Gosh, he's gullible.

Laughing with MARY and JESS.

You know what Owen really wants for you, Mary.

MARY. What?

HERB. No. It wasn't a question. You know.

MARY. *(Beat.)* To act again.

HERB. Yes. And I agree. It's where you really shine. Me, I've never acted a single scene, but I've watched thousands of performances here, and I've never felt as much energy radiating from the stage as when you're up there.
MARY. Thank you. I will, when I'm ready. And the ticket printer –
BETTY. Oh, hush about that damn ticket printer. Charlie can figure it out, dear. Don't let that little thing hold you back.
HERB. She's right.
MARY. I know.
    Beat.
I'll act again. For Owen.
HERB. And remember, you don't have to take my word for it. You'll see him, we'll make sure of it. Just you two. A proper goodbye.
MARY. Thank you. September 18th?
HERB. September 18th.
MARY. I can't wait.

    MARY smiles. HERB nods and smiles back. JESS and BETTY each put a hand on her shoulder. VINNY is still riding the high of his compliments. Thousands of emotions flood the air. Lights down.

Scene 3

Ghost light up. HERB sits in an armchair, waiting patiently. He looks offstage and smiles bittersweetly. OWEN enters and looks around. HERB stands up. When OWEN recognizes only HERB is there, he addresses him with a quote:

OWEN. "Time is the reef upon which all our mystic ships are wrecked." *Blithe Spirit*, Noël Coward.
HERB. I see you've had time to catch up on your reading.
OWEN. That one's about ghosts. Thought you'd appreciate it.
HERB. I do. Good choice.
OWEN. So? She coming?
HERB. She's on her way.
OWEN. And you're sure she'll actually – not like Betty claimed, but really really…?
HERB. Yes. She'll be able to see you. And hear you. Everything.
OWEN. Can I touch her?
HERB. *(Some of OWEN's humor rubbing off on him.)* Just make sure I'm out of the room first.
OWEN. No, I mean – You know what I mean.
HERB. Well, it's probably fine, but she should be the initiator. If you hug her first…
OWEN. What are they gonna do, kill me?
   He laughs at himself; HERB allows a polite chuckle.
HERB. How are you feeling? Scared?
OWEN. No. I was, but I've got the scared out of my system. And the anger. And sadness.
HERB. What's left?
OWEN. Horniness.
   Laughing again.
And, of course, my sense of humor.
HERB. They couldn't wrestle that away, huh?
OWEN. No, sir. Hey, and while my sentimentality's still around too, I wanna say – It's been a real privilege, sharing the afterlife with you, bro. I might've preferred a team of cheerleaders at first, but now, with everything in the rearview… I'm happy with how it turned out.
HERB. That means a lot. I've certainly enjoyed having you around,

too. You never took me up on spending a winter with me, and I'm sure you regret that, but these past four summers were – well, better than the previous forty-six. Thank you, Owen.

OWEN. Yeah, we've had fun, haven't we? Oh, and at the trial – I know you couldn't have talked them out of banishment…

HERB. I tried. I really did.

OWEN. I know. But – this "final goodbye" business – thanks for negotiating it for me.

HERB. I figured the judge still had a soul somewhere, deep down.

OWEN. Yeah. I just, can't say how much I…

He suddenly embraces HERB with a big hug. He doesn't cry, but some sadness and fear are still around.

I love you, bro.

HERB. Oh. I – I love you too.

OWEN breaks the hug, but keeps HERB at an arm's distance.

OWEN. Bro. "I love you, bro."

HERB. I'm not calling you…

OWEN. I'll take you with me. I'll insist they kill you too.

HERB. That's not how the legal system works –

OWEN. Come on, man, I read a play from the 1840s for you.

HERB. Which one?

OWEN. The one I quoted. The ghost one.

HERB. *Blithe Spirit* is from the 1940s.

OWEN. Whatever. It's all the same.

HERB. Well, at least you're not claiming Shakespeare wrote it.

OWEN. Duh. Shakespeare lived in the BCs.

Before HERB corrects him.

Kidding, kidding.

HERB. I should hope so.

He puts a hand on OWEN's shoulder.

I love you, bro.

OWEN. There it is! Gotta keep you young somehow.

Another hug. During this, MARY enters from the stage door. OWEN practically throws HERB aside and runs to MARY. This hug is much bigger.

Mary! Mary, Mary, Mary! Oh, please tell me you can actually hear and see and feel this right now!

MARY. Yes, Owen! I can! You're here!
> HERB takes this opportunity to exit. As he says this, OWEN breaks his hug with MARY and turns to acknowledge HERB.

HERB. See you around, my friend. I'll keep saving you a seat.
> OWEN smiles, waves goodbye, and turns back to MARY.

MARY. Owen, there's something – millions of things, I need to say –
OWEN. I'm gonna stop you right there.
> He takes MARY and kisses her passionately.

I should've done that when I met you on the wagon ride at Ms. Zackary's apple farm when we were five years old. I should've done it when you took a dodgeball to the face in gym class in 7th grade and you were self-conscious about your swollen lip. I should've kissed you at the Fourth of July party the summer before college. I should've kissed you in the cornfield, on the trampoline, under the old bridge, at the airport, in your bedroom, my bedroom, hell, Vinny's bedroom. I wasted my entire life not kissing you. I love you, Mary. I love you so Goddamn much. I have always loved you, and I will always love you, past all forms of time. It's me and you forever, Mary! Forever!

MARY. Oh, Owen! I didn't know it until you died, but you're my everything, my fate, my destiny. There is no end of time. Whatever life is, whatever we become and wherever we go, it's together. You and me. We're meant to… Meant to…
> Slowly, her giddiness turns to sadness as she looks deeply into his eyes. OWEN doesn't register this and embraces her.

OWEN. Meant to be! We're meant to be, Mary. Soulmates!
MARY. Owen…
> He finally lets go, sensing something wrong.

OWEN. Mary? What's wrong?
MARY. Your eyes.
OWEN. What about them?
MARY. They're – gray.
OWEN. Yes. That's true. If you haven't noticed, I'm all gray. Kind of a ghost thing. Didn't you see Herb?
MARY. Yeah. It's just…
OWEN. What? What's wrong with my eye color?
MARY. They used to be so bright, Owen. Bursting with color.
OWEN. I know.

MARY. You're really gone. You're gone.
OWEN. No – I'm still here! Look at me! And yes, sure, I'm getting killed again soon, but the way I see it, if there's one afterlife, isn't it more likely there's another? And whatever that is, I'll be right here. We'll find our way back to this. We will, Mary!
MARY. Owen. You're dead. And I'm alive.
OWEN. Yes. We've moved past that.
MARY. You have. I haven't.

Beat. OWEN doesn't know what to say.

God, it's dark in here.

She turns on the full backstage lights, changing the mood.

OWEN. I would've done that, but one weird thing – we can't do anything with lights.
MARY. Yeah, Herb mentioned that.
OWEN. Look at me, Mary.

He takes her shoulders.

I know it's a lot to process. If I was in your shoes, you bet I'd be freaking out right now. When I died, it took a long time to come to terms with it. I know this isn't ideal, Mary, but... You said it yourself, we're destiny. Fate. Soulmates. Maybe I said that one. But we both know it. There's no point fighting it.
MARY. Owen, I love you. I do. I love you, so much.

Beat.

But I need to move on.

OWEN tries his best not to appear hurt.

I don't <u>want</u> to, Owen, I <u>have</u> to. You've been gone over four years, and I'm – still here. I've still got my life to live. And I haven't been living it. I'm going through the motions, distracting myself with ticket printers and backstage jobs – and while you've been gone, I have, too. I'm not <u>here</u> anymore. I'm nowhere. I need to let you go.
OWEN. Let me go? Didn't we just say...
MARY. Yes, but – I mean, what do you want me to do, Owen? Kill myself? And then kill myself <u>again</u>, not even knowing if...? Once my time comes, of course, it's our destiny to – to love each other forever, but for now – I can't do that.

OWEN knows that MARY is right. He paces around, trying to find a loophole in the situation, but he can't.

Look, I'm not against trying to communicate with you. I wish we'd figured this out sooner. God, do I wish that. But it can't be the only thing I do. I can't spend the rest of my life trying to bring you back.
OWEN. God, Mary… You're right. I know you're right. Damn it, do I hate how right you are.
MARY. I'm sorry.
OWEN. No, don't be sorry… I want the absolute best for you. Above anything else, that's what I want. And I've watched you these past four years, so I know how much you're – not <u>you</u>. You're right. You need your life back.
MARY. I'm glad you understand.
He takes her hand.
OWEN. I'm not holding you back anymore, Mary. If you need my permission to move on, here it is. Once I'm gone, this time, look forward. Only forward. I'm in your future more than your past.
MARY. That's a lot to look forward to.
OWEN. It sure is.
They embrace again, this time with a different feeling, like they're propping up each other's souls. Finally:
MARY. It's a sunny day, you know.
OWEN. Is it? I don't get outside often.
MARY. Why not?
OWEN. Nobody holds the door open for me.
MARY. Here. I'll be nice.
MARY opens the back door and they exit the theater together, then sit on the back step of the theater, feeling the heat of the late summer sun.
What's it like, Owen?
OWEN. What?
MARY. Death. Dying.
OWEN. The actual – the moment of it, or everything afterward?
MARY. Both.
OWEN. Well, I'm sure it's different for everyone, depending on what takes you. At first it was awful, the worst feeling ever, but then it was peaceful. It felt "right." Like it was always supposed to happen. Like the universe was accepting me back into itself.
MARY. And the "ever since" part?

OWEN. Pretty soon after that, I sorta "woke up," but it was more of a gradual feeling of, I dunno, becoming aware of my new self. Like how we don't remember early childhood because we haven't grown into our consciousness yet.
MARY. I don't think that's the reason.
OWEN. Or whatever the reason is. Anyway, there was an accelerated version of that, and then I was, well, what I am now. A ghost.
MARY. Was there any orientation or anything?
OWEN. Nope. You just show up, bam, no guides, manuals, nothing. Figure it out on your own. I asked around about certain things, but everyone's just as clueless as anyone else. We've all got our opinions and we argue plenty, but we all showed up with zero knowledge of the situation and we're all figuring it out together.
MARY. A lot like life.
OWEN. Yeah. I guess it is. Luckily, Herb took me under his wing and showed me the ropes. He gave me a book that answered most of my questions.
MARY. Vinny read that. He considers himself a ghost expert now.
OWEN. What?! How'd he get his hands on it?
MARY. Herb, apparently.
OWEN. Boy, I've missed a few things, haven't I?
MARY. Guess so.
OWEN. Are Vinny and Jess official yet?
MARY. Oh yeah. They're pretty serious.
OWEN. Good for them.
Beat.
Hey, you're gonna audition again, right?
MARY. I will. But – not here.
OWEN. No? Why not?
MARY. I need something new. I can always come back.
OWEN. Sure. Yeah, you deserve to branch out.
MARY. You too. Go exploring.
OWEN. Maybe I will.
MARY. And stay out of trouble.
OWEN. I'll do my best. And hey, uh, make sure someone keeps that ghost light on, alright? For Herb.
MARY. He says you all hate it.

OWEN. Most of us do. But to be honest… It's something to keep us company. Something to come back to.
MARY. So it's not for Herb.
OWEN. No. It's for me.
They smile. Beat.
MARY. Are you scared, Owen?
OWEN. Of…?
MARY. Of – whatever's next? Are you – scared that it's nothing?
OWEN. A little. I'd be lying if I said otherwise. But, y'know – there's no end of time, right?
MARY. Yeah.
OWEN. Yeah. So it'll be something. And whatever that something is, my fear is balanced by excitement.
MARY. You're very brave, Owen. Honestly. I wouldn't be able to think of it that way.
OWEN. You will. I'm sure you will.
He puts his arm around her and she leans into his shoulder. He kisses her on the head. They look out at the sunny future.
Keep looking forward, Mary.
MARY. I will. I already am.
Lights down.

Scene 4

Lights remain down. It's after the after-party of the season's closing night. VINNY and JESS sneak in, a little drunk. JESS turns the full backstage lights on.

VINNY. Why'd you turn the big lights on?

JESS. To see where we're going.

VINNY. Haven't you been here long enough to know where you are in the dark? All you do is hang out here in the dark.

JESS. Fine, I'll turn 'em off.

She does. VINNY immediately trips on something. She turns them back on.

Well, whaddya know.

VINNY. *(Collapsing on the couch.)* Okay, to be fair, my spatial awareness is zero.

JESS. That's what five shots of vodka will do.

VINNY. You said that was water!

JESS. I did say that, yes.

VINNY. You little bitch.

Over the following, JESS starts clearing things off the stage manager's desk, then joins VINNY on the couch.

How long do you think we have?

JESS. They didn't even see us leave.

VINNY. But they'll notice we're gone.

JESS. They'll assume we went home.

VINNY. Without saying goodbye?

JESS. Well, we'll have more time if you stop talking.

They are just about to start kissing when MARY and BETTY barge in from the stage door, also a little tipsy.

MARY. You were right! They did sneak off!

BETTY. I knew you two wouldn't just disappear without saying bye.

VINNY. *(To JESS.)* See? We should've covered our tracks.

They get up and tidy themselves up. JESS subtly points to VINNY's crotch and VINNY sits back down quickly.

JESS. Sorry, it's become a little tradition of ours when a show closes.

VINNY. "Go out with a bang!"

BETTY. Excuse me, that's my niece!

VINNY. Sorry, Aunt Betty. "Go out with love."
MARY. We should let them continue their tradition.
BETTY. Sure, you lovebirds have fun, now.
JESS. No, you can stay. The mood's ruined already.
VINNY. Not for me.
JESS. Hush.
> *To everyone.*

Let's all say farewell together.
BETTY. Not farewell – just "see you next year."
VINNY. Except for Mary.
BETTY. Oh, that's right. But you'll visit, won't you?
MARY. Absolutely. This is home. I'll be back.
VINNY. When you've made it big.
JESS. She'll come back with a camera crew and a paparazzi mob.
MARY. You guys really think inflating my ego will help me?
VINNY. You're right. You suck at acting.
JESS. Worse than Lorraine.
MARY. Okay, too far.
> *They all laugh.*

BETTY. So, love, do you have a plan?
MARY. I have a loose plan. I kinda want to see where life brings me.
BETTY. That's very courageous. Definitely something to do while you're still young.
MARY. I know. My whole life is in front of me. I'm looking forward, from now on.
> *VINNY has started to collect a few items, including the book from earlier.*

JESS. No sense cleaning up, babe. Just save it for next year.
VINNY. I'm not cleaning, I'm taking a few mementos. Don't we need some decorations for our new place?
BETTY. What's this? A new place?
JESS. Yeah, I was gonna tell you tomorrow, but – we're moving in together! We found a cute apartment last week, it's very… cozy.
VINNY. What she means is "small."
JESS. Yes, that's always what cozy means.
BETTY. How sweet! Y'know, Jessie, if I hadn't brought you here…
JESS. Yes, I know. Not that those were your intentions, but thanks.

BETTY. I might've had it in the back of my mind. I've always wanted you to "keep it in the theater." And you've found a good one.

VINNY. Aw, thanks, Aunt Betty.

BETTY. And you have improved so much! Your stage presence, your monologues... And you sure saved us when you stepped in for Greg in *[musical]*!

VINNY. I did, didn't I?

BETTY. Yes! And I thought you couldn't sing!

VINNY. It was all about confidence. Once Herb told me I was the greatest actor ever born, I knew I could do anything.

BETTY. He really said that?

    A look at JESS, who smirks.

VINNY. Wait – He did, right? You wouldn't lie to me.

JESS. I think I'm gonna audition next year, Aunt Betty.

BETTY. My, you're just full of surprises! That's wonderful!

VINNY. Tell her what Herb said. Tell her.

JESS. I just want to save you from having to cast Lorraine.

BETTY. Oh, thank you for that, dear.

VINNY. Damn it, Herb was joking, wasn't he? You're all a bunch of liars. That's it. I bet Mary couldn't even see him!

MARY. No, I could.

JESS. She definitely could.

VINNY. Speaking of, why haven't we talked about how both of you can see the dead?! What are the freaking odds of that? I never heard of such a thing until this summer, and now both of you can do it? Is half of humanity hiding something from the rest of us?

JESS. Don't know what to tell you. I guess it's a coincidence.

BETTY. Not for you, dear.

JESS. What do you mean?

BETTY. It's in your genes, remember? Your mother could do it.

JESS. Oh, right. How do you know she wasn't faking it too?

BETTY. She wasn't. She didn't do it to impress people. She did it to learn – about life, death, everything in between. She would do these interviews with the dead, write down their answers to this, that, and the other thing. Any question she could think of, she...

    It's dawning on her.

Oh my... Oh my goodness!

JESS. What? What is it?
VINNY. *(Revealing the ghost book.)* This book!
BETTY. Yes! That book!
JESS. Wait, you're not saying…
BETTY. I am!
JESS. Mom wrote that?
BETTY. Let me see, dear.
   VINNY hands her the book.
Is there any identifying information here?
VINNY. There's a couple pictures at the end.
BETTY. It is her! Look, pictures with the headshots! That's her!
   Double-take.
She cropped me out of this one!
JESS. I can't believe this.
BETTY. Me neither! I was wearing my cutest dress for that picture!
   Off JESS's look.
Right, and I also can't believe this is her book.
JESS. Aunt Betty, I… I want to meet her. And Dad. Their ghosts, I mean. I want to try to track them down.
BETTY. Oh, that's wonderful! Yes, yes, let's do that. You'll love your mother so much, Jessie, she's just like you.
VINNY. Another mother! And maybe I'll be able to see her too!
JESS. Probably not, but I love your optimism.
   She notices MARY has gotten quiet and contemplative.
Okay, let's give Mary some time to say goodbye, shall we?
MARY. Thank you, Jess.
JESS. We'll see you before you leave?
MARY. Yes. I'm around for the next week or so.
JESS. Okay. Well, I guess this is just goodnight.
MARY. Yes. Goodnight, everyone. Thanks for a great season.
BETTY. You too, love. Glad you figured out that ticket printer.
MARY. Just in time to get a new one next year.
BETTY. That's life. Okay, kids, let's –
   She opens the stage door and yells.
Ah! There he is! Ms. Martin's cat! Right in the front row!
   She runs out, followed by VINNY and JESS. Cat noises are heard. MARY sits alone for a moment. HERB enters.

HERB. Can you see me?

MARY. Yes. I put the elixir in most drinks these days.

HERB. I sure hope that's safe for you.

MARY. Betty says it is. Then again – yeah, I should check into that.
>
> *They both laugh.*

Thanks for everything, Herb. I didn't expect this season to go the way it did, but – I'm glad you were here to help.

HERB. Of course. I like the company.
>
> *Beat.*

You know, if you're wondering whether I think he's –

MARY. I'm not.

HERB. No?

MARY. No. Well, of course, I am. But I'm trying not to focus on it. And I – I don't need to know if he's still around. If he is, great. If not, well... I can't do anything to change it. If we're meant to connect back up, someday, I'm sure it'll happen. But for now, I've got other things to do. Things for me.

HERB. I understand completely. I'm happy you're going somewhere new. It'll be good for you.

MARY. Yeah, it will.
>
> *Beat.*

Hey, what about you? Aren't you ever gonna travel, like other ghosts? There's other theaters out there, y'know – better theaters.

HERB. No. No, I've thought about it, but I don't need to, and I don't want to. I like it here. I like the way the floorboards creak when folks try to stay quiet backstage. I like the warm buzz of the summer crowds, and the chilling silence of the long winter. I like seeing familiar faces come back, and new faces joining the fray. I like seeing the whole process, auditions to tech weeks to matinees to closing nights. I like seeing folks screw up a line and try to find their place. It's my home, and it always will be. I don't need anything else.

MARY. That's very sweet. I'll make sure to come back when I'm dead, too. Maybe I'll keep you company.

HERB. Thanks. Next year will be pretty lonely without him.

MARY. I know how that is. Keep looking forward, Herb.

HERB. I will.
>
> *They smile, saying a silent goodbye. MARY goes to leave.*

Hey, aren't you forgetting something?
> *He points to the ghost light, which is off.*

MARY. Don't you hate it?
HERB. It's not for me.
MARY. Right.
> *She turns it on, then turns the big lights off.*

See you later, Herb.
HERB. See you, Mary.
> *She exits. HERB smiles, then starts walking offstage. On the way, he runs into a piece of furniture that seems to have "jumped out" at him.*

Owen, I swear to God...
> *He shakes his head, chuckles, and exits to the dressing rooms. Ghost light down.*

END OF ACT II

END OF PLAY

The Potluck Farce

A Play in Two Acts

by

Tucker Atwood

THE POTLUCK FARCE premiered as a self-produced production at Lakewood Theater in Madison, Maine in September 2024. It was produced and directed by Tucker Atwood, the stage manager was Charlie Staples, the lighting design was by Jake Junkins, the set design was by Tucker Atwood, and the costume design was aided by Cathie Starbird. The cast was as follows:

BENTLEY..Tucker Atwood
ELLA...Bianca Stoutamyer
RICHARD...Mike Clements
KITTY..Wendi Richards
WILL..David Shedd
MINNIE...Angelina Nichols
ANDREW..Matthew Stubenrod
SAM...Jake Junkins

SHORT SYNOPSIS

Andrew, a theater director, and his boyfriend Sam, a head chef, plan out a nice night for their parents to meet: dinner and a show. However, when Bentley, a local happy-go-lucky stoner, drops by with some pot brownies left over from his family potluck, the night takes an unexpected turn. With the help of Ella, a waitress he has a crush on, Bentley must keep Andrew and Sam from finding out that not only have their parents accidentally gotten stoned, but they are also all under the impression that Bentley is their son's boyfriend. What will win: order or chaos? It's a farce, you already know the answer.

CHARACTERS

BENTLEY — 20s. Perpetually stoned and friends with everybody, or at least thinks he is. Often gets common sayings/idioms mixed up.

ELLA — 20s. Waitress who initially doesn't want to deal with anything too far past her job description.

ANDREW — 20s. Theater director who hopes to direct something other than stupid farces someday. Sam's boyfriend.

SAM — 20s. Head chef, somewhat flamboyant with a slightly dark sense of humor. Andrew's boyfriend.

RICHARD — 40s to 50s. Andrew's father, an accepting and laidback dad; when stoned: mega chill.

KITTY — 40s to 50s. Andrew's mother, caring and full of love; when stoned: wild with laughter and hunger.

WILL — 40s to 50s. Sam's father, isn't a fan of his son being gay; when stoned, incredibly paranoid.

MINNIE — 40s to 50s. Sam's mother, bickers with Will frequently; when stoned, incredibly sleepy.

PROPERTY LIST

Plates/glasses/silverware
Cell phones
Dollar bills
Drinks that look like wine and whiskey
Towels
Broom
Wallet
Duck feathers
Lots of food, including (but could be substituted): a ziplock bag full of spaghetti, a plastic container of brownies, two pies, and various other food that can be humorously thrown about the stage

COSTUME NOTES

All characters start off dressed formally, with the exception of Ella, dressed as a waitress, Sam, dressed as a head chef, and Bentley, dressed very casually. In Act 2, some characters enter after being "in the lake." They don't need to be soaked, but should look somewhat wet. Also in Act 2, most characters end up in their underwear. The amount of skin shown is up to the director and comfort of the actors. The only two who do not strip down to their underwear are Sam and Andrew, who instead each put on identical maid outfits.

SET REQUIREMENTS

The play takes place in the dining room of a small, semi-formal restaurant, with a table center stage around which most action happens. There can be more than just this one table; however, it is implied that the audience consists of "the other restaurant patrons," so it is not necessary for more than one table to be onstage. There are four doors, leading to: the front entrance to the restaurant, a bathroom, a kitchen, and a back entrance to a nearby lake. There is also a bar/counter upstage which the audience cannot see behind.

LIGHTING AND SOUND NOTES

There are three sound cues of a cell phone ringing.

At the beginning of Act 2, there is a "dream sequence," during which Bentley wanders around the stage stoned. The general idea is shifting colorful lights, along with a sort of atmospheric sound – however, I will leave a good bit of creative interpretation up to the discretion of the director. As long as it's very strange.

During the chase scene near the end of Act 2, upbeat instrumental chase music definitely enhances the chase.

MISCELLANEOUS NOTES

On acting stoned: It would be ridiculous to require actors to have personal experience with being high, but they should at least have an understanding of what it looks like. There are certain stereotypes and tropes out there, some of which are true and some are not. Familiarize yourself with these and try to make the stoned behavior as believable as possible. Directors and actors can feel free to add little moments that typify stoned behavior – losing a train of thought, laughing at nothing, etc. – but do not add anything that a legitimately stoned person wouldn't do.

The actor playing Bentley, in particular, should be careful to avoid generalized stereotypes. Yes, he is forgetful and gets words mixed up, but he is not dopey or stupid. He may accidentally frustrate others, but above all, he is friendly, happy, and agreeable. For example, his friendship with Ella – he is not a stalker or a creep to her; he is respectful when she denies him. She certainly gets mad at him sometimes, but it's the same way you get mad at your dog for peeing on the floor. She does what she can to stop him from doing similar things in the future, but afterward she can't help but forgive him and clean up his mess. Though Bentley is not your typical "hero," he is the hero of this story, and therefore should be likable throughout.

On the food fight: It is tricky for several reasons to have food thrown around the stage and onto the actors. In the first production, here are a few things we did to ensure this worked well (and it did):
- Confine the food throwing to one particular area of the stage.
- No throwing at faces, in the direction of the audience, or near the walls of the set (if there are walls).
- Give each of the parents one food item, each in a different container/dish that they will recognize quickly backstage.
- Choose foods that are visually appealing when thrown and easy to clean up. The foods thrown in our production were: dinner rolls, big leafy lettuce, spaghetti, and angel food cake dyed in several different colors.
- The food fight was blocked such that the parents entered with their food and threw it at the opposite couple. The Ella - Andrew - Sam chase then led itself through the "line of fire" during which the parents paused throwing. Ella continued through, while Andrew and Sam got between the parents and, in their confusion, grabbed food from them and threw it back at them. Since the parents were in their underwear, their costumes were fair game, while we were careful not to get food on Andrew and Sam's maid outfits. However this gets blocked, just keep the costumes, set, and cleanup in mind.

ACT I

Lights up on a small restaurant, with a table center stage where ANDREW and his parents RICHARD and KITTY are seated. They have just finished eating, though some food remains on their plates.

KITTY. Wow, Andy, my goodness, that chef of yours can really cook! Don't you think, Dick?
RICHARD. *(Mouth full.)* Mmm. Delicious.
KITTY. I don't think I could eat another bite.
    Beat.
So what's for dessert?
    They all laugh.
ANDREW. Well, I'm glad you could make it.
KITTY. We'd never miss one of your shows, sweetie.
ANDREW. I meant dinner. This really means a lot to him. Thanks for fitting it in.
KITTY. Of course! A night at the theater just wouldn't be complete without dinner. And what a fine meal! You stick with this one, Andy, you'll never go hungry again!
ANDREW. That's the plan!
RICHARD. When are we finally going to meet the lucky guy?
ANDREW. Soon, don't worry. He'll be out here to say hi before the show starts. But people are still ordering, so it might be a bit.
KITTY. Well, I'm happy enough just to meet his food. Are you finished, dear?
RICHARD. Go ahead, Kitty.
KITTY. Don't mind if I do!
    She starts picking at RICHARD's leftovers.
RICHARD. *(Gesturing toward the audience.)* If these folks are just ordering now, won't they be cutting it close to showtime?
ANDREW. I think it's just apps and drinks at this point. Nobody in their right mind would order an entree half an hour before curtain.
RICHARD. Ah. Right, so, tell us about this show we're seeing.
KITTY. But no spoilers!
ANDREW. It's impossible to spoil a farce, Mom. They're pretty much all the same.

RICHARD. Farce – what's that again?

KITTY. It's a comedy.

ANDREW. *(With contempt.)* It's like a comedy. Like a comedy that's been given roller skates and pushed toward the orchestra pit. Mistaken identities, people acting like idiots, clothes taken off for no good reason... That sort of stuff.

RICHARD. Right. You've told me that before. I love those ones.

KITTY. Me too!

ANDREW. That makes two of you.

KITTY. What do you mean, sweetie?

ANDREW. Nothing, nothing.

> *He clearly wants to go on, but wants his parents to push him to it. They don't. Beat.*

RICHARD. Okay.

ANDREW. *(Refusing to let it go.)* It's just – very silly, over-the-top. Not much substance. I want to do plays that mean something, you know? Plays that make the audience think – have an impact on their lives, start a conversation for the ride home.

KITTY. Oh, sweetie.

> *She takes his hand.*

The last thing I want to do is have a conversation on the ride home.

RICHARD. That's true. Don't do that to us, son.

ANDREW. Very funny.

RICHARD. Thank you. Maybe next time we should go to tryouts.

ANDREW. "Auditions."

RICHARD. Sure. Well, if you dislike these plays so much, why are you directing one?

ANDREW. It was assigned to me. We didn't get a choice. This chick Marci who's also new this year, she gets to direct a drama.

KITTY. Oh, I hate those.

ANDREW. I love dramas! I live for dramas! That's where the real meat of it all is. Don't you remember when I came home from summer camp and put on a one-man show of *Angels in America* in our living room?

RICHARD. I sure do. That's when I knew you were gay.

ANDREW. Was it? Well, I wish you would've told me. Would've saved me a lot of awkwardness in high school.

RICHARD. Nothing can prevent awkwardness in high school.
ANDREW. True. Anyway, I just – I'd kill to direct a drama. And Marci – she's more of a "farce director," if you know what I mean.
RICHARD. Oh, sure, yeah, we know what you mean.
KITTY. Fucking Marci.
ANDREW. No, I like Marci, it's just that – I'm sorry, I'll shut up about it. Tonight's show is fine. I'm sure you'll laugh.
KITTY. Well, I do love to laugh!
ANDREW. Yes, everybody does, Mom.
RICHARD. You know, speaking of you being gay...
KITTY. Richard, you can't just start a sentence like that.
RICHARD. Oh. I'm sorry. Uh, let's see – so, you know how we've supported you through – through, you being – when you told us that you, and we – we told you we'd always love you no matter what –
ANDREW. Christ's sake, Dad, go back to "speaking of gay."
RICHARD. Thank you. So, speaking of you being gay, and the three of us <u>always</u> supporting each other, there's something your mother and I need to discuss with you.
KITTY. Oh, Dick, not now!
RICHARD. Why not?
KITTY. There are other people around!
RICHARD. Do you think they care about our lives?
KITTY. No, but they'll eavesdrop all the same! It's what I would do!
RICHARD. So what? Kitty, the world is getting more accepting of –
KITTY. How about we chitchat on the ride home, okay Andy?
ANDREW. Sure. But I'm kinda intrigued now.
KITTY. Then you'll have to live in suspense. Anyway...
Obviously changing the subject.
Wow, what a beautiful place for a theater! Look at that lake, Dick!
RICHARD. Mmm. Gorgeous.
KITTY. And all this, right next to the restaurant where Sam just happens to be the head chef!
ANDREW. Well, that wasn't a coincidence, we came here together.
RICHARD. Whoa, too much information!

> *RICHARD laughs at himself. Beat, until ANDREW and KITTY get his joke.*

ANDREW. Dad...

KITTY. Richard!

RICHARD. Sorry, sorry. Couldn't help myself. Ahem, uh, yes that is a nice lake, now that you mention it. Ever go swimming?

ANDREW. Not yet. Too busy. And Sam says my swimming trunks are too "last season."

RICHARD has stood up and is looking out the window.

You can go check it out if you want.

RICHARD. Shouldn't we get over to the theater?

ANDREW. You've still got some time.

Pointing toward the audience.

Besides, a party of eight just came in. They'll only get drinks, but they'll hold up the show regardless. Go on, take a look around.

RICHARD. Alright. Kitty, honey, wanna go check it out?

KITTY. That sounds delightful! One second.

She's taking a couple "last" bites of their food.

Didn't have lunch today.

ANDREW. They can box it up for you.

KITTY. No, no, it's fine. Just one more bite.

She takes three more bites. RICHARD opens the back door.

RICHARD. You wanna join us, Andy?

ANDREW. Thanks, but I'm gonna pop over to the theater. I like to chat with my actors before the show starts. Sort of a tradition of mine.

RICHARD. A little pep talk, eh?

ANDREW. No, it's usually just backstage gossip and last minute changes to the blocking.

KITTY. Well, if we don't see you, break a leg! Or whatever you're supposed to say to the director.

She exits, running into RICHARD as if their blocking was changed at the last minute.

RICHARD. We support your every endeavor, Andy.

ANDREW. I know, Dad. Thanks.

RICHARD. Which is why I don't want you to freak out about –

KITTY. *(Offstage.)* Dick, you better not be telling him our news!

RICHARD. I'm not! Oh, whatever. Talk to you later, kid.

ANDREW. Alright. Enjoy the lake!

He exits. ANDREW pulls out his phone and scrolls silently until ELLA, a waitress, enters from the kitchen.

ELLA. Aww, your parents left your show before it even started?

ANDREW. Good one. No, they're checking out the lake.

ELLA. *(Looking out the window.)* Look at 'em, they're so cute.

ANDREW. They're taken.

ELLA. Dang! Well, do they wanna take the rest of this home? I can go get a couple boxes.

ANDREW. No, that's alright. Here's my card.

ELLA. Thanks. Did they like everything?

ANDREW. Yes, they said it was delicious.

ELLA. That's a relief. Sam said if they didn't like it, he would've stuck his head in the oven.

ANDREW. Jesus, Ella. That's dark.

ELLA. He's the one who said it!

ANDREW. Mhm.

ELLA. *(Clearing glasses, but not the plates.)* His parents still haven't shown?

ANDREW. Not yet.

ELLA. How sad. They hate you.

ANDREW. They don't hate me! How could they hate me if they haven't even met me? They're probably just caught in traffic. As long as they're here before the show starts, it's fine.

ELLA. Would've been nice to have dinner with them, though.

ANDREW. Yup.

ELLA. Is that why you're grumpy?

ANDREW. Are you going to ring me up or what?

ELLA. I'll take that as a yes.

> She retreats to the POS system behind the bar. ANDREW sits in silence some more, then BENTLEY enters from outside. He is carrying a plastic container of brownies and a ziplock bag full of spaghetti.

BENTLEY. Hey hey hey, Andy Dandy! Long time, no time! What's going on, bro?

ANDREW. Hey Bentley.

> BENTLEY sits at the table next to ANDREW and instinctively puts down the brownies. Over the next few minutes, he casually eats from the ziplock of spaghetti, as well as the food off ANDREW's parents' plates.

Yes, go ahead, take a seat.

BENTLEY. Thanks man. Hey, shouldn't you be gettin' into costume? Show's gonna start soon.

ANDREW. The director doesn't wear a costume.

BENTLEY. Aw, gross dude!

ANDREW. Gross?

BENTLEY. Are you gonna warn the audience before you flash 'em?

ANDREW. I'll be wearing clothes, Bentley. Just not a costume.

BENTLEY. Y'know, when you really think about it though, aren't all clothes like a costume for the soul?

ANDREW just ignores this. ELLA returns with:

ELLA. Here's your card.

ANDREW. Thanks.

BENTLEY. Hey hey hey, Ella Bella! What's up?

ELLA. Hey Bentley. You're not eating off those plates, are you?

BENTLEY. Would you prefer I put it in the bag first?

He starts tipping the plates into his ziplock bag of spaghetti.

ELLA. No no no, stop! Andy – ?

ANDREW. What? My parents don't want it.

ELLA. Still, it's not his food. It's unhygienic.

ANDREW. It's Bentley. He could drink a gallon of arsenic and still ask for the old lace.

Beat.

Nobody? Really?

BENTLEY. Oh, yeah, I get it!

ANDREW. Thank you.

BENTLEY. 'Cause of my arson charges. Good one!

ANDREW. No, that's not – you have arson charges?

BENTLEY. Legally, I think I'm supposed to say "No."

He takes the last bite off ANDREW's parents' plates and hands the last one to ELLA. She clears the table and starts to walk back to the kitchen.

Hey Ella, what time does your shift end?

ELLA. Five minutes after you leave.

BENTLEY. Hah! Not the first time you've used that one. Anyway, I was thinking, you like movies don't you?

ELLA. Everybody likes movies, Bentley.

BENTLEY. That's not true. My aunt Becky thinks movies cause cancer. And sometimes I think she has a compelling argument.
ELLA. What are you getting at?
BENTLEY. Oh, just – my cousin Trevor's got a projector-screen setup thingy in his garage and he's gonna do a movie showing tonight. The whole family's gonna be there! Well, not Trevor's side of the family, but most of Becky's side. And get this: Dirty Uncle Nick is gonna be there, and he's got over twelve movies to choose from! I'm sure we'd find one you like.
ELLA. It's remarkable how the dates you invite me on sound less and less appealing each time.
BENTLEY. Aw come on, you'd love Dirty Uncle Nick! He really gets along with beautiful young women like yourself.
ELLA. Thank you. But no.
BENTLEY. Alright, message received. Just thought I'd shoot my shot. Can't play the game without missing the net. Or something.
ELLA. ...Okay.

She exits to the kitchen. ANDREW goes back to his phone while BENTLEY just looks at him, expecting a conversation to happen. After a couple beats:

BENTLEY. Great, you?
ANDREW. Hm?
BENTLEY. Oh, I just thought you might wanna ask how my day's going and whatnot.
ANDREW. Oh... No, not really.
BENTLEY. Hah, good one. So there I am, just on my way back from the old family potluck down at the pool hall. Got third place in cornhole and second place in spin the bottle. Charley's aunt won again this year, but I don't mind 'cause she looks good for her age. Oh, I've got some potluck leftovers here if you're interested!
ANDREW. No thanks.
BENTLEY. Suit yourself.

He takes a bite of a brownie, then continues:

Anyways, I'm biking back from the pool hall and see all those cars out there in the parking lot. None of 'em cops, so here I am, checking out the scene. Oh shit, there wouldn't be any undercover cops here, would there?

ANDREW. Actually, I was just talking to two of them. They were asking about your home address.
BENTLEY. They were?!

ANDREW smirks.

Ah, haha, good one. Anyway, seeing as it's a show night, and Ella's working, and me following the vibes of the universe and all that, I figured I'd stop in, catch the show.
ANDREW. What about your cousin's garage?
BENTLEY. Oh, Trevor won't get started with that till midnight or so. He's gotta feed the dogs first.
ANDREW. It's 7:30. How many dogs does he have?
BENTLEY. You want the short list or the long one?

He laughs, but ANDREW doesn't get it.

Hey, so if I'm goin' to the show, you wouldn't mind settin' me up with one of those compassion passes, would ya?
ANDREW. Companion passes?
BENTLEY. Yeah, those. Thanks, man.
ANDREW. No, I didn't say I would –
BENTLEY. Gosh, plays are so neat, aren't they? They're like movies that don't cause cancer. I hope tonight's one of them musicals.
ANDREW. It's not a musical.
BENTLEY. You sure?
ANDREW. I'm the director. I'm positive.
BENTLEY. Right, right. Well, what's the play then?
ANDREW. It's called *Nothing On*. It's a farce.
BENTLEY. A fart?
ANDREW. Farce.
BENTLEY. Oh, with an s.
ANDREW. Well, no, it's a c.
BENTLEY. Farc?
ANDREW. *(Exasperated.)* F-A-R-C-E.
BENTLEY. Hang on, let me write that down. Don't wanna embarrass myself in front of the patrons.

As he's searching for a pen, he spills spaghetti on himself. He finds a pen in his pocket.

Oh hey, I think this is Becky's pen. Whoops. Third time this week. Okay, spell it for me again. F-A-...?

ANDREW. What are you writing it on?
BENTLEY. My arm.
ANDREW. I didn't know people did that after middle school.
BENTLEY. Oh, and what do you do, carry a notebook around with you all the time?
ANDREW. No.
BENTLEY. Then how do you keep track of stuff?
ANDREW. I remember it? Sometimes put it in my phone.
BENTLEY. I used to do that, but it was confusing getting texts from myself. "Who is this?? Why are you telling me things from my past?" You know what I mean.
ANDREW. I do not.
BENTLEY. Anyway, F-A-...
ANDREW. ...R-C-E.
BENTLEY. *(Writing it on his arm.)* Ohhh, the C-E is what makes the "s" sound.
ANDREW. Yup.
BENTLEY. Cool. Y'know, I was an English major in high school.
ANDREW. High schoolers don't have majors.
BENTLEY. Well, it was the major language I spoke.
ANDREW. That's not... You are so...

Lost for words.

BENTLEY. Yeah, tell me about it, bro. So what's this <u>farce</u> about anyhow?
ANDREW. Oh, same old same old. Stupid disguises, slamming doors, secret love affairs, that sort of stuff.
BENTLEY. Ahh, nice nice. Like a porno.
ANDREW. Well, no, not quite.
BENTLEY. But kinda.
ANDREW. No, it's more like... Oh, what's a way I can put it in your terms... You know Scooby Doo?
BENTLEY. Bro, Scooby Doo is my fucking <u>jam</u>.
ANDREW. I thought so. You know when they're chasing the villain through the old mansion or whatever, and they keep running from one door to the next, zigzagging and falling down and all that?
BENTLEY. Oh, yeah. That's the gold standard of comedy right there.
ANDREW. Sure. Well, that's what a farce is. Nothing more than

foolish, nonsensical characters chasing each other around. Goofy physical humor, nothing to think about.

BENTLEY. And sometimes they go in one door and come out another! It's like, whoa, we didn't know those rooms were connected somewhere in the background!

ANDREW. You're actually getting it more than I thought you would.

BENTLEY. Cool, man. Sounds dope.

ANDREW. Thanks. I'm sure you'll like it.

BENTLEY. Yeah, I will. I'd still rather see a musical though.

> *ANDREW just smiles painfully. After a moment, SAM emerges from the kitchen, having just finished cooking. He sneaks up behind ANDREW quietly and gives him a loving hug over the shoulders. BENTLEY takes this opportunity to go to the bar and sift through other plates of leftovers.*

ANDREW. Oh! Hey, you.

SAM. Hi, darling!

> *He kisses ANDREW's head, then sits next to him.*

Well? How did it go? Do I have to stick my head in the oven?

ANDREW. Only if you think your parents might be in there.

SAM. What? They're not here?

ANDREW. Nope.

SAM. Oh my. Well, not a worry, I'm sure they're caught in traffic. They've been absolutely <u>dying</u> to meet you! Here, let me give them a call real quick.

> *He does. While he's waiting for an answer, BENTLEY sits back down with another plate of food.*

Hey there Bentley, didn't know you'd be around tonight.

BENTLEY. Me neither, man, I just rode the wave of destiny and here I am.

SAM. I see you're enjoying my mashed potatoes.

BENTLEY. *(With his mouth full.)* Fucking <u>exquisite</u>, bro.

SAM. Save room for dessert, I just made fresh pie!

> *He puts his phone down on the table.*

Well, they didn't answer. I guess they're dead.

BENTLEY. What?! You serious, bro?!

ANDREW. No, he's not serious. He's got a sick sense of humor.

SAM. Guilty! So, where are your folks?

ANDREW. They're checking out the lake. Figured it'd kill time faster than sitting around at the theater.

SAM. *(Looking out the window.)* Oh, I see them. Ohmygosh, they're so cute!

ANDREW. I can go get them, if you want.

SAM. No no, that's fine, I've still gotta clean up, especially if we're gonna make it to the show.

ANDREW. You don't need to clean up, you look wonderful.

SAM. I meant the <u>kitchen</u>. Are you saying there's something wrong with the way I look?!

ANDREW. No, I said the exact opposite! You look great!

SAM. I know, I'm just messing with you. Boy, someone's wound up tighter than his skinny jeans tonight, isn't he?

ANDREW. I'm sorry. I just – I really want things to go well tonight. And with your parents not here yet –

SAM. Andy, baby, don't you worry. My parents will love you, they've told me a hundred times. It's annoying, actually. They keep saying they can't wait to get some 1-on-1 time with you. And if, for some reason, things don't go exactly according to plan – we'll jump off a bridge together, alright?

ANDREW. You're not as romantic as you think you are.

SAM. So killing ourselves together wouldn't be romantic? Next you're gonna tell me *Romeo and Juliet* was a tragedy.

ANDREW. It was! Look, just – no dark jokes around my parents, alright? Let's take that off the table.

BENTLEY. *(Thinking he's talking about the plate he's eating off.)* No, I'm still working on it!

ANDREW. Not you!

SAM. Okay, darling. No dark jokes. I'll be good. And my parents will be good, and your parents will be good, and you'll be good. It's allllllll good, alright? This is going to be a simple, straightforward evening, and we're all going to love each other.

ANDREW. *(Calming down, softening.)* Okay. Yes, yes, you're right. It's going to be great.

SAM. Of course.

They kiss.

ANDREW. Alright. Well. I've gotta get over to the theater and settle a few scores.

SAM. Trouble in paradise?

ANDREW. No, just the woman playing the maid wants gas money or something. Shouldn't be too big of an issue.

SAM. Okay. I'll be over as soon as the kitchen is clean. And my parents will be here too, don't you worry!

ANDREW. *(A little worried.)* I'm not worried.

SAM. Great. I love you.

ANDREW. See you soon. Love you too.

> *They depart in their respective directions, looking back at each other with a smile. BENTLEY is left by himself, still eating. Beat.*

BENTLEY. Yeah, see ya dudes!

> *ELLA enters from the kitchen and sees there are now more plates on the table.*

ELLA. Where did those come from?

BENTLEY. Oh, I saw them just sittin' on the bar, figured you wouldn't want food goin' to waste.

ELLA. *(Watching him scarf down the food.)* Thanks... You know, we have a dishwasher position available.

BENTLEY. Really? You want me to work with you?

ELLA. *(Rolling her eyes.)* No, just letting you know you could do that without the other customers watching.

BENTLEY. Oh, I don't mind.

ELLA. They do.

BENTLEY. Do they? What do they care?

ELLA. Most people don't want to eat at restaurants where stoners wander in off the street and eat the rest of their meals for them.

BENTLEY. Y'know, there's people starving in Antarctica, Ella.

ELLA. *(A small laugh.)* You're hopeless. All done?

BENTLEY. *(One last bite.)* All done. Thank you, ma'am, that was mighty delicious.

ELLA. I didn't make it.

> *Referencing the brownies.*

What's this?

BENTLEY. Oh, just some leftovers from the family potluck. Why, you want some?

ELLA. Not in a million years.
While she cleans up, she happens to toss a napkin on them.
You going to the show tonight?
BENTLEY. Guess so. Got nothing better going on. Unless you –
ELLA. No.
BENTLEY. Sure, sure. Alright then, yeah, I'm going to the show. Andy says it's like Scooby Doo.
ELLA. I don't think so.
BENTLEY. *(Reading off his arm.)* Yeah it is, it's a... farce. See?
ELLA. *(Also reading off his arm.)* You had to write that down?
BENTLEY. I write a lot of things down. You should try it! It helps me remember important things I gotta do.
ELLA. *(Reading another spot on his arm.)* This one just says "Call." Call who?
BENTLEY. *(Studying the spot.)* Aw, shoot. Sometimes I forget to put the names. Whoops.
Just then, SAM's phone rings from the table.
ELLA. Whoa. That was weird. Maybe that's them.
BENTLEY. No, that's not my phone. I think it's Sam's.
ELLA. Oh, you're right. Here, I'll go get him –
BENTLEY. *(Answering the phone.)* Y'ello?
ELLA. Bentley!
BENTLEY. *(Signaling for her to be quiet.)* No, he's in the kitchen... Oh, he's your son? Well, that must make you his parents!... Well, yes, I guess that was obvious. Sorry... Uh, yeah, I guess you could say we're friends... Special friends?... Well, I'd have to ask Sam... Aww, he said that about me?... Gee, I never knew... Oh, uh, I'm not sure, I'll have to check –
To ELLA.
What's the name of this restaurant?
ELLA. Lakeview. You've been here how long, and you don't know –
BENTLEY. Shh.
ELLA rolls her eyes and exits to the kitchen.
Yes, it is Lakeview... Well, I just wanted to double check... What do you mean, I work here?... Uh... Lady, you're not making sense. Are you going through a tunnel?... Oh, you're here?
He looks to the front door and sees them. Waving:

101

Oh, there you are! Yeah, this is me! Come on in!

> *WILL and MINNIE enter from the front door. They are dressed formally as ANDREW's parents were, but are quite obviously not as thrilled about the prospects of the evening. They enter in the middle of a small argument, spoken quietly but with immense tension.*

WILL. I'm just saying, I specifically asked you if you wanted anything from the store, and you said no.

MINNIE. It doesn't matter, Will.

WILL. Obviously it matters, if you're gonna keep acting like a –

MINNIE. We'll talk about it in the car.

WILL. Then why did you give me the silent treatment the entire way here? How are we supposed to "talk in the car" if you refuse to –

MINNIE. Shut up. Just shut up. I'm tired.

WILL. You're always tired.

MINNIE. You're always tiring.

> *To BENTLEY, professionally.*

Good evening.

BENTLEY. Howdy, folks!

MINNIE. I just spoke with you on the phone, right?

BENTLEY. I know, I know – I'm shorter in person.

> *MINNIE and WILL don't know how to respond.*

You wanna take a seat? I think Sam's just cleaning up the kitchen, he'll be out in a jiffy.

MINNIE. Sure. Thank you.

> *They sit at the table with BENTLEY. WILL extends his hand.*

WILL. William. And my wife, Minnie.

BENTLEY. *(Wiping his hand on his shirt, then shaking their hands.)* Minnie, like the mouse?

MINNIE. That's right.

BENTLEY. That's hilarious!

MINNIE. Well, it's my name.

BENTLEY. *(To WILL.)* Hey, bro, why don't you go by Mickey?

WILL. Because that's not my name.

BENTLEY. Ah, you wouldn't get it.

WILL. No, I got it. Just wasn't funny.

MINNIE. We're sorry we're late, we got caught in traffic.

WILL. And had to make two trips to the store after work...

BENTLEY. Ah, no worries! You're too late for dinner, but just in time for the show.

WILL. Yes... the show.

MINNIE. We are so – excited – aren't we, Will?

WILL. Thrilled.

MINNIE. Is it funny?

BENTLEY. *(Thinking he's asking a rhetorical question.)* Depends – do you think <u>Scooby Doo</u> is funny??

 Beat.

WILL. I'm fifty-six years old. No, I do not.

BENTLEY. Oh.

MINNIE. The show isn't... Scooby Doo, is it?

BENTLEY. No, no. It's a...

 Looking at his arm.

Farce.

MINNIE. Oh, we love those, don't we Will?

WILL. Are they still serving drinks? I need a drink.

BENTLEY. You bet! Ella should be out here soon, she can hook you up. Or, here's what I do – see that bar?

WILL. It's in plain sight. Yes.

BENTLEY. Go ahead and sneak behind it and grab yourself a cold one, on me. Metaphorically.

WILL. I don't think I feel comfortable doing that.

MINNIE. Is Sam alright with you – sneaking alcohol?

BENTLEY. Oh – no, no, sorry. I don't drink alcohol. Just fruit punch.

WILL. Are you six?

MINNIE. Will, stop it.

BENTLEY. But go ahead, Sam won't mind. You're his parents, you can get away with it. Besides, they love having drunk audiences over there at the theater. The funnier your drink, the more you show! Or something.

 ELLA enters from the kitchen.

ELLA. Oh, good evening! I'm sorry, but we're done serving dinner.

MINNIE. That's alright.

WILL. Could I get a drink, at least?

ELLA. Sure. What'll it be?

WILL. Whiskey. Straight.
BENTLEY. Ooo, that sounded cool. Like James Bond.
ELLA. *(To BENTLEY.)* Let me guess – fruit punch?
BENTLEY. *(Making a brave decision.)* No, actually. I'll drink what he's having.
WILL. You mean "I'll have what he's having."
BENTLEY. Yes, that. I'll drink his drink.
WILL. ...No, you mean –
ELLA. *(Laughing a little and rolling her eyes at BENTLEY.)* It's alright, sir, I understand. And anything for you, ma'am?
MINNIE. Oh, no thank you. One drink and I'm out like a light. We're Sam's parents, by the way.
ELLA. Oh, how wonderful! So glad you made it.
> *She briefly wonders why BENTLEY is sitting with them.*

Do you – want me to go get Sam?
MINNIE. If it's no issue, sure –
WILL. No. Not yet. We need to have a word first.
ELLA. The three of you?
WILL. Yes.
ELLA. Without Sam?
WILL. *(Trying to get rid of her.)* Whiskey, straight, thank you.
ELLA. Okay... I think we're out of whiskey here at the bar, but there's more out back.
WILL. Great, thank you. And don't come back out till we call for you. This needs to be private.
ELLA. Yes, sir.
> *She exits hastily to the kitchen, a bit terrified of WILL, who is about to interrogate BENTLEY before MINNIE cuts in with a more indirect approach.*

MINNIE. So, I... might be the only one curious, but I have to ask. How did you and Sam meet?
BENTLEY. That's what you wanted to talk about?
WILL. Well, we need to make something clear –
MINNIE. Will, please. Ease into it, remember?
> *WILL shuts up, reluctantly.*

Yes. We want to get to know you a little.
BENTLEY. Okay. Alright. How did Sam and I meet? Uhh... Let's

see... Okay, yeah, yeah. So I was passed out in a movie theater, right, credits already done, lights coming back on, like waking up from a dream and realizing you're back in "real life," y'know. And then – y'know what, I think I <u>was</u> having this weird dream – yeah, I was, like, being chased by an eagle, this giant eagle, trying to find somewhere to hide but I couldn't, he was closing in on me – I mighta been in my boxers too, it was <u>weird</u>. Huh. Anyway, where was I?
MINNIE. Um... meeting Sam...
BENTLEY. Right! So then Sam comes in and wakes me up, tells me, "Hey, kid, we're closing." Boot the scoot, scram, y'know. He was nice about it, but professional. Real swell dude, I could tell right from the start. And let's see – oh yeah, I still had a couple bites of popcorn left so I gave him the rest. He mighta thrown it away, but still – he was cool.
MINNIE. Oh... Um, wow.
WILL. I don't recall Sam working at a movie theater.
BENTLEY. No?
MINNIE. And – I guess I thought it would've been more romantic.
BENTLEY. Romantic?? Nah. Hah, that woulda been weird. Now wait a minute, I think you're right, that wasn't Sam. Now that I think about it, I think that guy's name was Doug.
WILL. So... It wasn't our son?
BENTLEY. No. Nope, that was definitely Doug. He was cool, though, as I said. Still see him around once in a while. Mostly when I go to the movies. But they cause cancer, y'know, so I try and keep my distance.
MINNIE. I see. Well...
WILL. Okay, I'm done playing nice.
MINNIE. Will, let's just –
WILL. No, Minnie. Chitchat time is over.
    To BENTLEY.
Listen – we don't like what you've done to our son.
BENTLEY. What I've done?
WILL. We raised him with good, traditional values. He was a good kid. Played sports, worked with tools, dated girls... Somewhere along the way, he strayed from the course – and sure, some of it's his fault, but it's yours too.

BENTLEY. It's my fault that he's... ?
WILL. That he's...
    Whispering, as if he's afraid to say it.
That he's gay. Yes, it's your fault.
BENTLEY. Whoa. I turned Sam gay??
WILL. Yes. But we're putting an end to it. You listen to me – we're going to get along this evening, have a fine time, for Sam's sake. But after tonight, break his heart.
BENTLEY. You want me to break Sam's heart?
WILL. Crush him. I never want him to talk about or act upon his – his – <u>sinful</u> thoughts, ever again.
BENTLEY. Gee – I don't wanna be rude to the guy.
WILL. *(Pulling out his wallet.)* How much do you want?
MINNIE. Will, no, we can't –
WILL. Is this for the best, or is it not?
MINNIE. It – well, maybe, if you say so, but this isn't the best way –
WILL. Let me handle this, Minnie.
    Handing BENTLEY a few bills.
Here. There's – two hundred dollars.
BENTLEY. Is that the going rate for heart-breaking?
WILL. Yes! Break him! Break him into a million pieces!
    Taking BENTLEY by the collar. Very intimidating.
Tell me you'll do it! Tell me you'll break him!
BENTLEY. *(Scared, willing to say anything.)* Okay, okay! I'll break his heart!
WILL. *(Letting him go.)* That's a good kid. And this stays between us, you understand?
BENTLEY. Sure thing...
WILL. Good.
    Yelling to ELLA.
Okay, I'm ready for my drink!
BENTLEY. *(Intimidated into trying to make "adult conversation.")* So uh, what do you do for work?
WILL. *(Slightly taken aback and guarded.)* Shut up.
ELLA. *(Entering, warily, with two glasses of whiskey.)* Here you go.
WILL. Thanks. Here's a twenty, that should cover it. Come on, Minnie, let's go get our tickets.

ELLA. *(Referencing the drink.)* Oh, I'm sorry, but you can't take it with you. You'll have to finish it here.
WILL. Fine.
> *He gulps it all down at once and slams it back on the table.*

Thank you, ma'am. Tell Sam we're sorry we missed him.
ELLA. Okay. I'm sure he'll at least see you at intermission.
WILL. *(To BENTLEY.)* And I guess we'll be meeting your parents then too. Hooray.
BENTLEY. *(Completely puzzled.)* My parents??
WILL. Let's go, Minnie.
MINNIE. Alright. So nice to meet you. You seem like... quite the character. Sorry for his – forwardness.
WILL. I said, let's go!
MINNIE. Okay!
> *They both exit, beginning to bicker again on their way out. BENTLEY and ELLA watch them leave. Beat.*

BENTLEY. Why didn't my parents tell me they were going to the show?
ELLA. What exactly just happened, Bentley? What were you doing having a private conversation with Sam's parents?
BENTLEY. I dunno, but I gotta write this down before I forget.
> *Writing on his arm.*

"Break Sam's heart."
ELLA. What?! Why are you writing that?
BENTLEY. That's what they told me to do. Oh wait, that was supposed to stay between me and them. Uh, nothing, Ella! Nothing.
ELLA. No, tell me. You better not have just ruined the evening. Sam and Andrew are worried enough without you screwing it up even more. What just happened?
BENTLEY. Well, to be completely honest, I'm not sure. I was telling them about the movie theater downtown, then I sorta zoned out for a second... then out of nowhere, Pops there tells me I turned Sam gay and I gotta undo it! It's like, on one hand I'm flattered, but on the other, I don't wanna break his heart! I've only done it once before, and Becky's never forgiven me.
> *He takes a drink of the whiskey, but immediately spits it back into the glass.*

107

Eugh! This shit is disgusting!

ELLA. I'm sure some key pieces of this story are missing. What else did they say?

BENTLEY. Could I have some fruit punch?

ELLA. Bentley, think!

BENTLEY. I don't know! Uhm...

ELLA. *(Sensing his uselessness.)* I'm gonna go get Sam.

BENTLEY. No! No, they said they want tonight to go well.

ELLA. How is breaking Sam's heart going to help?

BENTLEY. I dunno. I guess – I guess I must've misunderstood them. Yeah, that's probably it. Okay, that settles it. I'm not breaking anybody's heart. I won't do it!

ELLA. How brave of you.

BENTLEY. I know.

    Beat.

Fruit punch?

ELLA. Fine.

    ELLA rolls her eyes and exits to the kitchen. BENTLEY goes back to eating his ziplock bag of spaghetti until RICHARD and KITTY enter, back from the lake.

KITTY. Well, what a darling little lake!

RICHARD. Yes, very nice. We should come here more often.

KITTY. Weren't those little ducks on the shore just charming?

RICHARD. Indeed.

    Noticing BENTLEY.

Well, hello there.

BENTLEY. Howdy, folks!

KITTY. Is Andrew around?

BENTLEY. Oh, yeah yeah, well – he just went over to the theater. Said something about "actors"?

KITTY. Yes, he said he would. Oh, wait! Are you here with him?

BENTLEY. I was a few minutes ago, yeah. He'll be back soon.

KITTY. No no, I mean, are you here "with him"?

BENTLEY. *(Oblivious again.)* ...Yes?

KITTY. Oh!

    She hugs him; RICHARD pats him on the back.

It's so nice to finally meet you!

RICHARD. Welcome to the family, "son"!
BENTLEY. Uh, yeah, you too!
> *He smiles awkwardly.*

KITTY. Oh – we're Andy's parents. Sorry, should've mentioned that! I'm Kitty, this is Richard.
BENTLEY. *(Shaking their hands.)* Oh, nice, nice. Gee, you're awfully friendly!
KITTY. Yes, I'm a hugger! Sorry if I came on too strong.
BENTLEY. No, of course not. You're much nicer than these other shitbags I was just talking to. I love hugs!
> *To prove his point, he enthusiastically hugs RICHARD.*

RICHARD. Alright, bring it in! Hey, I like this guy.
KITTY. We still have a few minutes before the show, don't we? Could we sit and talk for a second?
BENTLEY. Boy, everybody's chatty today. Sure!
> *All three sit down.*

RICHARD. Well, can I just say how much we enjoyed our meal tonight. Kitty couldn't stop eating!
BENTLEY. Tell me about it, bro, I get the same way! One bite turns into ten. Haha. It's actually becoming a bit of a problem...
KITTY. Well, with food this good, I can see why! How long have you been cooking?
BENTLEY. Me?
KITTY. Yes, you!
BENTLEY. Uh, well my roommate sophomore year taught me how to make spaghetti. As you can see, I'm pretty good at that.
KITTY. Oh, you're too modest.
BENTLEY. I am?
KITTY. Yes! Isn't he too modest, Richard?
RICHARD. Sure, but humility is a great attribute, son.
BENTLEY. Thanks. Well, you know what they say, it's not the heat, it's the humility!
RICHARD. ...Yes.
KITTY. So, I know this might be too personal, and no pressure at all, but – Andy just won't tell us. How did you two meet?
BENTLEY. *(Under his breath.)* God, this shit again?
KITTY. Sorry?

BENTLEY. Nothing, nothing. Just seems like everybody wants to know all about me tonight for some reason. Okay, Andy, let's see...

KITTY. It's alright, you don't have to –

BENTLEY. It was at a strip club. Skinny Mamas, about an hour and a half from here, maybe you know it. I used to go every Tuesday 'cause it was "Half-Off Corn on the Cob" night – though they don't do that anymore 'cause of the shucking incident of '19. Anyway, so I'm out on stage with two, two and a half, maybe three corn cobs altogether, dancin' my heart out, really feelin' the grooviness of time, y'know, and WHAM! I'm tackled right to the floor! Turns out they'd warned us about not getting on the stage, and my asshole friends never gave me the memo. And y'know who tackled me? Andrew – freakin' – Mulligan! I swear to God, that's how I met him! Crazy, right?!

> *A couple moments of utter confusion pass by, RICHARD and KITTY just looking at each other at a loss for words.*

RICHARD. Um... Andrew Mulligan?

KITTY. Our last name is Kelly.

BENTLEY. Ohhhh. Andrew Kelly? Okay. Hmm. Yeah, I don't really remember where I met him.

> *Beat. Nobody knows what to say. RICHARD starts to say something, then thinks better of it and just smiles. KITTY follows suit. BENTLEY sees them smiling and figures he's doing a great job, so he also smiles. ELLA enters from the kitchen.*

ELLA. Sorry, we might be out of your fruit punch –

> *Seeing RICHARD and KITTY.*

Oh! Hello again Mr. and Mrs. Kelly. How was the lake?

KITTY. Delightful! Absolutely delightful.

ELLA. Good to hear.

> *Sensing more awkwardness due to BENTLEY.*

Do you two – have your tickets yet?

RICHARD. Yes, Andy gave them to us earlier.

ELLA. Great. Well, the show starts in about fifteen minutes. Maybe it's time to head on over.

RICHARD. *(Joking.)* Doesn't look like a fifteen-minute walk to me.

ELLA. No, but you never want to be the ones sneaking in late!

RICHARD. Yes, those people are the worst. Don't worry, we'll make sure we're on time.

A side-eye at any audience members who came in late.

ELLA. Okay. Well – let me know if you need anything!

RICHARD. Thank you.

As ELLA starts to leave, BENTLEY absent-mindedly puts his feet up on the table.

Actually – one quick question – You do background checks, right?

ELLA. Yes, we do.

RICHARD. And the traditional hiring process? Resumé, references, experience?

ELLA. Of course. Why?

She subtly smacks BENTLEY on the back, causing him to put his feet back down.

RICHARD. No reason. Just checking. Thank you.

ELLA. Alright. You're welcome.

ELLA exits, trying to hint at BENTLEY to behave. He doesn't get it and waves goodbye to her.

BENTLEY. So, you folks like movies? 'Cause my buddy Trevor's got this whole big setup in his garage...

RICHARD. As we just discussed – it's probably time to head over to the theater.

BENTLEY. Oh yeah, the show! Forgot all about it. Okay, I'm just gonna hit the john real quick, I'll meet you over there.

RICHARD. Sounds great.

KITTY. Have your parents arrived yet?

BENTLEY. Y'know, this is the second time I'm hearing of my parents being here, and they never even told me. Can you believe it? Ah well, they must've forgotten. As they say, the apple falls all the way off the tree! Or something.

He starts toward the bathroom.

RICHARD. If I could just – I know we're in a hurry, but I wanted to let you know something, son.

BENTLEY. Yeah?

RICHARD. *(Getting all sentimental.)* I just wanted to say – it's been so long since we've seen Andy this happy. He's been through some rough times, as I'm sure he's told you. High school was <u>not</u> his gig, I tell you what! We could always tell there was something different about him, so when he came out, it was so – relieving, to see him finally accept himself. And now, to see how happy you make him...

He's tearing up.

It's just, very special. Thank you for being such a bright light in his life. He really loves you, and we really appreciate it.

BENTLEY. Gee, Andy loves me??

RICHARD. Well, yes! And, son – I know, not all love is forever. If anything happens to you two, we understand, of course. But please, do whatever you can to not break his heart, okay?

BENTLEY. I wouldn't dream of it! Andy's a cool dude, I don't see any reason to break his heart.

He writes on his arm to remind himself. Sotto voice: "Don't break Andy's heart..."

RICHARD. Wonderful. Okay, go on, go on, that's enough tenderness for one evening! Sorry to blabber on to you.

BENTLEY. No worries, my dude. See ya at the theater!

RICHARD and KITTY. Okay!, Bye!, etc.

BENTLEY exits to the bathroom, taking his ziplock bag of spaghetti with him.

KITTY. What a lovely boy. Are you alright, dear?

RICHARD. I'm just – so proud of Andy. He's finally found love.

KITTY. Oh, you're so sweet. Why aren't you this sappy about me??

RICHARD. I am! I love you, Kitty!

KITTY. I know. Calm down. I love you too, you crybaby. Ooo, did they bring out dessert?

While searching for more dinner, she discovers the brownies.

RICHARD. Why's it in Tupperware?

KITTY. You saw the boy. He's sweet, but as a chef, it seems he's got a few... <u>unique</u> practices.

KITTY is about to open the container, but stops as WILL and MINNIE enter. They are quietly bickering just as before.

WILL. Well, if you wanted an aisle seat, you should've told me.

MINNIE. I did tell you, you never listen!

WILL. That crowd size is pathetic, anyway – you can practically choose any aisle seat you want.

MINNIE. Maybe I will. And maybe it won't be next to you.

WILL. If only.
MINNIE. *(Noticing RICHARD and KITTY.)* Oh, hello there. Sorry, we just forgot our coats...
KITTY. Not a worry! Did we take your spots?
MINNIE. No, it's alright.
>*Beat.*

You don't happen to know if the chef is out of the kitchen yet?
RICHARD. You mean Sam?
MINNIE. Yes, Sam.
RICHARD. We were just talking to him! He just stepped into the restroom. Wait – are you his parents?
MINNIE. Yes, we are.
KITTY. Oh!!!
>*She instinctively hugs WILL and MINNIE.*

How lovely! We're Andy's parents!
>*Everybody starts shaking hands. RICHARD and KITTY are much more genuine than WILL and MINNIE, who remain terse and professional.*

ALL. *(Ad lib.)* Hello, nice to meet you, it's a pleasure, etc.
MINNIE. Well, we sat down with Andrew just a few minutes ago.
WILL. Yes, what an... interesting boy you have.
KITTY. Oh, you saw him? I was hoping we'd see him again before the show, but... oh well. At least we finally met Sam!
RICHARD. Yes, quite a nice fellow!
KITTY. I'm sure they make a great couple!
MINNIE. Mhm.
WILL. I need another drink.
MINNIE. You do not.
>*Back to KITTY.*

Well, you know, we just want what's best for Sam.
KITTY. Same here. We just want Andy to be happy!
MINNIE. Mhm.
KITTY. Yup!
>*A long awkward pause.*

WILL. Was Andrew homeschooled, by any chance?
KITTY. No, public school. Honor roll student!
WILL. Really? That's, well – what school?

KITTY. Pleasant Hill, about an hour south of here.
WILL. And they – they teach regular classes there?
KITTY. Regular?
WILL. The required classes that high schoolers should take?
KITTY. Yes, of course.
RICHARD. Are you implying something, Mr...?
WILL. Richard.
RICHARD. Mr. Richard? How funny! My first name is Richard. But please, call me Dick.
WILL. Gladly. No, I'm not implying anything. Where's the waitress?
RICHARD. She's in the back.
KITTY. She brought out dessert, though! Anybody else still hungry?
She leads everyone back to the table and offers the brownies around. Not wanting to be rude, everybody takes one over the following.
WILL. What's with the Tupperware?
RICHARD. We thought that was strange too.
KITTY. Charming. So charming!
RICHARD. Right.
WILL. Sure. Well, I just can't wait to see how <u>charming</u> this play is that your boy directed.
KITTY. Oh, Andy is so talented. I've never seen him do a bad play!
WILL. Well, you're his mother. You're obligated to say that.
KITTY. Of course, yes, but he really is very good.
WILL. So they've let him direct before?
KITTY. Yes.
WILL. ...At theaters with – good reputations?
MINNIE. Okay, Will, that's enough. Let's all just enjoy our dessert.
With huge tension in the air, everybody eats a brownie. Nobody says a single word the entire time. Several times, they begin to say something, but think better of it. Nobody has anything nice to say, so it's best to just keep quiet. After they've all finished, ELLA enters.
ELLA. Well, I see the parents are finally meeting! Everyone being nice to each other?
WILL. Yup.
MINNIE. Of course.

RICHARD. Couldn't be happier!
KITTY. What a pleasant evening!
>*More silence.*

ELLA. Okay... Looks like they're flicking the lights over there, that's your warning!
WILL. Finally.
MINNIE. Let's go.
RICHARD. Thanks for dinner!
KITTY. And what a lovely dessert!
> *WILL and MINNIE are in a hurry to get the night over with, so they exit promptly. RICHARD and KITTY share a look, "What's wrong with them?" They almost exit, before KITTY glances out at the lake.*

Oh, Dick, look at the ducks! Let me take a quick picture. Go ahead, save my seat.
RICHARD. Alright, honey. See you in a second.
> *KITTY exits toward the lake. RICHARD exits after WILL and MINNIE. ELLA has just cleared the rest of the plates from the bar.*

ELLA. Did she say dessert?
> *She's puzzled, but shrugs and exits to the kitchen. A few moments go by with an empty stage. Finally, BENTLEY enters nonchalantly from the bathroom and looks around.*

BENTLEY. Hello? Anybody? Gee, how long was I looking in that mirror? Ah well.
> *He gathers his things from the table, including the brownies. He starts to leave, then smirks and opens the container.*

Maybe just one more before the show.
> *He takes out a brownie and almost takes a bite. He does a double take, noticing some are missing.*

Uh oh.
> *He looks around the table, under the table, under chairs, in the audience, etc., then returns. More exasperated now:*

Uh oh. This – This isn't good.
> *WILL re-enters from the front door, in a hurry. BENTLEY instinctively puts the container behind his back.*

Nothing! Nothing at all!

WILL. What?

BENTLEY. Uh...

WILL. *(Grabbing his coat off the chair.)* Don't ever get married, Andy. You'll thank me later.

BENTLEY. Andy?

WILL. Remember: break his fucking heart!

> *WILL exits, slamming the door. Before BENTLEY can grasp anything, KITTY enters from the lake.*

KITTY. Those ducks are the cutest! See you at the theater, Sam!

BENTLEY. Sam?

KITTY. Again, so nice to meet you!

> *In a hurry, KITTY exits through the front door.*

BENTLEY. Boy, and I thought I was forgetful.

> *He shrugs, then starts to think about it. We can see him connecting dots in his head. After a few seconds, it all clicks.*

Oh shit. She thinks – and he thinks – and they all think – Oh shit!

> *He doesn't know what to do with himself. He paces the room, trying to figure out what's happening and what to do, until ELLA enters. She goes to the bar and pours a glass of wine.*

ELLA. Better get over there, Bentley. Show's just about to start, and we're closing up.

BENTLEY. Yeah, sure sure. Hey, uh, Ella?

ELLA. Fine, I'll pour you <u>one</u> glass, but the rest is mine –

BENTLEY. No, not the wine – But thank you, that's very generous.

> *He doesn't know which dilemma to start with. He starts with the brownies.*

But uh... Did you... Did you eat some of my leftover potluck?

ELLA. Those brownies? Like I said, never in a million years. They're probably filled with weed.

BENTLEY. They are. That's what a potluck is.

ELLA. That is <u>not</u> what a potluck is.

BENTLEY. It is for <u>my</u> family.

ELLA. I don't doubt that.

BENTLEY. Well, did you see anybody else come in and eat any?

ELLA. No. The only other people who ate at that table were Sam's parents and Andy's parents.

> *She is about to take her glass of wine into the kitchen but*

stops, then turns around slowly.
Bentley, please tell me they didn't eat your brownies.
BENTLEY. Um...
Still searching under everything.
There's still the possibility that four pieces got lost somewhere.
ELLA. Four pieces? You're missing exactly four pieces??
BENTLEY. I may not remember everything, Ella, but I sure do remember how much weed I have at any given time.
ELLA. *(Putting the wine on the bar to avoid freaking out and spilling it. Calmly, then aggressively:)* Do you realize how completely you might have just FUCKED UP, Bentley???
BENTLEY. Well, believe it or not – it's worse.
ELLA. How could it possibly be worse????
BENTLEY. Uh, well I'm not a hundred percent on this, but I think – it's a possibility that – maybe I gave the wrong impression –
ELLA. What?! Out with it!
BENTLEY. *(Afraid of the consequences.)* Andy's parents think I'm Sam. And visa verso.
ELLA. What?! How – What – Why – I don't – I don't even know where to begin. How could that have happened???
BENTLEY. I don't know! One minute I'm meeting Sam's parents and they're asking me about Doug from the movie theater, the next minute I'm telling Andy's parents about Half-Off Hot Dog night at Skinny Mamas.
ELLA. ...There have got to be more details you're leaving out here.
BENTLEY. Maybe! I can't keep track. I've gotta be honest, Ella, I've had a couple of these brownies today.
ELLA. Oh gee, I'm shocked.
BENTLEY. You can tell?? Oh God, do you think everyone else knows? I knew everyone knew!
ELLA. This is... No. No, I'm not doing this tonight. No, I'm going home, I'm taking a hot bath, I'm drinking a half bottle of wine, I'm putting on a movie, and I'm passing the hell out.
BENTLEY. Oh, Ella, you've gotta help me!
ELLA. I can't. You're screwed. Goodnight.
She tries to exit to the kitchen, but BENTLEY pulls her back.
BENTLEY. You have to! Not for me, for Sam! And Andy! They

deserve a pleasant evening, don't they?

ELLA. Bentley, this is not my fault –

BENTLEY. I know, I know. But – don't they?? Don't they deserve all the happiness?

ELLA. *(Beat.)* Yes, they do...

BENTLEY. Please, Ella. I messed it all up. I know that. I promise, if you help get me out of this – I'll never ask you out again.

ELLA. You gonna remember that promise?

BENTLEY. Which one?

ELLA. That's what I thought.

BENTLEY. I'm kidding! But seriously – Look, I'll write it down.

ELLA. You don't have to do that –

He scribbles onto his arm, then shows her.

BENTLEY. There.

ELLA. "Do not ask Ela on a date." You know, Ella has two l's.

BENTLEY. Oh, right. Sorry.

He fixes it and shows her. She sighs reluctantly.

You're my only hope, Ella. Please.

ELLA. I can't believe I'm doing this, but... fine. I'll help. I have no idea how, but... we'll figure this out.

BENTLEY. Oh thank you thank you thank you!!!

He goes to hug her, but she stops him.

Right. Sorry.

ELLA. Mhm. Okay, first step, I'm gonna go get Sam, and –

BENTLEY. No! They can't know. They're gonna hate me forever.

ELLA. They have to know! We need to get ahead of this, alright? As soon as they see their parents, everybody will know something's up.

BENTLEY. Then we have to keep them away from each other. We gotta create distractions – destroy the kitchen, go make the actors fight backstage – burn down the restaurant – !!!

ELLA. No. No no no. We won't be able to keep this away from them. It's better to just tell them right away. Maybe they'll have an idea on how to handle the situation.

BENTLEY. But they're just gonna blame me!

ELLA. They should! It's your fault!

BENTLEY. I know, but –

SAM enters from the kitchen, done cleaning up. BENTLEY

rushes over to him.

Nothing, Sam! Everything's fine!
>*Throughout the following, ELLA is internally trying to decide whether to play along or come clean.*

SAM. Why hello to you, too, Bentley. Say, be a dear and walk me over to the theater, will you?
BENTLEY. Nah, I'm not going. I decided that, uh, I just – really hate these shows. These – "farces."
SAM. Really? You're usually laughing more than anybody else!
BENTLEY. I fake it. Truth is, I have a much more refined sense of humor than everyone else in the audience, but I laugh along so they don't feel bad.
SAM. Okay, you know your truth, I'll know mine.
>*SAM tries to get past him, but BENTLEY blocks him and stalls, trying to think of a cover.*

BENTLEY. And, um, when, if, you go over there, I recommend not sitting with your parents!
SAM. And why not?
BENTLEY. Well, you don't wanna, y'know, give away any of the plot accidentally. And then, even at halftime, y'know, you should let them, uh, think about the show on their own terms. Away from you. Very far away from you.
SAM. Hah, no, that's alright. It's a farce, God knows they don't need to think too deeply about it. Besides, Andy and I gotta meet each other's parents at some point!
BENTLEY. Sure, sure. How about next week?
SAM. Bentley, you're a hoot. No, we've been planning out tonight for a while now. Why do you care?
BENTLEY. I don't! Nah, I don't care, man. You do you. It's just that, if it were my parents, I wouldn't want to ruin their evening by, like, talking to them or whatever.
SAM. What are you on about?
BENTLEY. Who's on about what? No, I'm just saying, the court is in your balls. Or something.
SAM. Okay, honey. Whatever you say.
>*He gets past BENTLEY after all. Holding out his arm:*

What about you, Ella? Care to assist the fine gentleman?

ELLA. Well, actually Sam...
   A look from BENTLEY, pleading with all his life.
SAM. Yeah? Something wrong?
ELLA. *(Suddenly breaking down in tears.)* Sam, I need some comfort right now. My boyfriend broke up with me.
BENTLEY and SAM. Your boyfriend?
ELLA. I've been trying to keep it together, but I just can't anymore. I need someone to talk to.
SAM. Well, gee, honey, I'm really sorry to hear that.
ELLA. Can we take a walk out by the lake? I just need to get out my feelings and – and – and –
   She begins bawling, really selling it.
SAM. The lake? Now?
ELLA. Please?!
SAM. Does it have to be me? I mean, I hate to be a stick in the mud or anything, but Andy and I –
   BENTLEY writes "stick in the mud" on his arm.
ELLA. I'm just in a really bad place right now... He was my everything, I'm completely heartbroken...
SAM. I can see that, sweetie, but –
BENTLEY. I could comfort you, Ella –
   He immediately receives an elbow to the gut.
Ugh, I mean – it's too bad I'm just another lousy straight guy who can't provide any help in a situation like this.
ELLA. Sam, please?
SAM. Seriously?
   She gives her best honest heartbroken look.
Well, fine, darling, whatever you need. I'll talk with you for a few minutes... But I'll have to explain to Andy –
ELLA. Bentley will let him know, won't you?
BENTLEY. *(Still recovering.)* Yes? Yes. Yeah, I'll let him know.
   Getting out his pen and writing on his arm.
What was your boyfriend's name?
ELLA. *(Angry at BENTLEY for not picking up her cover.)* Bentley...
BENTLEY. Really?? How many Bentleys do you know –
   Another elbow to the gut.
Oof. You're really taking this hard. Okay, I'll just write "boyfriend."

ELLA. Anyway, who wants to meet somebody at a play, when you can't talk to the person next to you the whole time? And besides, you already know what happens.
SAM. Oh but I <u>love</u> already knowing what happens! But, no. It's fine. You're my friend, and I'm here for you honey! I'll just want to be back for intermission, alright?
ELLA. Okay, but I am <u>really</u> sad.
SAM. Sure. Alright, let's... go to the lake, I suppose...
ELLA. Thank you, Sam. I appreciate it so much. Be right with you.
> *SAM exits first; before ELLA exits, she goes to the bar to get her wine. Whispering hastily to BENTLEY:*

You owe me! Now just keep Andy away from us.
BENTLEY. Okay. And Ella – Sorry to hear about your boyfriend.
ELLA. I made that up, you idiot!
BENTLEY. You did?? Wow, that was good. You got me. Wait, does that mean I have to make something up too?
ELLA. I don't care, just deal with Andy!
SAM. *(Off.)* Hey wait, has anybody seen my phone, it was – ?
ELLA. *(Cutting him off.)* Yes, I'm coming! I'm just so sad...
> *She looks at her glass of wine, decides it's not enough, and brings the rest of the bottle with her too. She gives one last look to BENTLEY, then exits.*

BENTLEY. Okay... Make something up... Deal with Andy...
> *BENTLEY sits down and starts thinking, thinking, thinking... After a few moments it seems he's thinking about something else entirely and has forgotten his initial intention. He puts his feet back up on the table and laughs at some joke he's just thought of. He's totally spaced by the time ANDREW enters.*

ANDREW. Hey Bentley, Sam around?
BENTLEY. Oh hey hey Andy Dandy! What's up?
ANDREW. Well? Is he?
BENTLEY. Is what?
ANDREW. Is Sam around? I just gave the opening speech, time to head over.
BENTLEY. Oh! Sam! Oh shit, I was supposed to, um, so – let's see –
ANDREW. It's an easy question, Bentley. Is he here or did he go to the theater?

BENTLEY. No!
ANDREW. No, what?
BENTLEY. He's not here.
ANDREW. So he already went over?
BENTLEY. No.
ANDREW. Then where is he?
> *BENTLEY tries thinking of an excuse. We can see the gears turning in his head, but nothing is coming out. Long pause.*

Bentley, please.
BENTLEY. What? Have I been talking too much?
ANDREW. You haven't said a single thing!
BENTLEY. Oh. Man, was that all in my head?
ANDREW. Bentley! Where – is – Sam?
BENTLEY. Sam! Right. He's – he's... sick.
ANDREW. Sick?
BENTLEY. Sick.
ANDREW. He seemed fine earlier.
BENTLEY. Yeah it was real sudden. His, uh, kidney burst.
ANDREW. What??
BENTLEY. Yeah, it was bad. He's on his way to the hospital right now trying to get a new one.
ANDREW. A new kidney?
BENTLEY. Yes!
ANDREW. I don't think kidneys "burst."
BENTLEY. Then what am I thinking of?
ANDREW. I don't know! What was wrong with him??
BENTLEY. Appendix! Is that something?
ANDREW. Yes, it is.
BENTLEY. Does it burst?
ANDREW. Sometimes, yeah.
BENTLEY. Really? Wow, I'm good.
ANDREW. Are you serious right now?? Did Sam's appendix burst?
BENTLEY. Yes, yes it did! But he's gonna ask for a kidney at the hospital, so you better go over real quick and correct him before they put in the wrong organ!
ANDREW. That's not how – Have you ever been to a hospital?
BENTLEY. *(Pointing to his elbow.)* Once, when I broke my spleen.

ANDREW. You have no idea how the body works, do you?
BENTLEY. Nope, but we'll cross that bridge when we burn it. You gotta get yourself to the dentist!
ANDREW. Dentist??
BENTLEY. Doctor! I said doctor.
ANDREW. I don't know what to believe right now. Sam? Sam?!
> *He goes into the kitchen to check for SAM. Meanwhile, BENTLEY starts to write on his arm and stops. ANDREW re-enters.*

He's not back there!
BENTLEY. Hey, how do you spell appendix?
ANDREW. I don't have time for this! Where is Sam?!
BENTLEY. I told you, he's... uh...
ANDREW. At the hospital?
BENTLEY. The hospital, yes! They're probably opening him up as we speak.
ANDREW. Bentley, look at me.
> *He forces BENTLEY to look him dead in the eye.*

If you're lying to me, for whatever reason, there will be hell to pay. Do you understand me? This is an important night for Sam and I, and I <u>need</u> it to go well. If you have anything to explain to me, now is the time to do it.
> *Beat.*

Well?
BENTLEY. ...Tell Sam I hope he feels better!
> *ANDREW stares BENTLEY down for another second or two, then makes an exasperated noise and hurries out the door with his keys. BENTLEY takes a deep breath. Then he looks back at his hand and ponders it for a second.*

"Don't ask Ella on a date"? Gee, why wouldn't Ella want to date me?
> *He shrugs, grabs a brownie, puts his feet on the table, and takes a bite. Lights down.*

END OF ACT I

ACT II

Lights up on the restaurant about an hour later, just before intermission of "Nothing On." The restaurant is noticeably in more distress; chairs turned over, tablecloths rumpled, etc. We begin with a "dream sequence" that takes place in BENTLEY's mind. Colored lights flash all around and atmospheric sound effects are played. BENTLEY is slowly wandering around the room, incredibly stoned and grinning from ear to ear, perhaps holding one of the chairs, charting it through the room like a plane. This goes on for a while, and can even be done while people are filtering back into the theater. Somewhere within the weirdness, SAM's phone begins ringing. BENTLEY thinks it is part of his imagination. After a couple of rings, the light show stops, the sounds stop, and we're back in "real life." BENTLEY is staring at the audience, rocking back and forth, smiling. Without answering the phone, staying right where he is:

BENTLEY. Hello?
    The phone keeps ringing.
Hell-ooooo?
    The phone stops ringing.
Hm. Must've been a wrong number.
    He shrugs and continues staring, lost in thought.
If there are infinite alternate universes out there, does that mean there's one where I don't <u>believe</u> in alternate universes?... And so, that version of me doesn't believe in this version of me?? And – is he right?! Am I even REAL?!?
    He shudders, then finds an Oreo in his pocket.
Aw, sweet! Secret snack!
    He eats the Oreo and laughs at himself while WILL and MINNIE enter. They are completely zonked. WILL is obviously not feeling well, and MINNIE is almost asleep.
WILL. I don't get it, Minnie, I had <u>one</u> drink.
MINNIE. Don't lie to me, I know how you sneak. You can't sneak one by me without sneaking one by me.
WILL. ...Are you sick too? Were we poisoned?!

MINNIE. No, just tired. I need a nap.
> *She flops down right onto the table center stage. This alerts BENTLEY, who turns around, sees the couple, and jumps.*

BENTLEY. Oh, fuck! I mean – gee whiz, howdy folks – Ma'am, I don't think you can do that.
MINNIE. *(Slurring, pretty much asleep.)* Is fine, made a reservation.
BENTLEY. Right. Carry on. Hello, Mr. Uh –
WILL. You!
BENTLEY. Mr. You?
WILL. What?
BENTLEY. No, he's on second! Hah!
WILL. You poisoned me!
BENTLEY. I did?? Where did I get poison?!
WILL. You're not really a theater director, are you?
BENTLEY. Oh, right, you think I'm Andy!
WILL. Aha! You're not Andy!
BENTLEY. Um, yes I am! Professional director of theaters, at your service. How did you like my play?
WILL. It's too late, you fraud! You just admitted it! You're not here for my son, you're here for me! You're undercover with the FBI, and you're working to infiltrate my – my undisclosed business!
BENTLEY. Whoa, do you do illegal business?!
WILL. I am not obligated to say anything! I'm onto you, buddy! You'll never get a thing out of me! You just tell your – You just tell – What – what was I just saying?
BENTLEY. *(Helping WILL jog his memory.)* Uh – illegal business, alternate universes, I'm undercover with the FBI...
WILL. Aha! I knew it!
> *He grabs at his head.*

Ach! The poison! It's in my head! I gotta get this out of me. I know – I'll go make myself get sick!
BENTLEY. Wait, sir – that won't help –
> *But WILL has already run into the bathroom. BENTLEY is about to follow, but he looks out the door and sees somebody coming, so his attention turns to MINNIE.*

Uh oh. Mrs. You, hey! Wake up!
MINNIE. Hmm? Room service?

125

BENTLEY. Yes, this is room service. Here to bring you to another room! C'mon, get up!

He helps MINNIE up. She falls awkwardly to her knees.

MINNIE. Willy – where's Willy?

BENTLEY. I beg your pardon?

MINNIE. Show me Willy!

BENTLEY. *(Backing away.)* We're not that kind of room service, Mrs. You!

MINNIE. Please, call me Minnie. Where's my husband, Willy?

BENTLEY. Ohh, thank God, I thought you meant – uh, nothing, Mrs. Mouse – he's in the bathroom, running away from the FBI.

MINNIE. ...Am I dreaming?

BENTLEY. Whoa, I never considered that. Maybe.

MINNIE. I should pinch myself...

BENTLEY. Wait! What if you wake up and it turns out I never existed in the first place? I could be a figment of your imagination! Don't erase me!

MINNIE. Okay, fine. I'll stay. But this dream is – I don't feel right...

BENTLEY. You're gonna be alright, Mrs. Mouse, alright? Just ride the wave, okay? Everything's gonna be fine. Here, do it with me.

He simulates "riding the wave." She follows along.

There ya go. Ride the wave, ride the waaaaave, perfect...

MINNIE. Do – do you have something to do with this?

BENTLEY. Don't we all have something to do with everything? They say butterflies cause hurricanes, y'know. Yeah, it's called the Hurricane Effect.

MINNIE. What? I – I can't ride a hurricane...

BENTLEY. No, no, that's a completely separate anomaly.

The front door starts to open. BENTLEY has brought MINNIE to behind the bar. He lets go of her there – she's too tired to stand on her own, so she just flops down.

And here's your new room! Enjoy your review, leave a stay!

BENTLEY quickly hides somewhere as RICHARD and KITTY enter. They are the complete opposite of WILL and MINNIE – handling the situation very well. RICHARD is mega chill, just smiling and nodding. KITTY is cackling and goofy dancing.

KITTY. Hahahaha, sardines! What will they think of next?! Ahahaha, oh Dick, I feel like I'm <u>thirty</u> again!

RICHARD. It's certainly been a while, eh Kitty?

KITTY. Ahaha! Look at you. I haven't seen you this bad since that Phish concert in – in – oh, where was it?

RICHARD. Where was what?

KITTY. Phish.

RICHARD. In the lake?

>   *They both roar with laughter. BENTLEY also laughs and forgets he's hiding.*

KITTY. Sam!!! Oh, you wonderful boy, you! Did you make those brownies yourself?

BENTLEY. Oh, howdy folks – Um, I don't know what you're talking about, I'm just a – director – no, FBI agent – no, chef – yes, a chef! And I don't use any sorts of extra ingredients.

RICHARD. Oh, come on now, son. We were young once. We know what was in those brownies.

BENTLEY. *(Nervous.)* You do? Gee, I'm so sorry –

KITTY. Sorry?! Shut the hell up, we love 'em!

BENTLEY. You do? So you're – you're okay?

KITTY. Okay?! We're on the mooooooon!!!

>   *She spins around wildly. RICHARD puts a hand on BENTLEY's shoulder.*

RICHARD. You know, I think I might have a job for you.

BENTLEY. A job? Dope! Oh, uh, I will have to disclose a few misunderstandings I've had with the law...

RICHARD. Not a worry, we've all got those.

KITTY. Dick, he's already got a job!

BENTLEY. I do?

KITTY. You're a chef here! And I think I'd like to order a second dinner, I'm starving!

>   *She squeals happily and goes into the kitchen without a second thought.*

BENTLEY. Wait, I don't think Sam would want you to go in there!

RICHARD. But you are Sam.

BENTLEY. Oh, that's right. Okay, right this way! Bone appetite!

>   *He follows KITTY to the kitchen. RICHARD goes to the*

>*window overlooking the lake. He smiles mindlessly until SAM's phone rings again. Casually, RICHARD strolls over and picks it up. He fakes sobriety pretty well.*

RICHARD. Hello?... Andy! Hey there, sport, your mother and I are loving your play!... And let me tell you, that boyfriend of yours is a keeper if I've ever seen one!... Yes, he's here... No, he's been here the whole time... Hospital?? What's wrong?... Oh. No, he seems fine to me... Bentley who?... Hm. No, I don't think I've met him... Okay, see you soon!

>*He replaces the phone on the table and goes back to the window. He suddenly gets the Phish joke.*

Oh! Phish, like the band! Ahahaha. Wonder how often they go swimming. Kitty! I'm gonna go back to the lake! Let's see if I can catch myself a jam band...

>*He starts taking his clothes off, preparing to swim, as he exits to the lake. KITTY and BENTLEY enter from the kitchen, each with an entire pie and a fork.*

KITTY. *(With her mouth full of pie.)* This hits the freaking spot! Did you make this, Sam?

BENTLEY. Oh – yeah, of course! Every day! You know what they say, a pie in the sky is worth two in the hand! Or something.

KITTY. You're a riot, kid. Oh, you spilled some.

>*She flips some whipped cream onto BENTLEY's nose.*

BENTLEY. Hey, you – !

>*He catches on.*

Oh. No, you spilled some! Take that!

>*He retaliates, flinging pie toward her. They both start running around the room, flinging pie at each other, making an absolute mess. They are having the time of their lives. After a few laps, ELLA enters from the lake, furious.*

ELLA. Bentley!

BENTLEY. *(Stopping in his tracks.)* Fuck.

ELLA. Bentley, what the hell is going on in here?!

BENTLEY. She started it!

KITTY. Who's Bentley?

BENTLEY. Oh, right. Not me! He's a – a dog! A stray dog who came in and ruined the place! What terrible luck!

ELLA. I'll have you know, I just had to push – <u>our friend</u> – into the lake, since somebody didn't keep track of where all of – <u>our guests</u> – have wandered off to!

BENTLEY. ...I think the dog went this way!

He runs into the kitchen, flinging pie at KITTY as he runs by. She gets him back and they both exit to the kitchen, giggling like school children. ELLA is about to follow them and rip their heads off, but WILL enters from the bathroom.

WILL. Stay back! I'm unstable and not afraid to use it!

ELLA. Sir, it's okay, everything's gonna be alright. You were given –

WILL. You poisoned me! You're a hitman! Sorry – hitwoman!

ELLA. No, sir – I'm a waitress –

WILL. Who do you work for?!

ELLA. This fine establishment here.

WILL. No! No, no, no! You know what I mean! Who sent you?!

ELLA. *(Noticing vomit on his shirt.)* Did you get sick? Oh, gross –

WILL. – Must've been Darrell, everybody knows he's wanted my position for years, and you'd have to be an idiot not to see his angle on this –

ELLA. *(Going to the bar to get some towels.)* Let me clean you up...

WILL. – He's probably here right now, watching us. Darrell! You can't fool me! –

ELLA. *(Finding MINNIE behind the bar.)* Um, isn't this your wife?

WILL. Minnie! Darrell hasn't gotten you yet!

MINNIE. *(Standing, yawning.)* Will you two shut up? I'm trying to ride the wave here, and you're making me seasick.

WILL. Minnie, there's not much time – Darrell's got us surrounded –

MINNIE. *(Sitting casually at the table, as if they're just having their morning coffee.)* Darrell from work?

WILL. Yes, Darrell from work!

MINNIE. He seems like a nice guy.

WILL. He's not! He's gonna kill us!

MINNIE. This dream is beginning to feel more like a nightmare.

ELLA. You're telling me. Okay, listen up you two –

WILL. No! You can't trick me!

ELLA. I'm not tricking you, I'm explaining what's going on –

WILL. Lies! It's all lies!

ELLA. I haven't even begun to –
WILL. Minnie, we can't trust her!
ELLA. *(Taking WILL by the collar.)* Shut up and listen to me!
WILL, terrified, shuts up.
Thank you. Now, in case Bent – I mean, Andy – hasn't told you yet: you were accidentally given a brownie with marijuana in it. This will pass. It's not forever. You are going to be okay. This was all a big misunderstanding and you'll be feeling better soon.
Beat.
WILL. *(Incredulous.)* DRUGS?! Darrell drugged me?!
ELLA. It wasn't Darrell – and as drugs go, it could be much worse –
WILL. NO! Nothing is worse!
Taking MINNIE in his arms, as if he's dying.
Minnie, I've always loved you!
MINNIE. *(Mistaking WILL's "always" for "used to.")* Oh, Will, I used to love you too.
ELLA. For the love of God –
Shaking WILL by the shoulders.
Dude! You're not dying, okay?
MINNIE. *(Thinking ELLA is coming onto WILL.)* Hands off my husband, bitch!
MINNIE tackles ELLA but humorously can't "take her down." The two are pushed closer to the bathroom door.
ELLA. BENTLEY, GET OUT HERE!!!
WILL. Minnie, I'll help you!
He moves towards them, stumbles, and all three fall into the bathroom in a weird tangle. SAM enters from the lake, dripping wet.
SAM. Ella?! Ella, what the hell was – Oh my Lord, my restaurant!
He rushes around the room, furious at the mess, unable to fathom what's going on. BENTLEY and KITTY enter from the kitchen, giggling and eating handfuls of various food.
Bentley!
BENTLEY. Oh! Hey there Sa... Sa... Sailor! Man overboard, huh?
SAM. Bentley, tell me what's going on this instant!
KITTY. Why do they keep calling you by the dog's name?
BENTLEY. Oh right, Bentley's the dog! Wow, what a mess he's

making! Quick, I think he went that way!

He pushes KITTY toward the lake, but SAM grabs him by the arm before he can leave. KITTY exits, though, squealing with excitement at the dog chase and oblivious that BENTLEY's no longer behind her.

SAM. Oh no you don't! Sit down! Sit!

BENTLEY. *(Sitting, obediently.)* Sam, there's a perfectly good explanation for all of this. Well, it's not perfectly good. I'm sure there's plot holes.

SAM. Just tell me the truth! This whole night has gone haywire! Ella's pushing me in the lake, my restaurant is a complete disaster, there's a man acting strangely out at the lake, that woman in the kitchen, I have no idea where Andy is – there are a lot of questions here, Bentley!

BENTLEY. Yes, and they all have answers! Where shall we begin? Let's see – so sorry about Ella pushing you in the lake, bro. I think it's 'cause she secretly has the hots for me or something, I dunno, she's complicated.

SAM. One, no, she does not have the hots for you, sweetie. Two, her pushing me in the lake is the least of my issues right now!

BENTLEY. Oh, good. Then I guess we're cool?

SAM. We are not cool!

BENTLEY. Right! So, um, oh! The woman in the kitchen was a health inspector! She has to test the food by the handful.

Noticing he also has a handful of food.

And so do I. And the man out at the lake was... Actually, I honestly have no idea. Was he having a good time, or totally freaking out?

SAM. Look, I don't care. All I want to know is what you have to do with this! Go on, start at the beginning.

Noticing his phone on the table.

Is this my phone?

BENTLEY. I dunno, want me to call it?

SAM. It's not lost, it's right here. Yes, this is my phone. How long has this been here? I'm calling Andy.

He does. While he's waiting for Andy to pick up, BENTLEY goes into his explanation.

BENTLEY. Okay, let's see, start at the beginning... So this morning, I wake up around, I dunno, 8:23. Y'know, a lotta people assume I sleep in, but I'm actually a bit of an early worm. Anyway, today we had our family potluck – we rent out the pool hall once a year, twice on leap years. So I'm getting ready for the potluck, and I've got some leftover trim from last year's harvest, right, and you know how I love to cook – not that I really know how to cook, but anyway – which reminds me, if you're hiring, I've got some neat ideas – like, what if we make a cake that's as big as this room? Now that would be something. And don't worry, I've got experience too – I'm basically a step away from soup chef at my uncle's church, which is actually just a reggae shop collecting tax money off a loophole, so but – uh... where was I?

SAM. *(Sighing and putting his phone away.)* Damn it, no answer. Yeah, I couldn't care less about whatever you're saying – Just tell me where Andy is if you know anything, which I'm assuming you do.

BENTLEY. Andy, right! He didn't answer because he's... uh...

SAM. Oh, shoot. He's at the show, isn't he? God, I hope I didn't just disrupt the entire theater.

BENTLEY. *(Getting an idea.)* The theater! That's it!

SAM. What?

BENTLEY. There was, uh, an accident – one of the actors fell and broke her, uh –

    Looking at his arm.

Appendix, and now the show can't go on without a replacement. Andy needs your help! You gotta get over there!

SAM. Broke her appendix? That doesn't happen.

BENTLEY. Right, right – burst, she burst her appendix!

SAM. If you keep lying to me, you're gonna be next week's special!

BENTLEY. Aww, you think I'm special?

    ELLA enters from the bathroom, dusting herself off from the struggle with WILL and MINNIE. She sees SAM and her eyes get wide.

ELLA. Sam! I'm so sorry about –

SAM. I don't care, honey, it's fine. Just tell me where Andy is! Bentley just spun this bullshit story –

ELLA. It's true! It's true! Whatever Bentley said is true.

SAM. Okay then – what happened, hm? What did Bentley tell me?

    BENTLEY is behind SAM, doing charades to ELLA.

ELLA. There was a... a crash? An accident? Mhm... In the parking lot? No, no – the theater? Yes. An accident at the theater – someone's stomach was hurt – no, their... heart? Lung? Kidney?
BENTLEY. *(Coughing.)* Appendix!
> *SAM turns around and BENTLEY shoves food into his mouth nonchalantly.*

ELLA. Appendix! Yes – an actor's appendix burst, and now you need to... to go dress up – to go get in their costume, and go cover for them! Yes, that's what happened!
> *BENTLEY gives a big thumbs up.*

SAM. ...Ella, have you gotten into Bentley's brownies?
ELLA. As much as I regret it, I'm completely sober.
BENTLEY. And so are your parents!
SAM. What? I didn't say my parents –
BENTLEY. Good, now get to the theater! You're about to have your shining moment on the stage! Lights, komodo, action!
SAM. I don't have the patience for any more of this. Fine. I'm going to the theater and looking for Andy. If you two don't clean this up by the time I'm back, I'm going full *Sweeney Todd* on your asses.
ELLA. Understood.
BENTLEY. Not understood, but go on. They need your help!
ELLA. Break a leg!
> *SAM exits in a huff.*

BENTLEY. Boy, is it just me or are we nailing this?
ELLA. It's just you. Okay, genius, get over to the theater. And go the back way so Sam doesn't see you.
BENTLEY. Why?
ELLA. You've gotta get an actor out of the show! Otherwise, our cover is blown.
BENTLEY. How do I do that?
ELLA. That's for you to figure out. I need to clean up. God, look at this place...
> *Fiddling around in his pocket, BENTLEY finds the $200 that WILL had given him earlier.*

BENTLEY. Whoa, when did I get all of this cash?
ELLA. That's perfect! Pay an actor to get off the stage!
BENTLEY. I dunno – Would an actor really put a performance in

jeopardy over... two hundred dollars?
ELLA. They don't get paid, I'm sure they're open to negotiations. Just sneak backstage and find the first one you can bribe.
BENTLEY. Wow, you're playing dirty! I like it!
ELLA. Yeah well, I don't.
BENTLEY. I bet you kinda do.
ELLA. Maybe a little. Now get out of here!
BENTLEY. Right. I've got a show to disrupt! Wish me a broken leg!
He exits out toward the lake.
ELLA. I already was.
She goes to the kitchen, opens the door, and sighs loudly at the state of things. Reluctantly, she goes in to start cleaning. RICHARD and KITTY enter from the lake, both dripping wet and in their underwear.
KITTY. Wooooo!!! Dick, I've never felt so alive!
RICHARD. Phish... is a band.
KITTY. Hahahaha!!!
RICHARD. Well, shouldn't we head back over to the theater at some point?
KITTY. For Andy's little play? No, I couldn't possibly focus on that right now. We'll catch it tomorrow. Oh, let's go dancing!
RICHARD. Where would we go dancing?
KITTY. Right here! Let's stand on the tables and dance like when we were young!
RICHARD. Be careful! How about a drink first?
He saunters over to the bar and checks out the selection while KITTY starts climbing onto the table.
KITTY. Yes, please, I am parched! My mouth is so dry, that whole lake wouldn't be enough to satisfy me.
RICHARD. I could be enough to satisfy you. Hehehe.
KITTY. Oh, Dick! Yes you could! Now that's an idea!
She gets off the table and runs to RICHARD. She embraces him warmly and passionately.
Dick, let's make secret love like when we were young!
RICHARD. Kitty, we could get caught!
KITTY. Yes, we could! How exciting, hmm?
RICHARD. (*Lowering her behind the bar, where the audience can't*

see them.) Here Kitty Kitty Kitty...
> *Over the following, their legs can be seen writhing around on the ground behind the bar. WILL and MINNIE enter from the bathroom, dazed and confused. WILL keeps looking in all directions nervously, while MINNIE's eyes are barely open.*

MINNIE. This is the craziest lucid dreaming I've ever...
WILL. Minnie, don't say anything. They've got this place bugged. I can't prove it, but I have reason to believe Darrell's got a $50,000 hit out on me! Look at all this. This isn't a restaurant, it's all fake! It's all just a carefully crafted <u>set</u> of some sort, designed to trap me!
> *MINNIE has fallen asleep at the table.*

I'm warm. God, is it hot in here or is it me? I'm so sweaty. Minnie, they've turned up the temperature to weaken us! Well, joke's on you!
> *He begins removing his clothing.*

I can handle the heat! Bring it on...
MINNIE. *(Briefly waking up.)* Yes, honey, you're right. They don't respect you at work. I know.
> *She drops her head down again.*

WILL. I need to get out of here. It's like a sauna. You can't trap me forever, Darrell! I'll show you! I'll exit your stupid set, you'll see!
> *He exits to the lake, screaming for freedom's sake.*

MINNIE. Yes, dear, two scoops of sugar, thank you.
> *After no answer, she picks her head up and notices he's gone.*

Oh, thank God.
> *She puts her head back down and goes immediately to sleep. ANDREW enters, out of breath, and starts looking around – though he does not see his parents' legs behind the bar.*

ANDREW. Sam?! Sam, are you here?
> *He notices MINNIE at the table and sits across from her.*

Excuse me, ma'am?
MINNIE. *(Lifting her head.)* Huh?
ANDREW. Have you seen the chef?
MINNIE. You have very pretty eyes.
ANDREW. Um – thank you – ?
MINNIE. But they're... too small for your face.
> *She closes one eye and reaches toward his face, trying to change her perspective.*

Just gotta zoom in on 'em –

ANDREW. Are you okay, ma'am?

MINNIE. Yes, fine – just dreaming.

ANDREW. You're not dreaming.

MINNIE. Tell that to your eyes.

ANDREW. Please, just tell me –

> *BENTLEY enters from the lake, laughing at a joke he's just thought of.*

BENTLEY. Oh man, I gotta tell that one to Trevor! He's gonna – Andy! Shit!

ANDREW. Bentley!

> *He races over to BENTLEY and takes him by the collar.*

Tell me what's going on, or you'll be the first person ever beat up by the gay kid!

BENTLEY. Okay, Andy, look –

MINNIE. I thought you were Andy?

BENTLEY. Oh, right! I am!

ANDREW. No, this is Bentley. I'm Andy. Who are you?

MINNIE. I'm – Who am I?

BENTLEY. She's just a very tired patron, and Bentley's the dog, and – what's that, I think I hear him barking! This way – here, boy!

> *He starts to run, but ANDREW stops him. MINNIE gives up on this conversation and goes back to sleep.*

ANDREW. No! Stay, boy!

BENTLEY. Yeah, I figured that wouldn't work twice. Oh wait, it didn't even work the first time...

ANDREW. Look – you're going to have to explain this whole comedy of fucking errors that's happening, but right now I only care about one thing – where is Sam?!

BENTLEY. He's, uh – Oh shit, where is he? I just saw him...

> *He reads something he's written on his arm.*

Right! The theater! There's been an accident at the theater!

ANDREW. Does it involve Sam? Because if not – I don't care!

BENTLEY. Yes, I'm sure it involves Sam somehow! Except right now I can't quite remember.

ANDREW. You're gonna remember, if it's the last thing you do!

BENTLEY. *(Panicking.)* Gosh, you're strong. Okay – right, yes – the

maid, from your play! Mrs. Crackett!
ANDREW. Clackett?
BENTLEY. Clockett, yes! She – all of a sudden – came down with a terrible case of stage fright! You'll have to play her part, 'cause she won't go on with the show! Oh, and at what cost! Somewhere around two hundred dollars, haha – Sorry, you wouldn't get that –
ANDREW. What are you talking about?! Are you being serious?
BENTLEY. No, I'm being Shirley! Hah!
ANDREW. Bentley, for Christ's sake, be clear with me – am I down an actor or not?
BENTLEY. I think so? Man, I was just over there, you'd think I'd remember – I'm feeling awfully forgetful tonight – Have you seen my spaghetti?
ANDREW. No – look, is Sam at the theater or not?
BENTLEY. Pretty sure, yeah!
ANDREW. Okay... If I can just find him, I'm sure we can figure out what's going on.
Noticing something out the window to the lake.
Is that man fighting a duck...?
BENTLEY. Yeah, the lake association ranger guy is here! Anyway, bye bye, good luck – I mean, broken legs!
ANDREW. *(Heading toward the front door.)* God, of all the nights for this to happen, it has to be when my parents are here – I hope they're at least having a good time...
BENTLEY. *(Noticing RICHARD and KITTY's legs behind the bar and quickly running over the stand in front of them.)* Yes, I can assure you, they're having a wonderful time!
We hear moaning coming from the parents.
ANDREW. What was that?
BENTLEY. Mmmmy stomach! I'm starving!
ANDREW. You're never starving.
BENTLEY. Hah! You got me there!
ANDREW shakes his head and exits.
Boy, that was a close one. Wait – if Sam is at the theater covering for Mrs. Brackett, and Andy is doing the same thing...
Beat, then a chuckle.
Heh, that'll be funny.

MINNIE. *(Stirring slightly.)* But you're Andy.
BENTLEY. Right, thanks for the reminder. And Bentley is the dog. I gotta write this down.
MINNIE. I didn't hear any barking.
BENTLEY. He only barks at dog frequencies.
MINNIE. Then how did you hear it?
BENTLEY. I'm half dog. Spiritually, at least.
MINNIE. Can I be half sloth?
BENTLEY. Half dog, half sloth?
MINNIE. No, half human.
BENTLEY. That's three halves. I may not have paid much attention in math class, but I know there's four halves in a quarter. No, four quarters in a half dollar. No, uh – What were we talking about?
MINNIE. Bedtime.
> *And she's conked out again. KITTY, happily exhausted, looks up over the bar.*

KITTY. I need a snack! Stay right there, and keep that "blindfold" on. Don't try anything new without me!
> *She stands awkwardly and stumbles toward the kitchen. To BENTLEY:*

Hey Sam, thanks for covering for us.
RICHARD. *(Unseen.)* I thought he was Bentley?
KITTY. That's the dog, Dick. Keep up.
RICHARD. *(Unseen.)* Dog?
BENTLEY. Dog dick?
KITTY. Anyway, thanks kid. Sure, it wouldn't have been the first time Andy's walked in on us, but it's best to save the embarrassment. He doesn't like it when we act all – <u>young</u> like this!
BENTLEY. Hey, I get it. I hope I'm still banging behind bars when I'm your age!
KITTY. Still? Honey, you gotta start first. Oh, burn!!! Hahahaha.
> *She roars with laughter at herself and exits to the kitchen.*

BENTLEY. Good one! Haha.
> *Once KITTY is gone.*

Man, if I don't find love soon, I'll grow old alone. And then I'll die.
> *He's sad for a beat, then finds his spaghetti under the table.*

Hey, there's my spaghetti!

ELLA. *(Entering, dragging KITTY with her.)* No no no! I just cleaned back there, I don't need you torpedoing the place again!

KITTY. Aw, just one more pie!

ELLA. No! You've had enough!

KITTY. *(Pointing out the window to the lake.)* What's that?

ELLA. Nice try, but you can't –

KITTY. No, I'm serious! There's a man out there, fighting the ducks! Wait – Sam, that's your father!

BENTLEY is distracted by his spaghetti.

ELLA. Sam, she's talking to you.

BENTLEY. Me? Right! My father! Um, no worries – he's just talking to them about life insurance.

KITTY. No he's not! He's chasing them around! Look, he's tearing out the feathers! I'LL SAVE YOU, DUCKIES!!!

She runs out the door to the lake. ELLA and BENTLEY watch silently out the window, and react accordingly as if KITTY and WILL are dueling with the ducks. Beat.

BENTLEY. Want some spaghetti?

ELLA. No, I want to go home and pretend like none of this ever happened.

BENTLEY. Oh, come on. Isn't this fun?

ELLA. This is your idea of fun?!

BENTLEY. This, and laser tag. C'mon, admit it, you're having fun!

ELLA. *(Beat.)* Okay, a little bit.

BENTLEY. Aha! I knew it. Hey, so I was wondering –

ELLA. No! Read your hand! "Don't ask Ella on a date"!

BENTLEY. No, not that. I respect boundaries. I was just wondering – if you could time travel, when in history would you go?

Beat. ELLA has no idea how to handle BENTLEY.

ELLA. Come on, Doc, let's get cleaning.

She exits to the kitchen. BENTLEY follows after her.

BENTLEY. Because if I could time travel, I'd go back to when we first started making dogs our pets, and I'd start teaching them English right away – that way, we'd be able to talk to them by now. I've been trying it with Trevor's dogs, but it's too late – dogs these days have already given up on talking. We gotta go back to the beginning...

He exits. MINNIE lifts her head up and sees she's alone.

MINNIE. Finally. Where was that bed...?

> *She wanders back to behind the bar. She sees RICHARD's legs and pauses.*

'Scuse me, is this bed reserved?

RICHARD. Kitty? I haven't moved an inch. Come, Kitty – Let me make you purr...

MINNIE. Sure, why not?

> *She shrugs and joins RICHARD behind the bar. Now it's their legs we see writhing around together. WILL and KITTY enter from the lake, covered in duck feathers.*

WILL. I don't care who sent you – it's gonna take more than a flock of ducks wearing wires to get my secrets!

KITTY. My goodness, you're a mess. Listen – nobody is out to get you! You're being paranoid!

WILL. That's exactly what someone out to get me would say!

KITTY. And where are your clothes?

WILL. I could ask you the same question!

KITTY. I was getting laid, not chasing ducks!

WILL. My God, where are my clothes?

KITTY. *(Finding WILL's pants nearby.)* What do we have here?

WILL. Hands off! There's private information in my wallet! No – I've given myself away! Give me those pants!

KITTY. Well, now I'm intrigued!

> *She reaches into the pocket of the pants and pulls out WILL's wallet. He chases her around the room, slipping on the water and food spilled all over, as she looks through the wallet.*

Let's see – Driver's license!

WILL. You can't prove anything!

KITTY. A credit card!

WILL. I'm holding it for a friend! I don't know anything about it!

KITTY. And a coupon to the Ice Cream Shop!

WILL. That's a classified document!

KITTY. *(Pulling out a ten dollar bill.)* Ooo, a tenner! Could you lend me this?

WILL. Give it back!

> *During the chase, RICHARD and MINNIE poke their heads above the bar to see what's going on. MINNIE's clothes have*

also been removed. They look at each other, look away, then double take.
RICHARD. AHH! You're not Kitty!
MINNIE. Do you want me to be?
KITTY. Dick! I told you not to move!
WILL. Minnie?! They've captured you!
He runs up to the bar and approaches RICHARD.
RICHARD. Now hold on, Mr. – ?
WILL. Richard!
RICHARD. No, I'm Richard.
KITTY. Dick, and Mr. Dick!
MINNIE. And I'm Minnie.
KITTY. So are they!
RICHARD. Good one, dear.
WILL. Shut up!
To RICHARD.
You slept with my wife!
RICHARD. No, she slept with me!
WILL. Do you work for Darrell?
RICHARD. I've got a friend named Darrell, but that's probably a coincidence.
KITTY. I slept with a Darrell in college.
RICHARD. But that was Darrell Mulligan.
MINNIE. Darrell Mulligan? Me too.
WILL. There's another Darrell?
MINNIE. Wait till you hear about the three Brads.
RICHARD. My brother's name is Brad.
MINNIE. I thought you looked familiar.
To WILL.
Boy, does he take after his brother.
Beat. WILL lunges at RICHARD, who darts away before WILL can get to him. RICHARD runs around the room and then out the door to the lake, followed closely by WILL, MINNIE, and KITTY, all in their underwear and shouting incoherently. Everything is peaceful for a moment, then ELLA and BENTLEY enter from the kitchen.
BENTLEY. No no no, I said if, note: if, dogs could time travel. I'm

141

not saying they can, although I've never seen any evidence they can't, but that's a whole different story. My first instinct would be to say no, they probably can't, but I saw this interesting video about what really happened on 9/11, and it really changed the way I approach the time traveling dog dilemma. Did you know –

ELLA. The Renaissance.

BENTLEY. What?

ELLA. I'm answering your question. The Renaissance.

BENTLEY. Why would a dog go to space? I didn't say he had, like, space helmets or anything.

ELLA. I'm saying, if I could time travel, I'd go to – I'm sorry, do you think the Renaissance is a planet?

BENTLEY. Are you saying it's not?

ELLA. The Renaissance was a time of rich culture and scientific progress in 1500s Europe.

BENTLEY. Oh. Well, I wasn't a European major in high school.

> *ELLA shakes her head in tired amusement and looks around the room.*

ELLA. God, every time I come in here, it's more of a mess. Here, let me get some towels and a broom.

> *She gets these items behind the bar.*

BENTLEY. And I'll take a fruit punch.

ELLA. No you will not. You don't deserve one.

BENTLEY. *(Sadly.)* Yes ma'am...

> *They begin the lengthy process of cleaning the dining area.*

ELLA. So, genius – you know Andy and Sam are going to need an explanation for everything tonight. Do we tell the truth?

BENTLEY. We've gotten this far without it. You know what they say, if it ain't fixed, don't break it.

ELLA. Then what do we tell them?

BENTLEY. It'll come to me.

ELLA. No, we need something planned out.

BENTLEY. Do we? Ella, hey, leave it to me. I got us into this mess, and I can get us out.

ELLA. Your specialty seems to be getting us further into trouble.

BENTLEY. Yeah well, y'know, sometimes you have to dig a hole deeper in order to get out.

ELLA. I can't picture a single scenario where that's true.
BENTLEY. Don't you believe in me?
ELLA. No.
BENTLEY. Why not? We've spun some pretty clever hijinks tonight, haven't we?
ELLA. Is that all you're calling it? Hijinks?
BENTLEY. You're having fun, remember?
ELLA. No, I'm – Sure, maybe, but mostly, no. I'm exhausted and stressed the fuck out and I just want to be home, taking a bath and sipping wine.
BENTLEY. Oh come on, you do that every night. Once in a while, you've gotta live a little! Where's your sense of adventure?? Have you ever had such a wild and crazy turn of events as what we've gone through tonight?
ELLA. No... Thank God...
BENTLEY. Isn't life so freaking boring sometimes?
ELLA. What do you mean?
BENTLEY. *(Throwing down his broom for emphasis.)* Life is boring! You know? You eat the same breakfast every day, go to dumb meetings you hate, go to bed each night exhausted and unfulfilled. And you've been doing it for so long, time feels bizarre and unreal, months go by in a blink – nothing new means the brain doesn't get stimulated, and you're so bored of waiting, breaking your back for your paychecks, buying groceries and doing laundry and wishing you were skydiving or on a roller coaster or hanging out with a dog. And you say, maybe someday – and you say it to yourself for years, years and years, and you say it about everything: Maybe someday. You distract yourself from the gray dull world you live in by dreaming all day about a bright shining hypothetical future, where you've made it, you're a success, you've worked your way to the top and you take jiu jitsu lessons and you've learned how to speak French and you climb mountains and write books and – but that's all "Maybe someday," and it'll never actually happen. It'll just give you enough hope to keep you complacent and distracted from your boring ass life where you have not made it, and you never will! Don't we all deserve, then, to just fuck around once in a while? Get some strangers stoned and pretend you're their son's boyfriend? Run around hiding them from

their kids? Isn't this a more memorable night than any of the other tens of thousands of nights you'll live? Isn't that why we live – to make every moment special? Is it? I honestly have no idea. Maybe I'm wrong. Maybe I'm all wrong...

Beat. ELLA starts to smile.

ELLA. No. You're not wrong. I mean, a lot of that seemed like your own personal problems being projected onto me and everyone else. But no, you make a good point somewhere in there.

BENTLEY. Really?? I made a good point?

ELLA. Yes. You've got a lot more going on up there than it seems, Bentley.

BENTLEY. What was it I said? I sorta blacked out just now. Here, let me write it down.

ELLA. Make every moment special.

BENTLEY. I feel like I said a lot more than that, but yeah that rings a bell. "Make every moment special."

ELLA. And y'know what – you're right. This has been a pretty fun night. I never want to do anything like this ever again, not in a million years, but it's fun. It's almost like being in one of Andy's plays.

BENTLEY. Yeah, a fart.

ELLA. Farce.

BENTLEY. *(Beat.)* That's it!

ELLA. Yes. Eureka.

BENTLEY. No, no! I have a plan! Well, not a plan, per se, but an explanation.

ELLA. You do? What is it?

BENTLEY. Can't talk, I gotta write it down before I forget.

ELLA. You're just writing the word "farce." And you misspelled it. There's a c, not an s.

BENTLEY. Oh, thanks.

ELLA. ...And it was already written right here. You could've just underlined it or something.

BENTLEY. Oh yeah, you're right. I'll just draw an arrow between the two. And just so there's no confusion, I'll put the word "life" above them.

ELLA. That, I'm sure, will add confusion. Why "life"?

BENTLEY. Because, Ella. Life is a farce.

He looks out the front door.
Okay, here goes nothing. It's die or do time.
He grabs ELLA's hand, comforting her. She doesn't pull back.
Trust me. I'm the master of chaos.
ELLA. I know. Somehow, I do trust you. You can do this.
BENTLEY. I love you.
ELLA. N – No – No...
BENTLEY. Sorry. Misread that. Okay, here they come!
ANDREW and SAM enter, both dressed as maids and furious. BENTLEY and ELLA try not to laugh.
ANDREW. You! You lying, scheming, idiot!
SAM. You've humiliated us for the last time!
ELLA. Looks like you did that yourself.
SAM. Stay out of this!
BENTLEY. Fellas, howdy howdy! So, what happened at the theater?
ANDREW. We both went on as Mrs. Clackett!
SAM. Nobody knew what the hell was going on!
ANDREW. We had to play it off as "twin maids"!
SAM. Saying the same lines! Twin maids with telepathy!
ANDREW. And when I tried to improv, Sam couldn't help me out!
SAM. I've never acted before! I'm sorry!
ANDREW. He ended up apologizing to the audience! Completely broke the fourth wall!
SAM. And they gave me pity applause! It was humiliating!
ANDREW. *(To BENTLEY.)* I don't know what you did, but you ruined our show, our evening, our parents' evening, God knows where they are... You've ruined everything, Bentley!
BENTLEY. Okay, okay, let's calm down... first of all, let me just say, that sounds like an absolute riot. It's a farce, right? Nobody cares if it doesn't make sense here and there. And breaking the fourth wall, everyone loves that! Right, [name of stage manager]?
STAGE MANAGER. *(Popping head onstage.)* That's right, [name of actor playing Bentley]!
BENTLEY. You see? If I was in the audience for your show, I would've given it a standing ovation!
They move in closer to him, threateningly.
And – and if I was in your show, y'know what I'd say right now?

ANDREW. What?

BENTLEY. *(Scooby Doo impersonation.)* Ruh roh, Raggy!

    The chase scene begins. Throughout, feel free to add figure-8 movements, door slams, and other farce tropes to the chase. BENTLEY runs into the kitchen, followed by ANDREW, who gestures for SAM to follow ELLA as she takes BENTLEY's cue and runs out the front door. Once they've all left, the parents enter from the lake. WILL has RICHARD in a headlock while KITTY and MINNIE are hitting each of them from behind, without much force. They all circle the room a couple of times, then their struggle takes them into the bathroom. BENTLEY re-enters from the kitchen and runs to the lake, followed by ANDREW. ELLA re-enters from the front door, followed by SAM, who grabs at her shirt and rips it off. She exits to the kitchen, closely followed by SAM. The group of parents re-enter from the bathroom, this time with MINNIE and KITTY grabbing each other's throats and WILL and RICHARD trying to separate them. WILL pulls KITTY away and RICHARD pulls MINNIE away. Everything stops for a moment as the two husbands swap their wives back. Then they all chase each other out the front door. ELLA enters from the kitchen and BENTLEY enters from the lake. BENTLEY sees ELLA without a shirt on and instinctively also takes his shirt off. ELLA runs into the bathroom, followed closely by BENTLEY. SAM enters from the kitchen and ANDREW enters from the lake. They meet up and silently wonder where the others are. ELLA enters from the kitchen (wait, those rooms are connected back there?) followed by BENTLEY. They see SAM and ANDREW and run back into the kitchen. SAM and ANDREW follow. The parents return from the front door, this time playing monkey in the middle with WILL's wallet. The game takes them into the kitchen. BENTLEY enters from the bathroom, sees his bag of spaghetti nearby, and fashions himself a spaghetti wig as a disguise. He sits at the table with his head down, hiding. ELLA, SAM, and ANDREW enter from the bathroom and chase each other around the room, none of them realizing

BENTLEY is sitting there. The parents enter from the kitchen, throwing various food at each other. In the midst of the chaos, the parents start throwing food at their own kids and pretty soon everybody is in their underwear and throwing food at each other. ELLA stands on a chair center stage and stops everything once and for all.

ELLA. Enough!!! Everybody, stop!
Everyone takes a moment to breathe and recover.
ANDREW. Bentley, what the hell is going on??
BENTLEY. *(Thinking his disguise is working, with a lower voice.)* Uh, I think he went that way!
SAM. Don't be stupid, we know it's you.
BENTLEY. Dang, you guys are good. Okay then –
He starts applauding enthusiastically.
Bravo! Huzzah! Hurray! Great show! Woooooo!!!
To ANDREW and SAM.
Okay, okay, I'm sure you two are wondering what's going on here tonight. Well, you see, all of your parents just <u>loved</u> Andy's play, uh, farce, so so much, that they decided to create, rehearse, and perform their very own farce! Yeah, all this running around and stripping and food fighting, it's all been carefully planned and perfected – that's why we've been trying to keep you away from your parents all night, to give them time to rehearse! You just saw the opening of, uh, "Sam and Andy's Parents Do a Farce After Seeing Andy's Farce and Being Really Proud of it, So Much that they Decide to Perform Their Own Farce as a Thank-You Present!" It's a working title. A farce to celebrate all farces! Ta da!
Beat. Nobody knows what to say.
...And we would've gotten away with it too, if it weren't for you meddling kids!
ANDREW. Bentley...
BENTLEY. Yes! And their dog!
SAM. Sorry honey, but – we don't believe you.
BENTLEY. No?
ANDREW. Not a single word.
BENTLEY. Oh. Which word should I have changed?
SAM and ANDREW step threateningly again to BENTLEY.

Why – Why don't you believe me?

SAM. You've been lying to us all night.

ANDREW. And you've ruined everything.

BENTLEY. Besides that.

RICHARD. *(Stepping in, to BENTLEY:)* Kid, let me handle this. You've done your part. Now it's time they know the real truth.

ANDREW. Dad, stay out of this...

RICHARD. Andy, remember your mother and I had something we wanted to discuss with you before the show?

ANDREW. Sure.

RICHARD. Well, here it is: Kitty and I are starting a dispensary. Now before you say anything, just know we've put a lot of time and effort into this process already, and we are confident we'll succeed. What happened here tonight was, we tested a few of our samples. And these folks, they wanted a sample too – doesn't seem like they handled it as well as we did, but that's my fault and mine only. We all just wanted to have a little fun at your show, that's all. We obviously went a little overboard, and we humbly apologize.

To BENTLEY.

Sam, I'm sorry we did this to your parents. They seem like very kind folks, and we didn't mean any harm.

Beat.

BENTLEY. You still think I'm Sam?

RICHARD. What?

SAM. ...I'm Sam.

RICHARD. You're – you're the one with Andy?

SAM. Yeah – You're Andy's parents?

KITTY. *(Hugging him warmly.)* Welcome to the family, other Sam!

ANDREW. *(Regarding WILL and MINNIE.)* Wait, then, are these your parents?

SAM. Yes. Mom, Dad, this is – Mom, wake up!

MINNIE, who had fallen asleep standing up, jumps awake.

Mom, Dad, this is Andy.

MINNIE. How do you do?

She dozes off again. ANDREW shakes her limp hand, then turns to WILL, who is still freaking out and has no idea what's going on.

WILL. Who do you work for?! Tell me! Did Darrell send you?!
ANDREW. No, sir – I'm dating your son.
WILL. Well, stop it! Get out of his life! You've ruined him!
ANDREW. Okay, this just took a different turn.
SAM. Dad, what are you – ?
WILL. You can't indoctrinate me! You can't make me accept this – this unnatural freak show! You're all fake – just a bunch of actors!

> *Beat. ALL except WILL turn to the audience, shrug, and return to scene.*

Darrell must've hired you, didn't he?! I'm onto you and your games! You'll never get my job, Darrell! You'll never get anything out of me! Minnie, now's our chance, run!

> *Without looking back, WILL runs out the front door, yelling in pure rebellion.*

MINNIE. Okay, see you at home.

> *Beat.*

Boy, say what you will about him, but he sure takes his job seriously for a vacuum salesman.
RICHARD. ...As you all can see, one of the side effects of our products is paranoia. We'll work on that.
ANDREW. *(Relieved.)* Dad – are you serious? You're starting a pot shop? Is that all that's been going on tonight?
RICHARD. Yes. I swear to you, that's all.
ANDREW. You're stoned right now?
RICHARD. Incredibly stoned, yes.
ANDREW. You're hiding it well.
RICHARD. Just like we did your entire childhood.
KITTY. Dick, he doesn't need to know that! Ugh, now that'll be a conversation on the ride home...
ANDREW. And – how is Bentley involved?
BENTLEY. Yeah, how am I involved?
RICHARD. This is Bentley? I thought Bentley was the dog.
KITTY. The dog never existed. Keep up.
RICHARD. Right. Um, Bentley is – is going to work for us. Isn't that right, kid?
BENTLEY. Really? Well, I don't really believe in the concept of "working," but if there's weed involved, then... sure! Y'know what

they say, do what you love and you never work a day in your life! Hey, I think I got that one right. Really hit the nose on the nail there.

RICHARD. So, Andy – I'm sorry for our behavior tonight. It's nobody's fault but ours. Please forgive us. We'll come see the show again tomorrow, clean as a whistle and sharp as a tack.

BENTLEY writes this on his arm.

ANDREW. Okay. Yes, I forgive you.

To SAM.

I feel bad about your dad, though...

SAM. Oh, please. I always knew he resented me for being gay. I'm glad it's finally out. But now I'll need somewhere else to live...

ANDREW. *(Almost too quick with it.)* Live with me! Please! Let's find a place together!

SAM. Yeah, darling? You sure you're ready for that? We're not gonna kill each other?

ANDREW. I've never been more ready for anything else. Besides, your cooking every single night? Yes, please!

SAM. Oh, I'm gonna spoil you rotten!

ANDREW and SAM hug. KITTY and RICHARD look at their son and new "son-in-law" with happiness.

ALL. Aww...

BENTLEY. We're like one big happy family!

ANDREW. Stay out of this.

BENTLEY. Right. Sure.

SAM. Okay, everybody, go find your clothes for heaven's sake. We're in public. You monsters.

Everyone looks at each other and registers they're all still in their underwear. They all scatter, ad libbing and locating their missing clothes. They all re-dress over the following.

My goodness, this place is a mess.

ELLA. Don't worry about it. Go home and get some rest, you lovebirds. This place will be sparkly clean in the morning.

BENTLEY. Aw, that's nice of you, Ella.

ELLA. You're going to be here too, Bentley.

BENTLEY. Oh, right. Yeah, I'm gonna make this place as clean as –

Sideways glance at his arm.

– as clean as a tack and sharp as a whistle! No, wait – as muddy as a

stick in the heart and a farce in the appendix! No, uh...
>*Trying to decipher what's written all over his arm.*

RICHARD. Hey, Andy, is your play still going? How about we go check out the end?

ANDREW. No no, it's okay. It really drags at the end once they stop running around in their underwear. Boring, cheesy, unrealistic ending. Trust me, you won't like it. Let's just go home and pretend tonight was a crazy wild dream.

MINNIE. *(Briefly waking up.)* Pretend?

SAM. Mom, I'll drop you and Dad off at home, but then I'm spending the night with Andy.

MINNIE. Fine. Don't tell your father.

SAM. I don't care about his opinion anymore.

MINNIE. Welcome to the club.

ANDREW. Wait – I just realized, Mrs. Clackett comes back on in the end! I've gotta get over there!

SAM. Oh, can I do it??

ANDREW. Are you kidding? You hated being onstage!

SAM. I can do better this time! The whole two-maids thing confused me, and when you started to improv, it threw everything off.

ANDREW. Me?! I didn't throw anything off!

SAM. I had the script in my hands, I knew what to say!

ANDREW. But we couldn't <u>both</u> say those lines!

SAM. Right, so let <u>me</u> do it!

ANDREW. It's my show!

SAM. Don't you love me?! Let me be the maid! Give me a chance!

ANDREW. No! I'm the maid!

SAM. I'm the maid!

>*They both exit quickly, racing each other over to the theater. The remaining parents follow after, curious to see what will happen. RICHARD gives BENTLEY a wink and a thumbs-up, while KITTY is sneaking out as much food as possible. Finally it is just BENTLEY and ELLA.*

ELLA. Alright. You all get home safe now!

BENTLEY. Well. As they say, all's well when ends smell!

ELLA. Something like that. I guess it <u>did</u> all work out.

BENTLEY. And I didn't have to figure out whose heart to break!

He scribbles those parts off his arm.
ELLA. Andy's dad really saved your ass, there.
BENTLEY. Yeah, he did. Just for that, I'm gonna share my secret spaghetti recipe with him. He won't regret hiring me!
ELLA. *(Starting to clean up.)* Man, look at this place.
BENTLEY. Looks like a good old family potluck happened here. If these walls could talk, huh?
ELLA. Hey, you got another one right.
BENTLEY. Yeah well, even a clock breaks twice a day.
ELLA. Y'know, you were right earlier too.
BENTLEY. Everything earlier, or just one thing?
ELLA. Just one thing.
She points to the phrase on his arm.
"Make every moment special." You were right.
BENTLEY. Huh. How about that. Yeah, yeah – make every moment special. Take notice, be present, do weird shit. These are my mottos.
Pronounced "mow-toes."
ELLA. I kinda like them.
BENTLEY. Yeah?
ELLA. Yeah. You gotta get some order into that chaos though.
BENTLEY. Maybe you need some chaos in your order.
ELLA. Maybe I do.
She finds another spot on his arm and crosses out one part.
BENTLEY. "Ask Ella on a date." Wow, that was smooth. When did you write that on my arm?
ELLA. You did, ya moron!
BENTLEY. Wow, I need to work on my penmanship. Oh, so uh, oh God I'm never good at this. Ella, do you – When I – And you – And when you – Do you – And, would you – When we –
ELLA. – Yes, I will go on a date with you. <u>One</u> date.
BENTLEY. Sweet! Think we can get out of here by midnight?
ELLA. Probably. Why?
BENTLEY. You're gonna love Trevor's garage! He's got it set up like a mini movie theater, but with tons of dogs! And Becky's making her famous artichoke pudding, and Dirty Uncle Nick – well, I'll make sure he keeps his distance. And if you see any mice, don't make eye contact. Oh, also –

ELLA. Y'know, Bentley, that really wasn't what I...
> *Beat. BENTLEY is so happy, she can't turn him down.*

Oh, what the hell. Sure, let's go to Trevor's garage thing.

BENTLEY. Oh yeahhh! Dang, this is so awesome. Hey, thanks for helping me out, Ella. Tonight would've been a total shitshow without you. Like wheels on hell.

ELLA. I know.

BENTLEY. *(Starting towards the kitchen.)* Okay, let's get cleaning, or we'll miss the previews!

ELLA. Bentley?

BENTLEY. Yeah?

ELLA. *(Smiling.)* I had fun tonight. I really did.

BENTLEY. Ella – the fun is just beginning!

> *He smiles and exits. ELLA watches after him for a second, then shakes her head chuckling. Her eyes fall on the table and under a napkin, where the brownies are. She looks back to the kitchen, back to the brownies, shrugs, and opens the container. She takes a small bite out of one of the brownies, replaces the lid, and exits into the kitchen. Lights down.*

END OF ACT II

END OF PLAY

Dance Again

A Play in Two Acts

by

Tucker Atwood

DANCE AGAIN premiered with the Belfast Maskers in Belfast, Maine in May 2022. It was produced by Meg Nickerson, directed by Tucker Atwood, the stage manager was Cassidy Small, the sound design was by Dominic Williams, the set design was by John Bielenberg, and the costume design was by Meg Nickerson. The cast was as follows:

```
BILLY.................................................................Scott Taylor
HELEN............................................................Robyn Tarantino
MAJOR JACK..................................................Andre Blanchard
MAJOR JOHN...................................................Jared Nickerson
DENNIS............................................................Tucker Atwood
LUCY.................................................................Autumn Stupca
LOUIE....................................................................Chris Hayes
SIMON..................................................................Erik Perkins
```

SHORT SYNOPSIS

A snowstorm forces soldiers from both sides of a war to seek refuge from a sweet aging couple living on the border of the two nations. As the hosts attempt to keep the soldiers from learning each other's affiliations, it becomes clear the couple is more involved in the war than expected.

CHARACTERS

BILLY — 50's to 60's. A caring and lively man, married to Helen. He was once a soldier but now lives a simpler life. He has seen plenty of bad in the world, but is somehow still optimistic. Loves telling stories.

HELEN — 50's to 60's. A thoughtful and compassionate woman, married to Billy. They met in the war as soldiers when they were young. She is generally upbeat, but gets a bit nervous in dangerous situations.

MAJOR JACK — 30's to 40's. A no-nonsense soldier and leader of Dennis and Louie. He considers himself a fighter, but also shows signs of a fun-loving side.

DENNIS — 20's. A quiet, attentive soldier who does not belong in the war. He is Louie's older brother and is in charge of him.

LOUIE — late teens to early 20's. A clumsy, foolish soldier who always finds a way to get hurt.

MAJOR JOHN — 30's to 40's. Another no-nonsense soldier and leader of Lucy. Very similar to Major Jack in appearance and personality.

LUCY — 20's. A reserved, strong-willed soldier who also does not belong in the war. She has attempted to escape in the past but has never been able to pull it off.

SIMON — 20's to 30's. A deceiving soldier, unaffiliated with the others.

PROPERTY LIST

Radio
Five guns, two of which with gloves "stuck" on
Five knives
A paperweight and/or other knick-knacks
Potatoes, half-unpeeled
Three bottles of whiskey
Seven shot glasses
A checkers set
Plates, utensils
Two ears of corn on the cob (cooked, or at least shucked)
A piece of cloth
Rope
Two notes on folded up paper
A bandana (script says purple; color could be changed)
A lantern
First aid kit
Ice, or a towel that could be "holding ice"
Six mugs

SET REQUIREMENTS

All of the scenes take place in the living room of an old rustic cabin. It is a fictional world, but one that could very well be real. There is no specific time period, but the cabin should appear to be from around the early to mid 1900's (no modern technology). The room is centered around a sofa and a coffee table. There is at least one other chair in the room. Other furniture and decorations are recommended but not required. There are four entrances and exits: outside, a kitchen, upstairs, and a basement. A staircase to the upstairs is not necessary, but could be included.

SOUND NOTES

At the beginning of each of the six scenes there is a short audio clip of an instrumental song, preferably songs that sound like they're from the 1940s or 1950s. Following each is a short recording of one or two voices on the radio.

COSTUME NOTES

The soldiers enter wearing uniforms. The colors of the uniforms are arbitrary. In the script it says "Blue" or "Red" but as long as the soldiers from opposite sides are wearing different colors, it doesn't matter. Once they've changed out of their uniforms, they all change into clothes owned by Billy and Helen, so their clothing for the remainder of the play should be similar to Billy's or Helen's clothes.

At the end of Act 2 Scene 2, Billy enters after a bear attack. This should be apparent somehow; perhaps a rip in his shirt and a bloodied shoulder or arm. In the transition between scenes, a sling or bandage should be put over his arm to show he has been "mended."

MISCELLANEOUS NOTE

A noted distinction between the Eastern soldiers and Western soldiers is the manner in which they eat corn on the cob. When the script mentions eating the corn "vertically" or "horizontally," this is the direction they eat the corn, not the way they are holding it. For example, eating the corn "vertically" means taking one bite, moving up, then taking another bite; it does not mean the corn is being held vertically. That would look very strange and out of place; the real distinction is meant to be subtle.

ACT I

Scene 1

Lights up on a rustic, comfortable living room in an old cabin. HELEN and BILLY, a sweet aging couple, are slow dancing to an old, instrumental, romantic song. It is clear that they have been together for a long time and have seen all facets of love. As the music fades out, BILLY and HELEN embrace while the RADIO ANNOUNCER's voice comes through the radio, very soft and important.

RADIO ANNOUNCER. ...A lovely little tune to start off the hour. It is now five in the afternoon local time, with the sun nowhere in sight. This is just a reminder that nobody should be traveling tonight due to what some are calling the "Snowstorm of the Century." Hundred mile an hour winds coming in from the north, with gusts from the east and west colliding and making quite a mess. Be careful out there, folks.
    BILLY and HELEN have settled down from their dance and now listen offhandedly while catching their breath.
Now in reference to last night's Battle of Turtle Cliffs, it appears the western army has gained the upper hand. Joining me now to discuss is Secretary James of the western nation.
JAMES. Good evening, sir.
RADIO ANNOUNCER. Now, what are your updates on Turtle Cliffs?
JAMES. Well, sir, last night the eastern army attempted to capture Turtle Cliffs. However, our soldiers, specially trained and perpetually alert, were able to successfully hold off the threat.
RADIO ANNOUNCER. The area remains under western control?
JAMES. Undoubtedly.
RADIO ANNOUNCER. How many casualties, if you had to estimate—
    BILLY shuts the radio off. He and HELEN sit down and rest for a moment.
BILLY. They don't play enough music.
HELEN. Oh, they used to.
BILLY. *(Thinking.)* No, they never have.
HELEN. What are they going to do, ignore it?

BILLY. No, 'cause then the war'd stop, and all those smart voices on the radio—
HELEN. —would lose their jobs, I know.
> Beat.

It wasn't always this bad. With the radio, I mean.
BILLY. Nope. Used to just be in the newspaper.
HELEN. Not that we'd read any of it.
BILLY. I did.
> Beat.

Y'know, me and my father—
HELEN. Oh, shut up about your father.
BILLY. I always try, but I never can.
HELEN. *(Beat.)* So, what are we having for dinner?
BILLY. *(Standing up and putting a foot on the coffee table, like a triumphant warrior.)* The blood of our enemies!
HELEN. *(Laughing.)* Oh, stop it.
BILLY. But, dear maiden, I must save you from the evils of the east!
HELEN. Like I'm the one who needs saving. What are you trying to do, finally put that knee out of its misery?
BILLY. Well, you keep refusin' to shoot it for me.
> *Settling back down, grabbing at his knee.*

So, let's see… We've got plenty of potatoes, don't we?
HELEN. We should.
BILLY. Potatoes and corn, then?
HELEN. Tonight, potatoes and corn. Tomorrow, blood of our enemies.
BILLY. There's the soldier I know. You gonna eat your corn the right way this time?
HELEN. Oh, you know you're the one who does it wrong. I can't see how anyone can eat their corn vertically.
BILLY. Blame my upbringing, I guess.
> *There is a sudden knock at the door. BILLY and HELEN look at each other in shock, wondering what to do. Whispering:*

Get in the kitchen.
> *She hurries to the kitchen but remains in the doorway. BILLY calls out nervously:*

Who is it?!
> Beat.

MAJOR JACK. *(Off.)* M-m-my n-name is M-major J-j-jack, s-s-s-sir. M-m-my m-men and I h-h-have b-been w-wandering around lost—
HELEN. Oh, he's freezing, Billy! Let him in.
> *BILLY rushes to the door and hesitates. He turns and gives HELEN a quick kiss, then goes back to the door. He takes a deep breath and opens it. Standing there are three men in blue military uniforms: MAJOR JACK, DENNIS, and LOUIE. They are pointing their guns at BILLY, but are also shivering and desperate to get out of the cold.*

BILLY. Well, howdy howdy how's it goin', boys? Bit of a chilly evenin', ain't it?
> *The men remain in shivering silence.*

Now, we sure would like to keep you warm tonight and make friends with you, so long as you put those weapons down 'round my wife, if you don't mind.
> *Their weapons slowly move down.*

Thank you. Come on in, and wipe those boots off. We're just about to get some potatoes and corn going. I'm sure you fellas wouldn't mind that, would you? We certainly wouldn't mind the company, gives us someone to watch the storm with. Please, fellas—
> *The three men have entered and BILLY has closed the door behind them, but their weapons are still held at the ready.*

—No battles goin' on in here, you don't have to worry. Just put 'em down.
MAJOR JACK. S-s-sir, m-my m-m-men and I h-have b-b-been g-given orders t-t-to—
BILLY. Well, I'm givin' you different orders. Trust me, I'm qualified. Leave those guns at the door, boys, and your only orders will be to come downstairs and sit by the woodstove with me and my wife. How's that sound? Potatoes and a warm fire, how 'bout it?
> *MAJOR JACK gives DENNIS and LOUIE silent permission, then looks back to BILLY. Slowly, MAJOR JACK lowers his shivering weapon to the floor, dropping it with a dull thud. DENNIS follows suit. LOUIE, trying desperately not to shiver too much, drops his gun on his foot. He starts jumping up and down in pain.*

LOUIE. Ahh G-G-Gaaahd, d-damn it, s-s-s-s-son of a b-bitch—

162

MAJOR JACK and DENNIS give LOUIE a look, like this shit happens all the time.
BILLY. Thank you, fellas. You alright there, son?
MAJOR JACK. H-he's f-f-fine, s-sir.
LOUIE smiles through obvious pain.
BILLY. Alright. Now, you must have knives on you. Let's have those on the floor too.
They hesitate, but reluctantly pull knives from their ankles and throw them on the floor as well.
Great. Well, now's we're all friendly, my name's Billy. This here's my wife, Helen.
HELEN. Nice to meet you.
MAJOR JACK. *(Offering a shivering hand.)* M-M-M-Major J-Jack. Th-these are m-m-my m-men, D-D-Dennis and L-Louie.
BILLY. *(Shaking all of their hands.)* Jack, Dennis, Louie. Nice to have you here, fellas.
MAJOR JACK. M-M-Major, s-sir.
BILLY. What's that?
MAJOR JACK. M-m-my t-title is M-M-Major—
BILLY. Oh, no titles here. No misters, majors, minors, lieutenants, doctors, jesters, whatever. I'm Billy, you're Jack.
MAJOR JACK is slightly offended but keeps quiet.
Hey Helen?
HELEN. *(Wary of the soldiers.)* Yes, dear?
BILLY. Could you get started on the potatoes while I show our friends upstairs? Maybe some coffee too? You boys like coffee?
All three nod enthusiastically.
HELEN. Sure, I can do that. I…
BILLY. What is it?
HELEN. Oh, Billy, I just…
BILLY. Just give us a second, fellas. Go ahead and take those uniforms off, they must be soaked.
BILLY leads HELEN out of earshot of the soldiers. While they are having this conversation, the three men begin taking off their uniforms. LOUIE's arm gets stuck in one of his sleeves and he requires DENNIS to help get it out. MAJOR JACK looks on with pity. BILLY and HELEN are whispering now.

Yes, I know. I know all your concerns right now, love.
HELEN. It's not concern, it's just… Oh Billy, what if they came here to hurt us? Or kidnap us? Or something?
BILLY. I know. I know. What if? Well, what if they're just simple humans tryin' to survive a brutal snowstorm?
HELEN. They could be, yes. But they're—they're wearing blue, Billy—
BILLY. I'll be okay.
HELEN. But won't they see something? Up there?
BILLY. It's all hidden away. They'd have to go diggin', and they wouldn't. Helen, love, these fellas are here for one thing: to still be here tomorrow. Doesn't matter what color they wear, they'll be sleepin' here tonight, warm and full of potatoes.
HELEN. Okay.
BILLY. Trust me. You know you can.
HELEN. I know I can.

> *Beat.*

So what can I do to help?
BILLY. Feed 'em! Trust me, you feed these fellas your famous potatoes and corn, hell, they'll see no point in the war. They'll all be goin' back east tomorrow skippin' along like schoolboys.
HELEN. I could do that.
BILLY. I know you can.

> *He kisses her and turns back to the trio.*

Great. Now, fellas, let's head on upstairs. Don't you worry, I've got plenty of warm dry clothes you'll all fit into—

> *Noticing MAJOR JACK's bulky frame, or LOUIE's small frame.*

Well, you can try anyway.

> *BILLY starts upstairs, the trio shuffling along behind.*

You know, my grandfather built this cabin when my father was a kid, 'bout nine or ten, he'd have him runnin' 'round here gatherin' wood and throwin' tools up to the roof and down again. Built it all in one summer, well, most of it that summer, still worked on the upstairs here into the fall…

> *He trails off as they all exit upstairs. HELEN looks up after them with forced optimism.*

HELEN. Oh, I sure hope this doesn't end up like last Christmas.

> *She moves toward the kitchen but stops at the weapons on the floor. She checks upstairs again, then turns back to the weapons with a solemn look. She recognizes them. She picks up MAJOR JACK's gun and examines it. She handles it, points it, etc.; it is obvious she has experience with it. Suddenly, there is another knock on the door. HELEN freezes, gun in hand. She looks upstairs as the knocking intensifies. She considers calling BILLY downstairs, but decides to handle the situation on her own. She pushes the other two guns and the knives underneath the sofa with her foot, then cautiously approaches the door. There is one more desperate knock. She takes a deep breath and opens the door, ready for anything, gun pointed straight ahead. Standing in the doorway are MAJOR JOHN and LUCY, pointing their own weapons right back at her. There are a few moments of understood terror before HELEN breaks it:*

Are you two looking for a place to stay warm tonight?

> *Still holding their weapons, MAJOR JOHN and LUCY silently nod in frozen pain. A few seconds pass as everyone considers the situation. HELEN really doesn't want to invite them in, but she feels compelled to. Finally, she puts her weapon down and steps aside.*

Well, what are you waiting for? Get in here. Wipe off your boots.

> *As MAJOR JOHN and LUCY enter, HELEN is taken back to see they're wearing red uniforms. This is clearly a potentially disastrous situation. HELEN does not stop them, though. She is nervous, but trying her best not to show it.*

What are you two doing, looking for a cold? Well, you found it! Come on in, drop your weapons at the door. First thing we'll have to do is get you out of those clothes, those uniforms must be soaked.

> *MAJOR JOHN and LUCY have entered but are still holding their guns.*

Oh, can't you put those damn things down for a night? Go on, like this.

> *She hesitates, but decides that she trusts them and places the gun she'd been holding on the floor. MAJOR JOHN and LUCY attempt to copy her, but they can't seem to get the guns out of their hands.*

MAJOR JOHN. M-m-ma'am, I th-think they're fr-frozen t-t-to our g-g-gloves.

HELEN. Oh my. Here, let me help.

> *Carefully, she approaches MAJOR JOHN and reaches for his gloves. He naturally wants to pull back, but allows her to slowly grab one glove and pull it off his hand. She repeats the other hand and stands there, holding a gun with two gloves frozen onto it, almost laughing. MAJOR JOHN holds his arms as if he's still holding the gun.*

Well, how's that for disarming?

> *LUCY cracks a smile, but MAJOR JOHN does not.*

Oh, I'm just kidding. Sorry. Here, let me…

> *HELEN repeats the process with LUCY's gun. She puts them all on the floor and pushes them under the sofa with her foot.*

There. Oh, I'm sorry, I haven't introduced myself. I'm Helen.

> *She sticks out her hand before realizing that a handshake won't work well. She waves awkwardly instead.*

MAJOR JOHN. M-M-M-Major J-John.

HELEN. Please, let's be friends. No majors, minors, any of that. My husband, Billy, he's upstairs, I'm sure he's got some clothes you could both fit into. You gentlemen just get those uniforms off and we'll—

> *LUCY pulls off her hat, revealing that she is a woman.*

Oh! I'm sorry. Well… I'm sure I've got some clothes for you, too, sweetie. What's your name?

LUCY. L-L-Lucy, m-ma'am. Th-thank you s-s-s-so m-much.

HELEN. Oh, it's nothing. I hope.

> *There are footsteps coming downstairs. MAJOR JOHN and LUCY are still partially in uniform and HELEN panics.*

Actually, before you get changed, I need to show you the kitchen. Quick, right in here. We're making potatoes, actually, maybe we can, uh—What are your favorite spices?

> *HELEN ushers MAJOR JOHN and LUCY into the kitchen as BILLY leads the three men downstairs. They are in new clothes and appear happier and warmer. As they get to the bottom of the stairs, LOUIE stumbles on the last stair and falls into DENNIS, who gives him a look. MAJOR JACK is only listening to BILLY.*

BILLY. …then when he was, oh, twelve or so, my father got himself a

job as a messenger of the war, runnin' back and forth under gunfire, reportin' casualties when he shoulda been studyin'. But anyway, as I was sayin', that sweater you're wearin', my father, he was up by Turtle Cliffs there, just down south a bit—
MAJOR JACK. We were just there last night, sir.
BILLY. Yeah yeah, I heard.
MAJOR JACK. We were working to… To stabilize Turtle Cliffs, sir.
BILLY. Stabilize, huh? Well anyway, I won't go on and on to you, but all's I was sayin' was my father, he was up there, past the edge of the woods, there, and in comes this bear! Now, I ain't ever seen a bear, can you believe it, I sure would like to someday, but my father—
HELEN enters from the kitchen and tugs at his sleeve.
HELEN. Billy, there's a bit of a, a situation—
BILLY. What? God, I can't ever finish one of these stories, can I? What's going on?
HELEN. Well… Could I talk to you, just the two of us?
BILLY looks at the trio, who all suddenly pretend to be interested in another part of the room.
BILLY. What's wrong, love? Look, I know these guys seem all tough and scary, but honestly, they're just lookin' for comfort. Give 'em a night here and—
HELEN. No, no, there's something else. I think I did something I shouldn't have.
BILLY. What? What'd you do?
HELEN. Well, I was down here on my own and, and…
Beat.
There was another knock on the door…
BILLY. We've got more visitors?
HELEN. Well, yes, but—
BILLY. *(To the trio.)* We've got more visitors!
HELEN. Billy!
BILLY. What?
HELEN. …They're wearing red.
BILLY. *(A moment of understanding. Whispering:)* Where are they?
HELEN. In the kitchen.
BILLY. Doing what?
HELEN. I don't know, peeling potatoes, I just gave them something to

167

do—

BILLY. Wait a minute, Helen, you're tellin' me we've got eastern soldiers admirin' our knick knacks in here and western soldiers peelin' our potatoes in the kitchen?!

She smiles apologetically.

Well ain't this a party! Let's bust out some whiskey, why don't we?

HELEN. Well, I don't know about that, but—

BILLY. Yes, this is a party for sure. Might as well turn that radio up and get the fire roarin', this is gonna be the party of the century! Just bring the others upstairs and get 'em out of their reds while I tell these fellas all about my father, will you?

HELEN. Your father? Don't you dare—Billy, I don't know if we should be doing this.

BILLY. *(Serious now.)* I know we shouldn't, Helen. But we need to. You know we can't choose sides.

HELEN. *(Also serious.)* You know you're not going to end the war tonight.

BILLY. I know I'm not.

He grabs her hand.

We both are!

All HELEN can do is smile. She knows as well as he does it's not going to happen, but she trusts him completely.

Now. I'm gonna bring these fellas downstairs, stoke the fire, get all nice and toasty. While we're down there, bring the other fellas upstairs and into some more of my clothes. God, they must be freezin', and you've got 'em peelin' potatoes, damn—

HELEN. Won't they see the blue uniforms these men showed up in?

BILLY. I've already hid the blues. Hell, it's not too late, I could sneak 'em into the fire…

HELEN. Oh, shut up.

Beat.

Okay. Okay, I'll bring them upstairs. I can do that.

BILLY. I know you can.

HELEN. One of them's a woman, you know.

BILLY. Really? Is she single?

HELEN lovingly swats at him.

Okay, I'm headed downstairs. I love you.

HELEN. I love you too.

BILLY. *(To the trio.)* Now, gentlemen, sorry about that—

They have been checking out a paperweight with forced enthusiasm; now that their attention has been brought to BILLY, MAJOR JACK hands the paperweight to DENNIS, who gives it to LOUIE, who drops it on his foot.

LOUIE. Ahh, Gaaahddamnit, son of a—

BILLY. You alright there, son?

MAJOR JACK. He's fine, sir.

LOUIE once again smiles through his pain.

BILLY. Right. Hey, I'm sorry I haven't brought you fellas down to the fire yet, right down here in the basement. C'mon, let's sit 'round and get so warm we sweat, how's that?

MAJOR JACK. *(DENNIS and LOUIE nod excitedly.)* We'd be delighted, sir. Thank you.

BILLY. Stop callin' me "sir." So anyways, where was I? My father, up there on Turtle Cliffs, so he's up there checkin' out the deer one day, no thought of bears at all, have you seen those deer up there? They're all over the place. Beautiful animals, aren't they? So he's sittin' there…

BILLY's voice trails off as he leads the trio downstairs to the basement. Just before he closes the door, he gives a wink and a smile to HELEN. She smiles back at him and waits a second or two before running into the kitchen. She re-enters with MAJOR JOHN and LUCY, who are still wearing their snow-covered uniforms and holding half-unpeeled potatoes. They are not as cold now.

HELEN. Oh, where are my manners? Here I've got you doing my chores, so sorry.

Taking the potatoes from them.

Wow, this is some fine peeling. Very good. Well, let's get you upstairs and into some warm clothes, how about that?

MAJOR JOHN. Thank you, ma'am. We are so grateful for your hospitality.

HELEN. Oh, please, I'm sure you'd do the same.

Leading them upstairs.

My husband's a bit smaller than you but you can squeeze, right? And Lucy, I've got plenty for you to wear. Do you like green?

LUCY. It's my favorite.

HELEN. Wonderful. So, uh...

Running out of things to talk about already.

My father, he, um...

Her voice trails off as they disappear upstairs. A pause, then BILLY swings the basement door open and enters, holding a bottle of whiskey.

BILLY. You boys just sit tight and warm up, I'll be right back!

He runs giddily to the kitchen and returns with four shot glasses cradled in his arms. As he approaches the basement door, he realizes he cannot open it. He tries to put the bottle of whiskey on top of the shot glasses, a recipe for disaster, before HELEN comes downstairs.

HELEN. Oh, be careful! Here, let me help...

She hurries to help him, then hesitates.

What's all this for?

BILLY. The fellas and I are gonna have a little toast, figured it'd buy you some time.

HELEN. They're already upstairs.

BILLY. Everything go well?

HELEN. So far, so good.

Beat.

Billy, what do we tell them? Won't they be suspicious?

BILLY. We turn up the radio and tell 'em they're here to dance.

HELEN. Oh, but won't they have questions? Or tell stories or something? I swear, if you tell them anything else about your father—

BILLY. We just have to be careful what we say. Get 'em focused on other things. Maybe we'll play a game of checkers or backgammon or somethin'. And, you know, steer the conversation. Hell, once we get some whiskey in 'em, that part'll be easy.

HELEN. Okay. It's just that, the war, you know, it's all anybody ever talks about. And soldiers, well...

BILLY. Then we get 'em talkin' about the north. Everybody hates the north.

HELEN. *(Almost instinctive.)* Fuck the north.

BILLY. There you go. I know it's gonna be tough, and maybe they'll find out eventually, but if they get to know each other before that happens... We'll see. You can't kill a friend.

HELEN. You can't. They might.

BILLY. Yeah, well, I'm hopin' my clothes rub off on 'em a bit. I washed 'em in peacemakin' soap, you know.

MAJOR JOHN and LUCY enter from upstairs wearing new sweaters. MAJOR JOHN's is comically ill-fitting and LUCY's is pretty and green.

HELEN. Hey there! Don't those look nice.

LUCY agrees, MAJOR JOHN does not.

Oh, this is my husband, Billy.

BILLY. Howdy folks!

Realizing he can't shake their hands with his arms full, he places the shot glasses and whiskey down on the coffee table, then extends his hand.

MAJOR JOHN. Hello, Billy. Major John, sir.

BILLY. *(Intentionally leaving out "Major" while they shake hands.)* Nice to meet you, John.

MAJOR JOHN. *(A bit offended, but not enough to say anything.)* This here's Lucy.

LUCY. Thank you so much. This is such a delight.

BILLY. Howdy, Lucy. Well, we're happy to have some company! Helen and I haven't had friends over in a while, have we dear?

HELEN. Oh, it's been a few minutes, at least.

BILLY. Yeah, well, what she means is, we've already got some friends downstairs by the fire. Hey, why don't I bring 'em up and we'll all have a drink together. How's that sound?

MAJOR JOHN. I'd be delighted, sir.

BILLY. Oh, cut it with the "sir."

Opening the basement door.

Hey fellas! Come on up and meet some friends of ours, will you? Let's have our whiskey up here!

HELEN. *(To MAJOR JOHN and LUCY.)* He's always just looking for an excuse to break out the whiskey.

MAJOR JOHN. *(Slight smile.)* I never need an excuse, ma'am.

BILLY. Ha! Now there's a guy with a sense of humor. My wife's been lookin' for one of those.

MAJOR JACK, DENNIS, and LOUIE enter from the basement.

> *LOUIE trips on the last step and falls face first onto the floor. DENNIS helps him up.*

LOUIE. Ahh, Gaaahddamn—
BILLY. Careful there, son. Watch that step, it's a doozy.
> *BILLY, HELEN, and even LUCY are trying hard not to laugh. LOUIE is now standing, the basement door has been closed, and everything is calm. The two groups are now facing each other, all in friendly sweaters, and everything is still for a few moments. MAJOR JACK is facing MAJOR JOHN. BILLY and HELEN watch on nervously. DENNIS and LUCY catch each other's eyes. LOUIE stares at a painting on the wall. MAJOR JACK finally approaches MAJOR JOHN and stands an arm's length away.*

MAJOR JACK. Who do you fight for?
BILLY. Who's fightin'? Fellas, let's turn up the radio and—
MAJOR JACK. Sir.
> *BILLY shuts up. Back to MAJOR JOHN:*

Who do you fight for?
MAJOR JOHN. *(Beat.)* I fight for God, sir.
> *Another beat. Finally, MAJOR JACK extends his arm.*

MAJOR JACK. Major Jack.
MAJOR JOHN. *(Shaking his hand, firm and strong.)* Major John.
> *A collective sigh of relief from BILLY and HELEN.*

MAJOR JACK. Where are you stationed?
MAJOR JOHN. Turtle Cliffs.
MAJOR JACK. So are we. Do I know you, sir?
MAJOR JOHN. Well, you do look familiar.
BILLY. Tonight, fellas, we're all stationed right here. By the end of the night, we'll all be familiar—
MAJOR JACK. Did you know the late Captain Hughes, sir?
MAJOR JOHN. Yeah, of course. I can't believe it took so long for us to—
BILLY. Say, why don't we take some shots and go piss up north, huh?
MAJOR JACK and MAJOR JOHN. Yeah, fuck the north.
> *They lock eyes and suddenly laugh together, big and hearty; approval has been made.*

BILLY. Alright. Helen, could you get us a few more shot glasses?

HELEN exits to kitchen. BILLY starts to distribute the glasses he's already brought out.

Everybody in?

MAJOR JACK. I'm not sure if Louie should partake, sir.

LOUIE. *(Brought back to reality.)* I can handle myself, sir.

MAJOR JACK. Louie, you can't handle a toad.

LOUIE. I promise, sir, I won't behave like last time. Besides, the wounds are just about healed up.

He shows off a scar on his hand.

MAJOR JACK. Dennis, keep an eye on him.

DENNIS nods in barely-hidden disappointment. HELEN re-enters from the kitchen with three more shot glasses. She passes them to BILLY, who distributes them.

BILLY. Fellas, I'd like to propose a toast. To the good men out there, fightin' for what they believe to be right. And God. Thank God everyone fights for God.

A small, knowing smile to HELEN.

May all the brave young soldiers out there find courage, strength, and forgiveness, or at least a flashlight.

He cracks up at his own toast.

And we must remember, all of us, no matter what's happening outside those doors, in here we are all friends. That's what's important. Tonight, we are all safe and happy and warm. And DRUNK!

ALL. *(Ad lib.)* Here, here! Yeah! Cheers!

They clink their glasses and down their shots. LOUIE chokes violently on his as the lights go down.

Scene 2

Lights up on the living room, now in a state of chaotic dancing. The radio is blasting some dancey jazz music, old and instrumental. Everybody is loose and happy. BILLY and HELEN are dancing together, surprisingly able to keep up with everyone else. MAJOR JACK and MAJOR JOHN clap their hands and try all sorts of half-successful steps, laughing at each other when they mess up. DENNIS is going crazy and LUCY is having a lot of fun but they are keeping their distance from each other for now. LOUIE is unseen. As the song dies down, MAJOR JACK and MAJOR JOHN slap each other on the back and each take another shot of whiskey. LUCY sits down happily. DENNIS remains dancing. The same voice comes back over the radio.

RADIO ANNOUNCER. ...Well, there's a tune to dance to if I've ever heard one. It is now seven in the evening local time, and the flurries seem to be just starting. Already about a foot of snow has fallen, and has made travel almost impossible. Several soldiers have been reported missing, with the Turtle Cliffs area seeming to be—
    BILLY rushes over to turn the radio off.
BILLY.   Well, fellas, where'd you learn to dance? The School of Mismatched Feet?
MAJOR JACK. I can't remember the last time I had this much fun!
MAJOR JOHN. You, sir, are hard to keep up with!
MAJOR JACK. Are you kidding? I was trying to follow you!
BILLY. Boy oh boy, what a time. You fellas should'a seen Helen when she was in her prime. Holy hell, could she go! Why, there was one time, now Helen won't want me tellin' this story, but I have to, sorry love—
    Suddenly there is a loud crash of pots and pans from the kitchen. LOUIE runs in holding several potatoes in one hand and an ear of corn in the other. He is very stressed out.
What's going on, son?! Is our dinner all over the walls?
LOUIE. *(A bit out of breath.)* No, sir—Well, maybe—
HELEN. I had a feeling we shouldn't have put you in charge.
LOUIE. I swear I've made this recipe before.
MAJOR JACK. The only recipe you know is the recipe for disaster.

Dennis, why aren't you—
> *DENNIS is still dancing away, too drunk to care about watching over LOUIE anymore.*

LOUIE. Could I have some help please?
BILLY. Not a worry, there, son, can't be any worse than last Christmas Eve.
> *With one look into the kitchen:*

Good Lord!!!
> *BILLY runs into the kitchen, followed by a worried HELEN, an excited MAJOR JACK and MAJOR JOHN, and LUCY, who stops in the doorway when she realizes that DENNIS is still dancing away. She smiles and watches as he, oblivious to her, turns up the radio and continues doing his previous dance, though the rhythm is much different. He gets really into it, thinking nobody is watching. Eventually he starts spinning around a bit and turns to face her. He almost jumps out of his skin.*

DENNIS. AHH!!!
LUCY. I'm sorry!
DENNIS. Holy shit.
LUCY. *(Laughing.)* I didn't mean to jump you!
DENNIS. It's okay.
LUCY. Really, I just, I was just on my way to the kitchen—
DENNIS. It's okay. I'm okay. I'm—
> *He sits down on the couch; he's pretty drunk.*

It's all good.
BILLY. *(Entering.)* What's the matter? Did I hear a—
DENNIS. I'm fine. Just humiliated.
BILLY. Oh, alright. No shame in dancin', son.
> *Sensing he should give DENNIS and LUCY a moment together, he yells into the kitchen:*

Everybody stay in here and keep cleanin'! Look, we've still got corn on the walls, and potatoes on the ceiling…
> *His voice trails off as he exits back to the kitchen.*

LUCY. *(Beat.)* I'm Lucy, by the way.
DENNIS. Dennis.
> *He throws his hand out real fast.*

Nice to meet you, Lucy.
LUCY. *(Shaking his hand.)* I like your dancing.
DENNIS. Oh, no, that wasn't really <u>dancing</u>, per se. It's just—You know, I think I've had too much whiskey.
LUCY. So you can't dance sober?
DENNIS. No. Well, yeah, I can. I mean, I'm not <u>great</u>, but I can, I just… I haven't danced in a while.
LUCY. Yeah, me neither.
DENNIS. All this fighting and everything.
LUCY. Yeah.
DENNIS. *(Beat.)* I hate it. Can I say that?
LUCY. Me too.
   Sitting down on the other side of the couch, facing him.
I was beginning to think I was the only one.
DENNIS. Jack's always talking war like it's the best thing in the world. His father died in the war, grandfather died in the war, so on and so forth.
LUCY. John talks about murder like it's a fact of life.
DENNIS. Well, it is.
LUCY. I know. I just…
   She smiles, despite it all.
I prefer to dance.
DENNIS. Me too.
LUCY. I can tell. Where did you learn those moves?
DENNIS. Are you kidding? Those weren't moves.
LUCY. They were… something.
DENNIS. Well, I do know a few moves, you know.
LUCY. Like what?
DENNIS. *(Drunk-bragging.)* I can waltz.
LUCY. You can waltz?
DENNIS. Like a broken pendulum. Yes.
LUCY. Well. Why don't you show me?
DENNIS. I will. Two conditions.
LUCY. Yes?
DENNIS. I require a waltzing song.
LUCY. Let's see what's playing.
   She moves to the radio, which brings her closer to him.

What else?
DENNIS. I require a waltzing partner.
LUCY. I'll go get Helen.
DENNIS. No! I mean, well, she's probably busy, right?
LUCY. *(She has found a song fit for waltzing.)* Well, you're going to have to ask somebody else, I suppose.
DENNIS. *(Standing up triumphantly.)* Lucy, would you care to waltz with me?
LUCY. Sorry, I don't know how.
DENNIS. Oh, what the hell…
LUCY. I'm kidding. C'mon, let's dance.

They smile and slowly, awkwardly assume the position. He is pretty drunk but he gets most of the steps right and they laugh when they mess up. At one point DENNIS steps on LUCY's foot.

DENNIS. Oh, sorry!
LUCY. That's alright.

She intentionally steps on his foot for "revenge"; they both laugh. They fall into a rhythm and all thoughts of wars and storms have vanished. Eventually the song dies down and they finish with a flourishing spin and a laugh. They remain close as a slower song follows the waltz. They are now slow dancing, with her face resting on his shoulder. Something special is happening.

DENNIS. Lucy, I, uh…
LUCY. Yes?
DENNIS. *(Almost laughing.)* Where have you been all my life?
LUCY. Whitestone Valley.

DENNIS pauses the dance. A beat, then he backs away.

DENNIS. *(Almost a whisper.)* Whitestone Valley?
LUCY. Yeah. Where are you from?

He doesn't answer.

How close were you to Whitestone?

Still no answer.

Dennis, what's the matter?
DENNIS. *(Scared to say it.)* Willow Lake. I'm from the shores of Willow Lake.
LUCY. Willow Lake…? There must be more than one, the only one I

know of is… Oh my God.

> *It hits them both at the same time. DENNIS moves quickly to the other side of the room and starts pacing.*

DENNIS. Goddamn it.

LUCY. Fuck.

DENNIS. Lucy, I can't—We can't—

LUCY. I know.

DENNIS. I mean, it's just— Fucking hell, what have I done?

> *The song, still playing, doesn't quite fit the situation anymore. LUCY turns it off.*

LUCY. Dennis… I don't think I can fight anymore.

DENNIS. I've said that for three months. We have to.

LUCY. I can't. I can't go out there tomorrow and pull my trigger if I know you and Jack and Louie are on the other side. Can you?

> *DENNIS stops pacing. LUCY moves closer to him.*

Did you feel what I did just now?

DENNIS. Lucy, we're soldiers.

LUCY. We're better dancers.

> *Moving closer to him, now about a foot or two away.*

Did you feel it too?

DENNIS. *(Beat.)* Yes.

LUCY. I know. I just wanted to hear you say it.

> *A moment of connection.*

DENNIS. Fuck it.

> *He kisses her passionately; she obviously kisses him back. They are wrapped up in each other when BILLY enters. He is surprised but very happy for them. He tries not to watch for too long, but they keep going. Eventually, he takes a step or two back into the kitchen and, a bit offstage:*

BILLY. John, you butter the corn! Jack, keep Louie away from the stove!

> *He emphasizes this last part.*

I'm going into the living room now!

> *It works; DENNIS and LUCY stop kissing and face him, a few feet away from each other and as innocent as can be.*

Oh, hey there friends! Sorry to interrupt your chattin', but dinner's just about ready! Come on in and grab your plates!

He turns to go back to the kitchen.

DENNIS. *(Hesitating, then, bravely:)* Billy!

BILLY. Ah, he speaks! What is it, son?

DENNIS. *(Beat.)* Sir, I'm not sure how to say this. We just—Well, I'm sure you know, but—

BILLY. Oh, I get it, yeah, don't worry son, there's a spare bedroom you can use upstairs if you want. Just don't be too loud about it, alright? These boards get squeaky.

DENNIS. What? No, no, that's not—Well, if you're offering—

LUCY. Sir, we know. We're on different sides of the war.

BILLY. *(Checking in the kitchen; nobody has overheard.)* Well, you haven't killed each other yet, I see.

DENNIS. No, but sir, if either of our superiors find out—

BILLY. I know. Trust me. But look, I've got it all under control, alright?

LUCY. How?

BILLY. *(Thinking of how to put it.)* Can I tell you a little story?

LUCY. Sure.

BILLY. *(Yelling into the kitchen.)* Don't come in here yet, keep cleanin' or something'!

Back to DENNIS and LUCY.

You ever hear about William Thomas?

LUCY. Of course.

DENNIS. I've never heard of him.

LUCY. He's a legend where I grew up.

BILLY. Really?

LUCY. Yeah. His disappearance is still talked about today.

BILLY. How about that? Anyways, this man, William, they say he was fearless. Marched his men into battle with the confidence of a rabid dog sniffin' a squirrel. Truthfully, though, he was scared as hell every time he set foot out there. What I heard, he even shit his pants once or twice. That doesn't matter, though, anyways he fought for years with the mindset of, "I'm a soldier, Goddamn it, I'm a fighter." That sort of thing, y'know, and he fooled himself into taking it on as an identity. It became the only thing he knew about himself. All his past, his days playin' horseshoes and swimmin' at the lake, it was all some distant dream. All there was, was fightin'. So, he's in this bloody mess up north, up by Coyote Mountain, you know it? And he gets caught off guard by these northern soldiers hidin' there near the summit. Now, William Thomas was no retreatin' man. Sure, his men were in no position to win, shootin' uphill and all, but he never took no for an answer. Well, turns out he should've. Half his men were killed there, bodies spread out all over that mountainside, bakin' their guts in the late afternoon sun, and there he lay, a bullet lodged in his knee, another in his shoulder, no sign of backup. Northern soldiers on their way to slit his throat, he could hear 'em. Couldn't do much about it. All he does is tilts his head back, stares up at the sky turnin' orange in the twilight, and accepts his death. Wishes he'd at least seen a bear once or twice, but otherwise no regrets. Just then, in comes a savior, an angel it seems, and he's just about passin' out when she fixes him up a bit and drags him to safety in some tall undergrowth. They hide out for the night on the mountain. She keeps him alive, brings him water, stops his bleedin' and all that. The mornin' sun pops up and he notices two things. First, that this savior is the most beautiful woman he's ever met. I mean, absolute babe, you know? Second, she's wearin' blue. Goddamn it, she's an eastern soldier. He panics for a bit before she calms him down, says she's not gonna hurt him. And there they sit, surrounded by northern soldiers on some far-off mountaintop, keepin' quiet for their lives, dirt and sweat packed on their faces, uniforms stained with dried blood, and right there they look into each other's souls and discover the one thing that might stop the war. Love.

 Beat.

Boy, was the sex painful though!

 He cracks himself up. The story is done, and though the ending was a bit unexpected, LUCY and DENNIS are completely entranced. Finally, LUCY speaks hesitantly.

LUCY. You're William Thomas? <u>Major</u> William Thomas?
BILLY. *(Disgusted at "Major.")* Yeah, I'm afraid so. Helen and I ran off—Well, limped off is more like it, and I guess I "disappeared" then. It's been, oh, thirty years or so.
DENNIS. So, Helen was a soldier too?
BILLY. Sure was. I thank God every day I never came face-to-face with her out there.
LUCY. I guess—I guess I just assumed you were dead. Most people do.
BILLY. Well, I might as well be, back home. Haven't been back since.

> *He's pretty sad about this. LUCY and DENNIS are sympathetic toward him. HELEN pokes her head in.*

HELEN. Billy, what's the big holdup? The food's getting cold and the boys want to play checkers.
MAJOR JACK and MAJOR JOHN. *(Offstage, ad lib.)* Yeah, checkers! Whiskey! C'mon, Billy!
BILLY. Yeah, we'll be right there, sorry.
> *HELEN retreats to kitchen.*

Now, your superiors don't need to know about this. Me, I think maybe if we get 'em to like each other even more, they won't even care.
DENNIS. That's quite a risk, sir.
BILLY. What else have we got?
> *DENNIS and LUCY have no answer.*

Alright. Who wants to eat? We've got so many Goddamn potatoes in there we could feed an army. Hell, <u>two</u> armies!
> *He laughs at himself and exits to the kitchen. DENNIS and LUCY look at each other nervously and follow. Lights down.*

Scene 3

Lights up. Everybody is just finishing their corn and potatoes, and spirits are high. A slower, peaceful song is playing on the radio. MAJOR JACK and MAJOR JOHN are in the middle of a game of checkers, the board set out on the coffee table. Throughout the following scene, they are playing the game while talking. When one says something like "King me" he is referencing the game. LOUIE is sitting in between them, eating and watching the game with enthusiasm. DENNIS and LUCY sit on opposite sides of the room but make eye contact every three seconds or so. There aren't enough seats for everyone so BILLY and HELEN are standing while eating, which is a bit tricky. As the song dies down:

RADIO ANNOUNCER. ...A delightful little tune to wrap up the hour. It is now eight o'clock local time, the snow still coming down in buckets out there. Local officials have put out a message to stay indoors at all costs, possibly due to a report of eighteen missing soldiers from the north—

ALL. *(Ad lib style, not simultaneous.)* Fuck the north!

RADIO ANNOUNCER. —who were known to be near Turtle Cliffs at the time of their disappearance. Joining me is Senator Lee of the eastern nation, whose men were at Turtle Cliffs last night—

LEE. Yes, a resounding success, sir, if I may—

BILLY rushes to turn off the radio. MAJOR JACK and MAJOR JOHN are both about to comment on LEE, but BILLY interjects before they have a chance.

BILLY. So up there at the Cliffs, you must'a had a great view of the Pine Sky Mountains, didn't you?

MAJOR JACK. Oh, beautiful spot, yes. King me.

MAJOR JOHN. Yeah, I've done lots'a huntin' up there.

MAJOR JACK. Really? That's quite a trek.

MAJOR JOHN. No, not really. Grew up pretty close by.

MAJOR JACK. What? That doesn't make sense, how could you have grown up—

BILLY. Yeah, I used to go hikin' up there all the time. Probably these

days I'd prefer the switchbacks, but I used to like those big tough climbs, Eagle's Nest or somethin' like that.
MAJOR JOHN. No good huntin' there.
BILLY. No, but the views are just mind-blowin', it's really somethin' special up there.
MAJOR JACK. *(To MAJOR JOHN.)* So what do you hunt?
MAJOR JOHN. Deer, mainly.
MAJOR JACK. Beautiful animals.
   Beat.
Have either of you ever been over to Coyote Mountain, up north?
BILLY. Oh yes. Lifetimes ago.
MAJOR JACK. I used to hunt deer there all the time.
BILLY. The hikin's alright, too, you know.
LOUIE. AHH, GAAAHDDAMNIT!
   He hits himself in the leg in frustration.
Bit my tongue, son of a bitch...
MAJOR JACK. You'd bite your ass if it wasn't behind you.
   To MAJOR JOHN.
We just picked him up a few months ago. Doing a bit of a favor for his family. Didn't want him on their farm anymore.
LOUIE. I set the chickens free.
MAJOR JACK. Among other things, yes, all the chickens were set free, at least for a few hours or so. Poor things got mangled by wolves. Big, bloody, feathery mess.
MAJOR JOHN. Wolves? Jesus, where was that? I never seen a wolf west of here. King me.
MAJOR JACK. Oh, obviously it was east of here.
MAJOR JOHN. East of here? But—
BILLY. Yeah wolves are tricky, so anyways, chickens, huh? You ever seen any bears, Louie?
LOUIE. Yes, sir.
BILLY. Well I'll be damned. What'd you do?
LOUIE. Honestly, sir?
BILLY. Quit callin' me "sir." Yeah, honestly, what'd you do?
LOUIE. Well, I tried to hide in a tree.
   Beat.
But I fell out of it.

BILLY. Damn, and the bear? What'd he do?
MAJOR JACK. King me.
LOUIE. Dennis killed it.
BILLY. That so?
> *To DENNIS.*

You killed a bear, son?
DENNIS. I hope I never have to again.
BILLY. Probably you'll never get the opportunity. Y'know, I never seen a bear before. What are they like?
DENNIS. They're big, and beautiful.
LOUIE. *(To himself.)* Fucking scary.
DENNIS. Just the most magnificent thing you'll ever see. Natural fighters, too.
BILLY. Unlike the rest of us, huh?
> *Beat.*

How'd you get to be lookin' after Louie here?
DENNIS. He's my brother.
MAJOR JACK. Louie's not allowed anywhere without him.
BILLY. Why's that?
MAJOR JACK. He gets all… Oh, I don't know…
DENNIS. Unpredictable.
LOUIE. Last time I was alone, I broke my arm. And somebody else's leg.
BILLY. Somebody else's? I thought you said you were alone?
LOUIE. I thought I was.
MAJOR JOHN. Well, let's all watch our limbs 'round you, son!
> *To MAJOR JACK.*

Where did you say you been stationed? I would'a thought I'd remember you three. King me.
MAJOR JACK. Oh, we've been down by the outskirts of the Willow Woods.
MAJOR JOHN. Jesus, how long you been in enemy territory?
MAJOR JACK. What do you mean?
> *LOUIE starts to choke on a bite of potato. DENNIS hits him in the back a few times and eventually LOUIE stops choking.*

LOUIE. Son of a bitch. Thanks.
MAJOR JACK. *(To MAJOR JOHN.)* What about you, where have you

two been stationed?
MAJOR JOHN. Well, actually there were four of us.
Beat; it's hard for him to say this.
We lost two men at Turtle Cliffs last night.
MAJOR JACK. Damn shame. Sorry to hear.
Beat; it's hard for him to say this too.
We lost one. Well, kept him alive all night. Passed early this morning.
MAJOR JOHN. May God be with you.
MAJOR JACK. Thank you, sir. And you.
LOUIE. I really liked Carl.
MAJOR JACK. I know, Louie. We all did.
Everybody is very solemn. BILLY doesn't like it.
BILLY. Say, why don't we bust out that second bottle of whiskey?
MAJOR JACK. Oh, I'll never say no to that.
MAJOR JOHN. I'll be askin' for whiskey on my deathbed. King me.
BILLY. Great. Here, let me go downstairs and get it; Helen, love, could you get these plates outta here and gather up those glasses?
HELEN. Aren't we running out of whiskey?
BILLY. Still got a couple bottles down there. Probably last us the next hour or so, right fellas?
Excited responses from MAJOR JACK and MAJOR JOHN as he passes by them and opens the basement door.
I'll be right back, don't do anything too excitin'!
He exits to the basement. As HELEN is collecting everybody's plates, LOUIE accidentally drops his plate on the floor when he tries to pass it to her.
LOUIE. Ahh, Gaaahd—
HELEN. Don't worry about it, sweetie. Anybody need anything in the kitchen?
MAJOR JACK. There's more corn, isn't there?
HELEN. We've got plenty, yes!
MAJOR JACK. Could I have an ear?
MAJOR JOHN. I'd love one too, thanks.
HELEN. Of course, just give me a minute to get it off the cob—
MAJOR JACK. That's alright, no need goin' to the trouble. I'll eat it right off the cob, that's fine. King me.
MAJOR JOHN. Same here. Thanks.

HELEN. Well alright. I'll be right back.

She exits to the kitchen with the plates. The game of checkers is getting noticeably tense and attention is now silently on MAJOR JOHN, who must make his next move.

MAJOR JOHN. *(With LOUIE on his right and DENNIS on his left.)* Looks like you've got me surrounded here, Jack.

MAJOR JACK. Better be careful with this move.

MAJOR JOHN. Think I could pull off a big surprise though.

MAJOR JACK. Not unless you've got a secret weapon I don't know about. Your back's up against the wall.

MAJOR JOHN. You just wait.

He finally makes his move.

MAJOR JACK. You're right, didn't see that coming. I've got two over here, though, so—

He makes his move.

MAJOR JOHN. Damn it. Well, this might be it.

LUCY. John, I think I see a way you can—

HELEN enters from the kitchen with two ears of corn.

HELEN. Here you go, I buttered them up for you and everything.

MAJOR JACK. Thank you so much, Helen.

MAJOR JOHN. Thank you. And thank you so much for your warm hospitality this evenin'. We really appreciate it.

MAJOR JACK. We owe you our lives.

HELEN. Oh, you don't owe us anything.

MAJOR JACK and MAJOR JOHN both smile and start eating their corn as HELEN continues chatting. MAJOR JACK eats it horizontally, while MAJOR JOHN eats it vertically. It takes a few bites for MAJOR JOHN to notice, but when he does, a switch flips.

You know, we haven't had a positive experience with soldiers in a long, long time. I'm just so happy you found your way here. I always feel happier when I'm helping—

MAJOR JOHN. What are you doing?

MAJOR JACK. What?

MAJOR JOHN. How are you eating your corn?

MAJOR JACK. *(Showing him the ear.)* Like everyone else.

MAJOR JOHN. Vertically?

MAJOR JACK. No... Wait a minute, are you—
> *MAJOR JOHN realizes a half-second before MAJOR JACK. In one swift move, MAJOR JOHN throws his corn aside and rushes over to MAJOR JACK, picking him up by the collar and pulling him up off the couch. Before MAJOR JACK can think about what's happening, he is pinned up against a wall, and MAJOR JOHN has a knife to his throat. The checkers game has been tossed aside, game pieces flying everywhere.*

MAJOR JOHN. You son of a bitch, you killed my men last night! You're eastern, aren't you?!
MAJOR JACK. *(Struggling.)* Go to hell! I'll kill you too—
HELEN. Billy! Billy, come quick!
MAJOR JOHN. My God, how did I not see this?
MAJOR JACK. Dennis! Do something, man!
MAJOR JOHN. Lucy, stop him!
> *DENNIS and LUCY stare at each other in terror, frozen. LOUIE attempts to come to the rescue but trips over the coffee table. BILLY enters from the basement. The following lines are more or less simultaneous:*

HELEN. Stop it! This isn't worth fighting over!
BILLY. Whoa, hang on! Stop! John, stop!
MAJOR JOHN. You killed two good young men last night, two brave young men!
MAJOR JACK. Screw you! Dennis, help! DENNIS!
LOUIE. Ahh, Gaaahddamnit, my shin, son of a bitch!
> *Suddenly there is another knock on the door, and everyone immediately shuts up. Another knock, and slowly BILLY walks over to the door, keeping an eye on the situation. He opens it. Standing there is a nearly frozen soldier, wearing a purple uniform and not holding any weapons. This is SIMON.*

SIMON. S-s-s-sir, p-please, I-I-I b-b-b-beg of y-you—
BILLY. Who are you, son? Where are you from?
SIMON. Fr-fr-from th-the n-n-n-north, s-s-sir.
> *BILLY looks back on the current situation unfolding. MAJOR JOHN has loosened his grip on MAJOR JACK but is still holding him against the wall. DENNIS and LUCY have met up in the middle of the room, clutching onto each other. LOUIE*

rubs his shin. HELEN is almost in a state of shock. BILLY looks back at SIMON and calmly gestures for him to wipe his shoes and then come in. Lights down.

END OF ACT I

ACT II

Scene 1

Lights up. There is obvious tension in the room, most of it directed toward the center, where SIMON is tied to a chair with a cloth over his mouth. Throughout the following scene, he groans in pain every few minutes. Behind him is BILLY, with MAJOR JACK and MAJOR JOHN on either side of him. HELEN is near the kitchen with a knife in her hand. DENNIS is behind MAJOR JACK and LUCY is behind MAJOR JOHN, each of them looking at each other nervously. LOUIE has picked up the game of checkers and is playing a game against himself. A happy little tune is playing on the radio, sweet and simple. As it dies down:

RADIO ANNOUNCER. ...A cute little ditty to lighten up the mood on this dark, stormy night. It is now ten o'clock local time, and visibility has practically reached zero out there. Search and rescue teams have been told to stay indoors for the next six hours, though several soldiers are still believed to be missing. We only hope they are able to find safety on this tragic night. Joining me once again is Secretary James of the western nation, who is reporting that the west has taken control of Willow Lake.
JAMES. That's correct. Our men are brave, sir, and fight justly for God. After their success at Turtle Cliffs, we knew that—
BILLY turns the radio down.
BILLY. Sorry fellas, we can't send him back out there with that forecast.
MAJOR JACK. How the hell do you expect me to let this happen? I'm not sleeping five minutes with him in the house.
BILLY. Stay awake, then. I won't sleep five minutes knowin' he's out there freezin' to death.
MAJOR JACK. *(Begins pacing.)* This is bullshit!
MAJOR JOHN. *(To BILLY.)* Sir, you have to understand, these soldiers from the north—
MAJOR JACK. *(To MAJOR JOHN.)* You don't know shit about them—

MAJOR JOHN. What the hell do you mean? Why, I've—
BILLY. Hey! HEY!

> *MAJOR JACK and MAJOR JOHN are nose-to-nose with fury.*
> *BILLY calmly steps in between them.*

Remember our agreement?

> *Beat.*

Come on, now.

> *MAJOR JACK and MAJOR JOHN each take one step backward, maintaining a certain distance between them.*

Good. Now, boys, I'm sorry, I really am, and you can all go out there in the mornin' and blow each other's brains out. Yeah, John, I know all about these northern soldiers. Trust me, I understand plenty. But like it or not, he's stayin'. We're gonna keep him right here, he's not goin' anywhere, one of us'll stay with him all night, nothin' to worry about. He won't even be able to scratch his nose 'til the mornin'.
MAJOR JOHN. But sir, wouldn't it be easier to just kill him now? It's just that—
MAJOR JACK. What do you mean, you understand plenty? What else are you hiding?
BILLY. What are you talkin' about? Nothin'—
MAJOR JOHN. Can't we break his arm at least?
MAJOR JACK. Billy… Is that short for something?
BILLY. What?
MAJOR JACK. Is your real name William?
BILLY. My name's Billy, Jack.
MAJOR JACK. Your legal name. What is it? Is it Billy?

> *No answer.*

Or is it William?

> *Still nothing. BILLY looks to HELEN, who grips her knife nervously.*

Are you William Thomas?

> *A silent confirmation.*

MAJOR JOHN. My God.
BILLY. Now, listen, the man I am now is not who I was in the war, okay? I have never been further from—
MAJOR JACK. You're William Thomas…
MAJOR JOHN. Oh my God. Sir, you were my idol growing up. Wow.

Shaking his hand vigorously.
What an honor. Thank you for your service, Major William.
BILLY. Don't you ever call me Major again, John.
MAJOR JACK. You're Major William Thomas...
BILLY. Now Jack, please, let's just talk for a second here—
MAJOR JACK. You killed my father, you son of a bitch. You fucking killed my <u>father</u>, you—
> *MAJOR JACK tackles BILLY to the ground. He gets a punch or two in before MAJOR JOHN rushes in and pulls MAJOR JACK off BILLY, pinning him to the ground. MAJOR JACK pushes and kicks at MAJOR JOHN until he frees himself; MAJOR JOHN falls off to the side. MAJOR JACK moves back toward BILLY, but is immediately detained by DENNIS and LOUIE, each of them taking an arm.*

Fuck you! Let me at him—What are you idiots doing, let me—
BILLY. *(Still on the floor.)* Jack—
MAJOR JACK. You son of a bitch—
BILLY. Please, just let me say something.
> *MAJOR JACK begins to calm down.*

I know your pain, Jack. I know exactly how you're feelin'. You know, I was sixteen when I entered the war, and I was seventeen when my father was killed. He was ten feet away from me. Bright, sunny day, cool breeze, warm afternoon, beautiful. Just beautiful. We got ambushed, never saw it comin', and in one moment the man I idolized all my life had a hole in the middle of his forehead. Now, yes, I did kill the man who shot him. I did exactly what you want to do right now. But Jack, I didn't feel any better. I killed dozens of men over the next seven years, and not a single one made me feel any better than I did in that last moment I had with my dad.
> *All is still for a moment. MAJOR JACK is still furious but is not about to break away. MAJOR JOHN has recovered and is standing in front of LUCY.*

LOUIE. Maybe we should dance again.
> *MAJOR JACK gives LOUIE a look, then removes his arm from his grip in disgust. DENNIS lets go of the other arm, and MAJOR JACK regains his composure. He is still angry, but no longer in attacking mode. The mood is starting to relax.*

HELEN. Maybe we should all just go to bed.

MAJOR JACK. I'm not sleeping five minutes—

HELEN. Then you'll lie there and look up at the ceiling.

BILLY. You know, that's a good idea. If you fellas are headin' back out there tomorrow, you're gonna need some good rest, won't you? There's space upstairs, you can sleep in our bed for all I care, and there's a couple cots downstairs.

MAJOR JOHN. *(Referencing SIMON.)* We'll need to have somebody stay here and watch him. Sir, I'm certainly capable of—

BILLY. No, not you.

>*Beat.*

Lucy can do it.

LUCY. Me? With him? Why me?

BILLY. Because I know you're not gonna kill him unless you have to. The rest of these guys, I'm not so sure.

LOUIE. I could do it.

BILLY. Sorry, son, but... No. I remember the chicken story.

LUCY. Yeah, I'll do it. I can watch him.

BILLY. Thank you.

>*To MAJOR JOHN.*

How 'bout the two of us head downstairs? You haven't sat next to the fire yet, have you?

MAJOR JOHN. No, sir.

BILLY. Great, you'll love to sleep next to it. You and me, we'll get it nice and roarin'. Helen, love, could you take the rest upstairs?

HELEN. *(A look to MAJOR JACK.)* Well, maybe. Oh, I don't know.

MAJOR JACK. I'm not going to hurt you, ma'am.

BILLY. If he's hurtin' anybody tonight, it's me. But that's not gonna happen, is it?

>*No answer.*

Jack, I need your word or my wife ain't gonna trust you. And if she doesn't trust you, you're out in the blizzard on your own.

MAJOR JACK. I'm not going to hurt anyone.

>*Regarding SIMON.*

Except maybe this piece of shit.

BILLY. As long as he stays right there, that's not necessary. Come on, John, let's head downstairs.

MAJOR JOHN. Okay. Lucy, yell for me if anything goes wrong up here.
LUCY. I will. Goodnight, Major John.
MAJOR JOHN. John. Just call me John.
LUCY. Goodnight, John.
MAJOR JOHN. 'Night, Lucy.
 To HELEN.
Thank you for your hospitality, ma'am.
 To MAJOR JACK, gravely.
I'll see you tomorrow.
BILLY. *(As he opens the basement door and ushers MAJOR JOHN down.)* Hey, we've still got a couple bottles of whiskey down here, too. Boy, this is gonna be fun.
 To HELEN as he exits.
Keep these fellas here for a bit before you send 'em upstairs. I'll be right back with one of those bottles. John, you and I get to split the other one, how's that sound?
 He exits. There is an awkward silence.
LOUIE. That means they get more whiskey than us.
DENNIS. You can have my share.
 LOUIE is pleased enough by this.
HELEN. Well, did any of you ever expect this to happen when you woke up this morning?
 Beat.
Me neither.
 Beat; half-jokingly:
Thanks for not killing my husband, Jack.
MAJOR JACK. *(Barely audible, but honest.)* I'm sorry, ma'am.
HELEN. Oh, I know how the war can be. He's all I've got, though, you know.
MAJOR JACK. *(Regarding SIMON.)* What are we going to do with him tomorrow?
HELEN. Send him out when it's safe, I guess.
MAJOR JACK. I'll be right behind him.
HELEN. Now Jack, there's no need to be like that. He hasn't done anything to you.
MAJOR JACK. He would if he had the chance.

HELEN. He won't.

> *Beat. BILLY enters, carrying a bottle of whiskey with a few sips taken out.*

BILLY. Howdy, folks. Whiskey was a bit overflowin', I had to take a couple swigs.

> *He hands the bottle to HELEN.*

Make sure they drink enough to forget the war, love.

HELEN. There isn't enough whiskey in the world.

BILLY. I've never heard anything more true.

> *BILLY reaches into his pocket and subtly removes a handwritten note, folded up. He moves over to DENNIS and shakes his hand, secretly giving him the note.*

'Night, Dennis. Hope you take care to remember that story I told you...

> *Moving over to LOUIE.*

'Night, Louie. I sure would like to see you get your own chicken farm someday.

LOUIE. I'd prefer goats.

BILLY. Goats, then. Sure.

> *Finally, to MAJOR JACK.*

Jack, I know how much you'd like to kill me—

MAJOR JACK. It's not going to happen, sir.

> *Shaking his hand.*

Goodnight. Thank you for letting us stay here this evening.

BILLY. Maybe you'll do the same for someone else someday. Goodnight.

> *As he approaches LUCY, he pulls out another note from his other pocket. He slips it into her hand during their handshake as well.*

Nice meetin' you, Lucy. Thanks for keepin' watch up here.

LUCY. Thank you for your warm welcome, sir.

BILLY. Can't anybody stop calling me "sir"? I'll be downstairs, holler if someone's killin' somebody.

> *Kissing HELEN on the cheek.*

'Night, love. Everything will be okay.

HELEN. Goodnight. I love you.

BILLY. I love you too.

> *To the three men.*

If I come up here tomorrow and Helen's got herself a new boyfriend, we'll certainly have to settle a few things.

He laughs at himself and exits downstairs.

HELEN. So, who wants to be my new boyfriend?

Beat.

Oh, I'm kidding. C'mon, let's go upstairs. We've got plenty of blankets and pillows—

MAJOR JACK. Ma'am?

HELEN. Yes, Jack?

Through the following conversation, DENNIS and LUCY look at their respective notes but are too nervous to open them. LOUIE goes back to the checkers game.

MAJOR JACK. You're eastern, aren't you?

HELEN. I'm not anything anymore.

Beat.

But yes, I was.

MAJOR JACK. Did you ever know Charles Sanders?

HELEN. Oh, yes. We weren't too close, but we were stationed together once or twice. Fierce soldier. One of the strongest I'd ever seen. But, he had a soft spot. I remember he was one of the only soldiers I'd ever seen stare at the stars.

Beat.

He was your father?

MAJOR JACK. Yes, ma'am.

HELEN. I'm very sorry, Jack.

MAJOR JACK. It was a long time ago.

Beat.

Your husband…

HELEN. I know.

MAJOR JACK. How did you forgive him?

HELEN. I don't think I needed to forgive him. I needed to forgive the war itself. What it had done to everyone. What it's still doing.

Beat.

People are people, Jack. Sometimes it's a lot simpler than we think it should be.

MAJOR JACK is silent but attempts to understand. HELEN gives a look to DENNIS and another to LUCY. Each of them

hold their notes from BILLY, dying to know what they say.
Alright, let's go up.
LOUIE. Can I bring the checkers?
HELEN. Of course.
LOUIE gathers up the board and some of the pieces and follows them upstairs.
MAJOR JACK. He has no idea how to play.
HELEN. We can teach him. It's not that complicated.
MAJOR JACK. He thought it was the same thing as chess until earlier tonight.
They all exit, with DENNIS drawing up the rear, eyeing LUCY nervously. She waves as he exits and stares at the spot where he just was. She looks to SIMON, who silently begs her to untie him. She feels sorry but disregards him. She sits down on the couch and slowly unfolds the note BILLY had given her. As she reads it, her eyes widen. She stands up, excited, and begins pacing, checking upstairs once in a while. She keeps the note in front of her, reading it over and over again as she paces. Finally, DENNIS rushes downstairs with his own note clasped in his hand.
DENNIS. You read it?!
LUCY. Four times now, yes.
DENNIS. What do you think?
LUCY. It's our only chance.
DENNIS. We should do it?
LUCY. Yes. How much time do we have?
DENNIS. I don't know. Louie asked Jack the difference between checkers and chess. I think we have a few minutes.
LUCY. Do you think we can find it?
DENNIS. I think so. Let's see—
Reading from his note.
Follow deer trail two miles, turn left, follow river one mile to the cabin.
LUCY. What? Let me see that.
Taking his note.
Mine says turn right.
DENNIS. Right?!
LUCY. *(Reading from her note.)* Follow deer trail two miles, turn right,

follow river one mile to the cabin.
DENNIS. Shit. What do we do?
LUCY. Should we go talk to Billy?
DENNIS. *(Hearing commotion upstairs.)* We don't have time. We need to go, now.
LUCY. It's brutal out there. Shouldn't we do this tomorrow? It says to sneak off tomorrow.
DENNIS. We'd never make it without being seen. This is our only chance. Lucy—
    Taking her by the shoulders.
I'm not going to die for Jack. Not him, not Louie, not the east or west. If I'm dying for anybody, it's you. But we're not going to. We're going to find that cabin, tonight. Billy says there's two weeks' worth of food, there's wood for fire... We can hide out there until we get a nice clear night, then we make a run for it down south.
LUCY. South?! Dennis, you can't be serious—I mean, yes, I'd love to, but—
DENNIS. Then let's do it.
    Someone is coming downstairs.
Lucy, we need to go. Now.
LUCY. *(Beat.)* Okay.
    DENNIS takes her hand and they run out the front door just as MAJOR JACK enters from upstairs, followed by LOUIE and HELEN.
MAJOR JACK. Dennis? What the hell— Dennis!
    The three of them stop near the bottom of the stairs and survey the room.
Where's Lucy?
HELEN. Oh dear.
MAJOR JACK. Lucy! Dennis!
    He checks the kitchen.
Where the hell are they?!
HELEN. Oh, I sure hope they haven't—
    SIMON begins groaning in an attempt to get their attention. He seems to have something to tell them.
MAJOR JACK. You shut the hell up.
HELEN. Wait, he could probably help us.

MAJOR JACK. He'd help us more if he'd choke on that cloth.
HELEN. Come on, Jack, he's just a man. He's tied up, he's helpless, he's not going to hurt anybody.
MAJOR JACK. Ma'am, with all due respect, I disagree.

SIMON continues groaning. HELEN looks from him to MAJOR JACK and back again. She has a decision to make. Finally, she moves over to SIMON and pulls the cloth off his mouth. MAJOR JACK is ready to attack if needed.

SIMON. Thank you, ma'am. Thank you so much.
HELEN. Where are they, son? Where'd they go?
SIMON. They mentioned a cabin. A cabin by a river.
HELEN. Oh Lord, oh no—
MAJOR JACK. What? What is it?
HELEN. They must've—Billy must've told them—
MAJOR JACK. Are they outside?
SIMON. They ran out just before you came downstairs.
MAJOR JACK. Louie, come on.
HELEN. Jack, no! Wait, let's talk about this—!

MAJOR JACK pushes past her and runs out the door. LOUIE runs after him and slips in the entryway, falling flat on his back.

LOUIE. *(Gingerly standing up and following MAJOR JACK at a much slower pace.)* Son of a bitch…

He exits.

HELEN. Oh no, oh this can't be happening—
SIMON. I'm sorry, ma'am.
HELEN. I should get Billy.

She rushes to the basement door.

SIMON. Ma'am, please! Wait.
HELEN. *(Spinning around.)* What?
SIMON. Ma'am, my arm. I think it's broken. I'm in so much pain.
HELEN. I can't help you. I'm sorry.

Turning back to the basement and almost exiting.

SIMON. Please, I beg of you! I'm quitting the war!

HELEN stops.

I'm quitting. Today. I had already made my decision when I got here. You have to trust me, ma'am.

He groans in pain, louder than before.

HELEN. Son, you know I can't—
SIMON. You've saved northern soldiers before.
This makes HELEN pause.
I knew it was you. I knew it. You saved two of my uncles on Coyote Mountain. You wore eastern colors but you ran around saving soldiers on every side.
No response.
You're called the Angel of Coyote Mountain. You're a legend, ma'am.
HELEN. How do you expect me to believe you?
SIMON. You wore blue bandanas, didn't you? You used one to stop my uncle's leg from bleeding out. I have it, the bandana. It's in my pocket. Take it out.
HELEN hesitates but slowly moves over to him and reaches into his pocket. She takes her hand out quickly.
Other pocket. Sorry. Lucy is very pretty, isn't she?
HELEN shakes her head in disgust and proceeds to his other pocket. In shock, she pulls out a blue bandana.
HELEN. Oh my God...
SIMON. That's it, isn't it? That's yours! My God, I'm meeting the Angel of Coyote Mountain. Ma'am, it's an honor.
HELEN. What's your name, son?
SIMON. Simon. My name is Simon.
Beat.
Ma'am, I know how opposed you are to the war. I am too. I was forced to join when I was eighteen, and I've hated it ever since. I've never seen the point to all this fighting.
Loud groan. Referencing a painting he has noticed on the wall.
I always wanted to be a painter.
HELEN. Me too.
She hesitates, then rushes over to him and makes the executive decision to untie his hands. His arms fall limply to his sides as she moves to his legs. Finally he is free.
Now, I'm not sure exactly how much we can fix your arm tonight, but I do have a few things to keep it from getting worse.
She starts moving toward the stairs. SIMON reaches down to his feet; at first it appears he is just checking that his legs are untied, but then he pulls a knife from around his ankle. He

stands up and, with both arms in perfect healthy condition, points the knife at HELEN.

Simon, what are you—?

SIMON. My family is going to be so proud of me.

HELEN. What the hell—? Billy! BILLY!

She continues yelling for Billy as she runs into the kitchen, deliberately knocking down chairs in SIMON's way as he runs after her. He follows and there is a loud crash in the kitchen. HELEN re-enters with a frying pan, followed by SIMON, who is holding his head in actual pain. He corners her and puts the knife in his belt as she swings the frying pan at him a few times. He dodges successfully and in between two swings rushes to her, knocking the pan from her hand. He pulls his knife out and has it to her throat as BILLY and JOHN enter in a rush from the basement.

BILLY. Dear God, no! Helen!

HELEN. Billy, he tricked me! Billy—

SIMON. Shut up! You.

To BILLY.

William Thomas. I'm finally going to kill William Thomas.

BILLY. That's fine, son, just let my wife go and you can get your revenge, or whatever. Just, please, my God, let her go. I'm the one you want.

MAJOR JOHN. *(Unbelieving, under his breath.)* God, <u>fuck</u> the north.

SIMON. Shut up, all of you! Nobody move. I've been dreaming of this day since I was eighteen, and it's finally come. You see, this all goes back to—

Suddenly LOUIE enters, running, and again slips in the entryway. This time he falls right into SIMON, who is effectively pushed down to the ground. As LOUIE and SIMON disappear behind the couch, HELEN is released and runs over to BILLY's protection. Sensing his opportunity, MAJOR JOHN rushes over, pulls LOUIE off SIMON, kicks SIMON's knife away from him, and begins to absolutely beat the shit out of SIMON. Since SIMON is behind the couch, we cannot see him, but he yells in pain. Ad lib style:

Ah! God, please, stop! Fuck you! Stop it! Ah, Goddamnit! Fuck!

BILLY stands near the basement door, his arms stretched out in front of HELEN, protecting her. LOUIE watches in inspired terror. Suddenly, MAJOR JACK rushes in from outside and takes in the scene. He moves over to the fight and sees the victim is SIMON. He immediately joins MAJOR JOHN in beating the shit out of SIMON, whose cries eventually fade away. MAJOR JACK and MAJOR JOHN continue working together, punching away, as the lights go down.

Scene 2

Lights up. HELEN is sitting between MAJOR JACK and MAJOR JOHN, who are a bit friendlier now but are still fueled by hate. They each have a bottle of whiskey in their hands. BILLY is pacing behind them. SIMON is nowhere to be seen, but his knife is being played with by LOUIE. An intense instrumental fades out, and the RADIO ANNOUNCER comes through once again:

RADIO ANNOUNCER. ...And we have just crossed over into tomorrow, twelve o'clock midnight local time now. The flurries are actually beginning to calm down, with visibility creeping back up. Search and rescue teams are preparing to be sent back out into the wilderness, and several soldiers have been found in the last hour, some frozen to death. Our prayers are certainly with the families. Coming up we have a—
 BILLY shuts off the radio and continues pacing.
BILLY. I think I should go out there.
HELEN. Billy, love, it's too dangerous.
BILLY. It is for them, too! And they don't know it out there like I do.
 Looking out a window.
I'm just havin' a hard time believin' they'd have found the cabin. I really do think I wrote the wrong direction in Dennis's note.
MAJOR JOHN. Lucy's tried to ditch a few times.
MAJOR JACK. Dennis has never done anything like this. Never had the confidence.
BILLY. Let's hope all his confidence is in her.
LOUIE. He's coming back, right?
 Nobody knows what to tell him.
Right?
 He cuts his finger on the knife.
Ahh, Gaaahd—
BILLY. I'm goin' out there.
 He starts gathering warm clothes, a lantern, etc.
HELEN. For God's sake, Billy, you can't.
BILLY. I've got my big coat, I'll bring a light, I'll be fine. I know it out

there. Storm's clearin' up, I'll find 'em.

HELEN. You don't even know which way they went!

BILLY. I'll take my wrong directions first and if I don't run into 'em I'll turn 'round and head to the cabin.

HELEN. You're talking about walking four or five miles, in this snow and all...

BILLY. Done it before. I can do it.

HELEN. You used to.

This stops BILLY in his tracks.

Love, you used to be able to do this sort of thing. I know that. But now, well—

BILLY. I'm old, I know. Just say it.

HELEN. It's not that you're old, you're—Well, you're not as young as you once were, is all.

BILLY. Yeah, yeah, I know. But this is too important to consider that. This is love. I'm sure you understand.

She does.

I'll be careful. I promise. When we took everybody in this evening, I committed to helpin' these brave young men and women survive the night. And that's exactly what's gonna happen.

He kisses her.

I love you.

HELEN. I love you too.

He starts to exit.

Billy—

He turns to face her.

I trust you. I know I can.

BILLY. You know you can.

He smiles and exits, his lantern in front of him.

HELEN. Oh, why didn't he just give them a map?

She looks over to MAJOR JACK and MAJOR JOHN, who drink their whiskey in discontent.

Don't you two care at all?

MAJOR JACK. Frankly, no.

MAJOR JOHN. They want to go freeze themselves to get laid, so be it.

HELEN. Those are your friends! <u>Your</u> soldiers!

MAJOR JACK. He's no soldier to me anymore.

203

MAJOR JOHN. Didn't seem like he ever was.
MAJOR JACK. Sorry, who took Turtle Cliffs last night?
> *MAJOR JOHN stands up, followed quickly by MAJOR JACK. HELEN shoves herself in between them.*

MAJOR JOHN. Screw you, you know just as well as I do who won that battle.
MAJOR JACK. So you've accepted it?
MAJOR JOHN. You're losing reinforcements and everyone knows it. Once we've drained you of everything you have—
MAJOR JACK. With what? You've got nothing capable of making a dent.
MAJOR JOHN. Trust me, this war is just beginning—
MAJOR JACK. You better hope for your sake it's about to end—
HELEN. Shut up, shut up, shut up! Shut up! Do you know what the hell you're fighting about?!
> *They are too shocked to say anything.*

No, go on, tell me.
> *Nothing.*

How exactly did the war start? Go back, fifty, a hundred, two hundred years, tell me what started it all. Yes, go on and on about the borders and freedom and revenge, whatever it's about, it doesn't matter! It's not your war anymore! You fight and plot and kill for the sake of some vague idea of west or east or north or whichever. Don't you see how similar you two are? Hell, I can't even tell you apart. You've got the same hairstyle for Christ's sake. You waste your time talking passionately about what's right and wrong when none of it matters! You're trying to settle a matter of words with destruction and heavy artillery! You drown out each other's arguments with bullets and cannons! The borders have no real significance anymore, don't you realize that? You say you're protecting family, then you go kill somebody else's brother or sister. When will you get it in your head that you can't kill someone just for living somewhere else?
> *HELEN is breathing heavy and in a rage; now she starts to calm down. Nobody says anything for a few moments.*

LOUIE. I just want to go home.
HELEN. Oh, sweetie...
> *HELEN moves over to LOUIE and gives him a big hug. He*

starts to cry.
LOUIE. I'm sorry for fighting, ma'am.
HELEN. You didn't know what you're doing, sweetie. You were just doing what you were told.
LOUIE. I shouldn't have tackled that man earlier.
HELEN. The man from the north?
    LOUIE nods.
Well, actually, that was a good thing. He was trying to hurt us.
LOUIE. Did we really have to tie him up and throw him in the snow?
HELEN. *(Beat.)* Yes. We did, actually.
    She takes his head and makes him look at her.
You saved my life, Louie. You're a hero.
LOUIE. I am?
    He stops crying.
I saved your life?
HELEN. Yes, you saved my life. Thank you, so much.
LOUIE. *(Wiping his nose.)* I'm gonna be a doctor someday, you know.
    MAJOR JACK rolls his eyes; he's heard this before.
HELEN. A doctor?
LOUIE. I'm gonna save somebody's life every day.
HELEN. And you're going to be a hero every day.
    Beat.
MAJOR JACK. Louie, do you even know how to read?
    HELEN gestures for him to shut up; he does.
HELEN. You're going to be a doctor someday, Louie. A wonderful doctor.
LOUIE. Thank you, ma'am.
MAJOR JACK. *(Under his breath.)* God help us.
    HELEN sits LOUIE down. He is now smiling through his tear-stained eyes. She walks back over to MAJOR JACK and MAJOR JOHN.
HELEN. If you two don't want to make peace, so be it. When the morning comes, go back out there and kill each other as if none of this ever happened. I don't care. But under this roof, you're friends. My husband and I have provided you with safety and comfort, and I don't want a bloodbath for a thank-you gift. You need to forgive each other. Be friends.

> *Beat; MAJOR JACK and MAJOR JOHN look at each other, sizing each other up.*

Jack, remember, I knew your father. Yes, I know what he would do in this situation. But I think it says something that you haven't done it yet.

> *Beat.*

You fight for God, don't you?

MAJOR JACK. I do.

HELEN. Well, I am of the opinion that God does not need to be fought for. You may think differently, and that's fine, but this is my house. My land. Right on the border of east and west, right and wrong, however you think of it. The rules are different here. God works differently here. And I think, right now, the best thing you two can do for God is shake hands, say you're sorry, and sit the hell down until my husband comes back with your soldiers.

> *Beat.*

Don't make me count to three.

> *MAJOR JACK looks to MAJOR JOHN and reluctantly sticks out his hand. MAJOR JOHN shakes his hand after a moment.*

Don't forget "sorry."

MAJOR JACK. I'm sorry, sir.

MAJOR JOHN. So am I, sir. Sorry.

HELEN. Great. Now give me that whiskey.

> *She forcefully takes the whiskey bottle from MAJOR JACK and hands it to LOUIE, who is happily surprised. To MAJOR JOHN:*

You too.

> *She takes the other bottle from MAJOR JOHN for herself. She holds it out for LOUIE to clink bottles with her; he does so with great joy.*

To your future doctorate degree, son!

LOUIE. Yes!

> *They each take a big drink from the bottle. LOUIE chokes and coughs violently; HELEN coughs a bit too but handles it better.*

HELEN. God, that's horrible.

LOUIE. *(After he has recovered.)* I'm gonna go find Dennis!

HELEN, MAJOR JACK, and MAJOR JOHN. *(Ad lib.)* No, no, you probably shouldn't. Stay here. Don't go out there.

>*Suddenly DENNIS and LUCY enter, each of them with an arm around BILLY, who can barely walk and is bleeding badly. Even with his injuries, BILLY makes sure to wipe his shoes before entering.*

DENNIS. Help! He needs help!
LUCY. He needs first aid!
HELEN. Billy! What happened?! What's going on?
DENNIS. A bear. There was a bear.
BILLY. I saw a bear, Helen! Fuckin' monster...
HELEN. *(Suddenly thinking very quick.)* Get him on the couch, lay him down!
>*They do.*

Jack, there's a first aid kit in the bathroom upstairs!
>*MAJOR JACK exits upstairs in a rush.*

John, there's ice in the kitchen!
>*MAJOR JOHN exits to the kitchen in a rush.*

Dennis, Lucy, find me some old rags or something!
>*DENNIS and LUCY exit upstairs in a rush.*

Louie, the whiskey!
>*LOUIE rushes over and stubs his toe on the coffee table.*

LOUIE. Ahh, Gaaahddamnit—
HELEN. Quick, Louie!
LOUIE. *(Handing her the whiskey.)* Let me help, I want to be a doctor!
>*Back to his stubbed toe:*

Son of a bitch!
BILLY. I'm gonna be okay, Helen. I will.
HELEN. Save your breath, love. I know you will. Now drink this.
>*BILLY takes a swig of whiskey.*

BILLY. I've been thinkin' 'a Coyote Mountain a lot tonight.
HELEN. I know. Stay still.
BILLY. You know, I always wanted to see a bear.
HELEN. Yes, love, I know. You've done it.
BILLY. I think I'd rather die by bear than by soldier.
HELEN. You're not dying, love, unless you don't shut up!
BILLY. *(Closing his eyes.)* God, am I glad I married the Angel of Coyote Mountain.
HELEN. God, am I glad I married the man who wouldn't shut up.

Louie, you want to be a doctor?

LOUIE. Yes, ma'am!

HELEN. Here's your first patient.

> *All at once, MAJOR JACK enters with first aid; MAJOR JOHN enters with ice; and DENNIS and LUCY enter with the uniforms they had arrived in. Everybody gives their items to HELEN, who hands a few of them to LOUIE. She takes a deep breath and begins saving BILLY's life, with LOUIE faithfully by her side. Everybody else watches on with bated breath. HELEN downs the last gulp of the whiskey.*

Let's get started, Doctor.

> *Lights down.*

Scene 3

Lights up. It is early in the morning, just before dawn. BILLY is resting on the couch with HELEN dozing off beside him. BILLY is all bandaged up and seems to be on the mend. They are the only two in the room, which is barely lit. A soft melody plays on, longer than any of the other songs. HELEN wakes up toward the end and looks sleepily at BILLY. She holds his hand and smiles. As the song dies down:

RADIO ANNOUNCER. ...A beautiful delicate song to wrap up this early hour. It is now six in the morning local time, and it appears we'll have some clear skies at some point today. Somehow we have made it through the storm, and locals are just getting ready to head out and see the new white world that awaits. Joining me once again is Senator Lee of the eastern nation. Senator, any updates?
LEE. Yes, sir, I have it in good authority that the east has captured Whitestone Valley. It appears our success at Turtle Cliffs has—
 HELEN turns off the radio as she hears DENNIS and LUCY coming downstairs. They are just waking up and a bit groggy.
HELEN. Goodmorning.
DENNIS. 'Morning, ma'am.
LUCY. How is he?
HELEN. Oh, he's fine. He will be, at least.
LUCY. Thank goodness.
HELEN. Maybe I should get some coffee going.
DENNIS. I can do it.
HELEN. Thanks, that would be a great help. Kettle's right on the stove, coffee's in the cupboard. We might have a bit of milk left, if you like it.
DENNIS. Thank you, ma'am.
 DENNIS exits to the kitchen.
HELEN. Splendid boy, isn't he?
LUCY. He is.
 Sitting down.
I feel silly, though. I just met him. I can't possibly know him well enough to...
HELEN. That's what I thought too.

LUCY. So how did you know it was right?
HELEN. I didn't. All I could think was "What the hell am I doing?" over and over again. Drove myself crazy. But he was so brave, so funny, so... I hadn't seen a look of humor on any soldier's face before him. There he was, dying on a mountaintop in the middle of a war, and he laughed like it was any other day. So I just told myself, "Well, if this is it, then I'm happy. If not, he'll be dead soon anyway."

She chuckles to herself.

LUCY. He's a really great guy.
HELEN. I know.

Beat.

What's next for you?
LUCY. I'm not sure.
HELEN. Well, what do you want to do?
LUCY. I don't know. I'm too tired, and my head hurts too much to think about it.
HELEN. Then what is your heart telling you?
LUCY. To run away.

Beat.

But it's been telling me that for years now...
HELEN. You just haven't had anyone to run away with.
LUCY. I guess.

Beat.

I'm going to miss this place.
HELEN. Oh, you're always welcome back. Besides, we don't have anyone to live here once we're gone.
LUCY. You never had any kids?
HELEN. We knew they'd just join the war. We didn't want to add to all of that.

Beat.

I wish we had, though. Maybe we could've raised them in a certain way that they'd never wanted to fight. I don't know. Do you want kids?
LUCY. Maybe someday. I haven't had time to think about it.

BILLY is starting to wake up.

BILLY. Don't listen to her. Kids ruin everything.
HELEN. Hey there, love. How'd you sleep?
BILLY. I had a dream about my father.

HELEN. Yeah? What was happening?
BILLY. He was actually a bear in disguise. His whole life. Everybody knew about it. It was awful. And weird.
   DENNIS enters with two mugs of coffee.
DENNIS. Goodmorning, sir.
   He hands one mug to LUCY and one to HELEN.
BILLY. Mornin', son.
DENNIS. How are you feeling?
BILLY. I feel like dancin'! Just give me a few days.
DENNIS. Can't wait. Coffee, sir?
BILLY. I think another shot of whiskey would do me some good.
HELEN. Sorry, love, we're all out.
BILLY. Well, coffee it is. Helen, could you and Lucy go get it? I want a word with the lover here.
HELEN. Of course.
   She kisses him on the forehead.
Don't tell him about <u>everything</u>, okay?
BILLY. Oh come on! Not even that night down by the river?
HELEN. <u>Especially</u> not the night down by the river. God, he'd never look at me the same way again.
   She turns to exit to the kitchen with LUCY. As they exit, she whispers to LUCY:
You should know about it though. So we got down there around dusk, and we had the place to ourselves all night…
   They exit.
DENNIS. Good to see you alive, sir.
BILLY. Good to be alive. You know, I wouldn't be here without you.
DENNIS. Neither would I.
BILLY. Boy, you were sure blown off course, weren't you?
DENNIS. We couldn't see a damn thing. Just wandered around aimlessly, no sign of the trail, clutching each other close just for a bit of warmth. Thought we were about to die. God, was I scared as hell.
BILLY. I know the feelin'.
DENNIS. I know.
   Beat.
You're a great man, Billy.
BILLY. Thanks.

Beat.
You know what I was thinkin' 'bout when I came across that bear?
DENNIS. What?
BILLY. I was thinkin', "Wow, a bear!" and then he tore into my arm. Broke my favorite lantern and everything. Anyway, after that, all I could think was, "If only Helen could be here to see this with me." I couldn't think of anything else in the world other than havin' her by my side, right then. And I saw you two instead, runnin' at me. I thought, "Goddamn it, I guess they're good enough."
He chuckles to himself.
Thanks for savin' me.
DENNIS. You're welcome, Billy.
BILLY. *(Beat.)* Son, I know I don't have much authority to tell you what to do. Hell, we just met last night. But by God, if I was in your shoes... You know what I would do?
DENNIS. What's that?
BILLY. I'd quit the war and get laid already.
He chuckles again, then stops because it's too painful.
You know what I mean. Get married, fall in love, enjoy a new life with Lucy. Forget about all this. Leave it behind.
DENNIS. I just met her last night. I already feel, I don't know, foolish, for even thinking about—I mean, she's wonderful, it's just that—How do I know...?
BILLY. What? How do you know what?
DENNIS. How do I know that I'm doing the right thing?
BILLY. Son, anything you do without a weapon in your hand is the right thing.

DENNIS nods and smiles. He is about to say something but the basement door swings open, with MAJOR JACK dragging LOUIE into the room. LOUIE is shaking his hands in pain. MAJOR JACK is back in his uniform, but LOUIE is still in his borrowed clothing.

MAJOR JACK. Just in case anyone's wondering, no, we should not leave Louie in charge of the fire.
LOUIE. Sorry, sir. It didn't look that hot.
BILLY. Mornin', Jack.
MAJOR JACK. Goodmorning, sir. You look a lot better than you did

last night.

BILLY. You should see me in a dress.

HELEN and LUCY enter from the kitchen with two cups of coffee each.

HELEN. I thought I heard more voices. Here you go.

She gives her mugs to MAJOR JACK and LOUIE; LUCY gives hers to BILLY and DENNIS.

How'd you sleep?

LOUIE. Wonderful, ma'am.

MAJOR JACK. Would've been better if you hadn't tried cuddling so much.

LOUIE. *(To HELEN.)* I get clingy when I sleep.

DENNIS. You have to just let him cuddle, sir.

MAJOR JACK. No, I certainly do not.

Getting serious now.

Besides, I guess this is the end of the line for us.

LOUIE. What do you mean, sir? You're not quitting too?

MAJOR JACK. No, Louie. I'm not.

A deep breath; to HELEN:

I've thought a lot about what you said, ma'am. And I guess you're right in a few places.

Beat.

But I can't quit. I'm sorry.

HELEN. I understand, Jack.

MAJOR JACK. I'm a soldier. I fight for a living, and I live to fight. I don't know much else, and I feel like I'd be living a lie if I wasn't out there fighting for what I believe in.

HELEN. We'll agree to disagree, I guess.

MAJOR JACK. Thank you, ma'am.

To BILLY.

Sir, I'd like to thank you for your generosity. We came here with our lives on the line, and you saved us. My men and I appreciate your warm welcome very much, and if there's anything I can do to pay you back, just let me know.

BILLY. I think you owe me a bottle or two of whiskey.

MAJOR JACK. *(Laughing.)* Trust me, if we see each other again, I'll get you enough whiskey to make a bear weep.

BILLY. I can't wait. Jack...
MAJOR JACK. Yes, sir?
BILLY. *(Sitting up a bit.)* I'm sorry.
> Beat.

I'm sorry I killed your father.
MAJOR JACK. It's the war, sir. I understand.
> *Shaking his hand cautiously, careful of BILLY's injuries.*

I forgive you.
BILLY. That means a lot. Thank you.
MAJOR JACK. On an unrelated note, I believe my weapon is somewhere around here...
HELEN. Oh! Under here...
> *She and MAJOR JACK find his gun and knife underneath the sofa, where they have been since the men first arrived.*

MAJOR JACK. Thank you, ma'am.
> *To DENNIS and LOUIE.*

Gentlemen, it's been an honor. I hope you know I respect your decision to remove yourselves from the war.
DENNIS. You do?
LOUIE. Aren't we traitors?
MAJOR JACK. Not to me. But, actually, yeah, now that I think about it, you probably are. Technically. I'd lay low for a bit if I were you.
DENNIS. Yes, sir.
MAJOR JACK. So, what's it going to be? You're running off with Lucy, and Louie's just coming along?
DENNIS. *(Giving a look to LOUIE, who has just spilled coffee all over himself.)* We'll have to figure that part out.
MAJOR JACK. Fair enough.
> *MAJOR JOHN enters from upstairs, rubbing his eyes.*

MAJOR JOHN. Everybody awake already?
> *To BILLY.*

How are you, sir?
BILLY. I'll be runnin' around by noon.
MAJOR JOHN. Good to hear.
> *MAJOR JOHN is now about an arm's length from MAJOR JACK, who is holding his gun but couldn't be more peaceful.*

Is this it?

MAJOR JACK. This is it.
MAJOR JOHN. Once we're out that door…?
MAJOR JACK. Yeah.
MAJOR JOHN. Okay.
MAJOR JACK. Just give me a, I don't know, twenty minute head start, will you?
MAJOR JOHN. Which way will you be headed?
MAJOR JACK. North.
MAJOR JOHN. I'll go south, then.
    Extending his hand.
I respect you, sir.
MAJOR JACK. Likewise. May God be with you.
    He crosses to the door, opens it, and stands in the doorway. He takes a deep breath, then dashes out without a glance back.
BILLY. *(Beat.)* Don't kill him, John.
MAJOR JOHN. I'll do everything in my power not to, Billy. He's a friend.
    BILLY and HELEN look successfully at each other. They've done it; they've (temporarily) stopped the war. They smile to DENNIS and LUCY in their embrace, to LOUIE in cleaning up his spilled coffee, to MAJOR JOHN in his preparation to re-enter the battlefield. BILLY grabs HELEN's hand and squeezes it tight. Lights down.

END OF ACT II

END OF SHOW

Nobletiger

A Play in Two Acts

by

Tucker Atwood

NOBLETIGER received a staged reading with the Belfast Maskers in Belfast, Maine in January 2024. It was produced by Tucker Atwood. The readers were as follows:

NICK..Dominic Williams
KASEN..Tyler Johnstone
KYLIE..Abby Boucher
TRACY...Autumn Stupca
BRAD..Erik Perkins
ERICA...Katie Glessner

SHORT SYNOPSIS

As humanity and life as we know it crumbles to a disappointing end in the background, a father, his two kids, and a pizza delivery woman gather around to watch the final baseball game ever. They are protected only by a pair of bodyguards hired through (and quite obviously sponsored by) iZon, the only company still in existence. With the apocalyptic end drawing nearer, this family has simply stopped caring about their impending doom, choosing instead to focus all their time and energy on our beautiful national pastime. Natural disasters, wars, annoying advertisements – blah blah blah, can't you see the game is on?

CHARACTERS

KASEN — early 20s. A baseball nerd who lives and breathes statistics and doesn't have much interest in anything else.

KYLIE — early 20s. Kasen's sister, who is sooooo much cooler than Kasen, but is also stuck at home watching the game.

NICK — 40s. Kasen and Kylie's father, a former baseball pitcher who drinks and yells at the TV to relive his glory days. A bit gruff and passionate, but ultimately well-meaning.

TRACY — 40s. A pizza delivery woman who is temporarily stuck watching a game she knows nothing about.

BRAD and ERICA — 20s to 40s. Two bodyguards of the family who frequently advertise iZon products. They talk and act like heavily scripted characters in a cheesy apocalyptic movie.

PROPERTY LIST

Beer bottles
Water bottles
Pizza
Helmets/protective gear
Oxygen masks

COSTUME NOTES

Kasen, Kylie, and Nick are dressed casually, perhaps with baseball jerseys or hats. Tracy is dressed like a pizza delivery woman. Brad and Erica are the only characters whose clothing would suggest the "end of days" is near, but it's a sort of commercialized, thinly veiled "sexy" version of it. Their clothes are ripped and scant, and their skin is somehow dirty and glistening at the same time.

In Act 2, Kasen, Kylie, Nick, and Tracy are wearing torn up versions of what they were wearing in Act 1. Their hair is also much messier, and they all have minor cuts/bruises all over their bodies.

SET REQUIREMENTS

The set appears to be a middle-class American living room. In reality, it's an underground bunker attached to other nearby bunkers through an intricate tunnel system. However, the only indication of that is the front entrance, an airtight steel door, behind which lies incredible danger and destruction. Once inside that door, one would think they're in a typical home. On one side of the room is a hallway that leads to bedrooms, a kitchen, a bathroom, etc. A couch center stage is pointed directly at the audience, where a television-like appliance is presumed to be (i.e. when characters are watching TV, they're looking at the audience). There are also a couple of chairs and various furniture – you know what a living room looks like.

LIGHTING AND SOUND NOTES

There are several moments where vague disasters or wars are implied to be happening nearby. During these moments, a "warning system" will go off, which should consist of a loud warning sound and perhaps some flashing lights, though the lights are not necessary. Often, along with the warning, we hear rumbling, explosions, screaming, and an assortment of other horrifying sounds coming from outside the front entrance. It's not anything specific; it just needs to sound like the world is ending.

There is also a momentary spotlight on Brad and Erica at one point, though this is not entirely necessary either.

MISCELLANEOUS NOTES

There are descriptions of the stage "shaking," "rumbling," and even being "turned sideways." As cool as it would be to have the technical resources to make this possible, it is likely not possible or convenient to actually move the stage. Therefore, the actors should convey any implied shaking or movement through their actions. The sounds of terror and possible flashing lights mentioned before will make these movements more believable.

The actors and director do not need a working knowledge of baseball, but please make sure you pronounce everything as a baseball fan would. For example, many acronyms are simply spelled out by their letters, but WAR is pronounced like the word "war," not spelled out "W-A-R" like other acronyms. When in doubt, you can likely find a pronunciation online. The only statistic mentioned in this play that does not currently exist in real baseball is xwOBAwRC+, but it's just a juxtaposition of two real statistics: xwOBA (pronounced "x - WHOA - BAH") and wRC+ (pronounced "W-R-C-plus").

ACT I

Lights up. KASEN sits upright on the couch, seemingly staring into the distance. KYLIE hangs over the side of a chair, also staring into the distance. They are both slowly moving their arms through the air in front of them. It looks strange. What they're really doing is scrolling through "feeds" on devices implanted in their eyes with projected screens only they can see. This is our future. For a few moments, neither of them say anything. They mindlessly scroll, half-chuckling at something unseen now and then. Finally, KASEN appears to "send" something to KYLIE, who receives it immediately. She scoffs.

KYLIE. No, thank you.
KASEN. Come on. It'll take two and a half minutes.
KYLIE. No. It's dumb.
KASEN. That's what you say when you're scared you're gonna lose.
KYLIE. I am not.
KASEN. You're not what?
KYLIE. I'm not gonna lose.
KASEN. Ah, so you will play.
KYLIE. No, I'm – I meant, if I was to – Shut up. It's dumb.
KASEN. Come on. It's just a fun little thing. Nothing too crazy.
KYLIE. Then what's the point? Make it worth my while.
KASEN. How would I do that?
KYLIE. *(Beat.)* Thousand bucks.
KASEN. Oh, I wasn't going to put any money on it –
KYLIE. Why not? Pussy.
KASEN. Why do you have to talk like that?
KYLIE. Deal or no?
KASEN. *(Beat.)* Sure. Easy money.
KYLIE. Yup. For me.
KASEN. Have you forgotten I've lived and breathed baseball my whole life?
KYLIE. Have you forgotten I struck you out sixteen times in little league?
KASEN. My On-Base-Percentage against you was .385!

KYLIE. Only 'cause I plunked you whenever I got bored.

KASEN. Anyway, whoever was the better player is irrelevant. These predictions are based strictly on knowledge. And I know more about baseball than you could ever dream.

KYLIE. Good thing I'm dreaming about more exciting things.

There is no sound effect, but both react to a notification popping up in front of them.

KASEN. Nice, the pizza's here.

KYLIE. Wait, let's make Dad do it.

KASEN. Why? You know he's clueless with this.

KYLIE. Exactly. It's hilarious. DAD, PIZZA'S HERE!!!

KASEN. *(Tracking KYLIE's predictions as she's making them.)* What the – Holy cow, Kylie, these predictions are awful!

KYLIE. What? Why?

KASEN. A single apiece for Olivo and Velasco – they're in the middle of the lineup for a reason, they get <u>extra</u> base hits. Not many singles. Six runs total before the 5th inning, okay, that's not bad. Wait – <u>three</u> walks for Baker?? He's got a terrible eye! He doesn't walk!

KYLIE. I don't know what to tell you. He will today.

KASEN. Right. Eight strikeouts for Bannerman, fine, that's realistic enough. Four double plays? I guess you trust the infield defense more than I do... Fastest pitch, Mistretta? He's not a power pitcher, and both bullpens have some fast throwers. Kone, Diggs, Williams – heck, I'd even take Bannerman over Mistretta for that one.

KYLIE. But Mistretta's cuter than all of them.

KASEN. Come on, take this seriously.

KYLIE. Didn't you say "easy money"?

KASEN. Well, yeah, but make it a challenge. Oh, you must be joking – two extra base hits for Solano? He's a contact hitter!

KYLIE. Wish he'd make contact with me. Have you <u>seen</u> his eyes?

KASEN. Objectively, yes, they are nice eyes. But –

NICK enters from the hallway. He is from a generation that doesn't understand new-age technology as well – he is also looking at a screen projected in front of him, but knocking into furniture and very distracted. He has a beer in one hand which spills a bit every time he scrolls.

NICK. Why can't either of you let them in?

KYLIE. Sorry, mine's broken.

NICK. Right. Like you can live without it. I see you waving around.

KYLIE. It's called <u>scrolling</u>, Dad.

NICK. Kasen, bud, can't you do this for me?

> *KASEN looks at KYLIE, who responds with extreme silent peer pressure.*

KASEN. Mine is broken too?

NICK. You're both Goddamn awful at lying. Okay, fine – I'll do it myself. Is it the little icon with the eyeball on it, or the camera?

KYLIE. Camera.

KASEN. No, don't listen to her, that's your, well, your camera. You want the one with the door on it.

NICK. Red door?

KASEN. I don't know, what update are you on?

NICK. I just want my pizza! Why are you making this so difficult, the game starts in – when does it start?

KASEN. Eleven minutes.

NICK. Then quit making me do this, I don't want to miss the pregame! Turn it on, will you – Hello? Hi! Sorry!

> *He suddenly realizes he's in the middle of a "phone call." He stares straight ahead, obviously talking face-to-face with somebody. To KASEN and KYLIE.*

Wonder how long this phone call's been going.

> *Back to the screen.*

Yes, this is him. Nick. Yes. Okay, yup, I saw that – I'm letting you in, yeah, I just don't know what button to – My kids are assholes, y'see – Gold door? Okay. I see it. And – there. There. There? What am I doing wrong?

KASEN and KYLIE. Double tap.

NICK. Right. Okay. Double. Tap. Hurray!!! Okay, see you in a minute. Oh, don't worry about them – they're our bodyguards. But we got 'em from iZon and they're also, whatever-you-call-em, the social marketers or whatever.

KASEN and KYLIE. Influencers.

NICK. Influencer marketers. Yeah. They'll try to sell you this or that, just tell 'em "No thank you." Okay, see you.

> *He "hangs up."*

You know, we'd have the pizza by now if you two didn't like to see me fail at this techno-shit.

KYLIE. Worth it.

She makes a swiping motion.

There. I submitted my predictions. Happy?

KASEN. Yes, I am. 'Cause I'm gonna win an easy thousand bucks.

NICK. Thousand bucks? What's this now?

KASEN. The prediction contest I sent you. Did you see it?

NICK. Oh, I thought that was spam.

KASEN. It was from me.

NICK. And? You know how easy it is to pretend to be somebody you're not these days?

KASEN. Okay, well, I'm telling you – it's from me. Are you gonna fill it out? You have to fill it out before the game starts.

NICK. Fine, but you didn't mention this "thousand bucks" part of it before. Sure changes things.

KASEN. That's just something Kylie insisted on.

KYLIE. Makes it more interesting.

NICK. You bet it does.

He's been trying to find it, but can't.

Okay, I give up. Where is this thing?

KASEN. I'll just resend it to you.

He does.

There. Did you get it?

NICK. Yeah… And you're sure this is you?

KASEN. *(Beat.)* Yes, it is me.

NICK. Just checking.

He starts filling out predictions, with wild and unnecessary hand movements to make sure he's doing it right.

KYLIE. *(Reacting to the TV.)* I hate all this pregame stuff.

KASEN. What's wrong with the first pitch?

KYLIE. Not that.

NICK. It's the national anthem.

KYLIE. Bingo.

NICK. 'Cause she hates America.

KASEN. I'm sure she doesn't <u>hate</u> America.

KYLIE. No no, I do.

NICK. Y'know, it wouldn't kill you to show some damn respect for your country. You kids don't know how good you've got it. Y'know, if we were in one of them other countries, we'd be living above ground. You wouldn't want that, now, would you?

KYLIE. More likely we'd be dead.

NICK. Exactly. So don't take this for granted! Kasen, bud, you like the national anthem, don't you?

KASEN. Well, it is a tradition.

NICK. And a damn good one at that. It ain't baseball without the national anthem.

KYLIE. *(Sarcastically.)* And it ain't America without baseball.

NICK. *(Not sarcastically.)* Hallelujah.

KYLIE. Then what will we call all of this tomorrow?

KASEN. Tomorrow?

KYLIE. Well, if this is the last game…

NICK. Quit it. I don't need to be reminded that. Where's that pizza?

KASEN. I heard the Tunnel's a little backed up today.

KYLIE. Jessica said they found three bodies near the South Bend, and they were <u>hideous</u>.

KASEN. … But she still slept with them?

KYLIE. What?

KASEN. Y'know, because – Jessica's a slut.

KYLIE. Stop it. Jessica is not a slut.

KASEN. She kinda is.

KYLIE. Dad? You're gonna let him call Jessica a slut?

NICK. Kasen, be nice to your sister. Kylie, she is too a slut.

KYLIE. Dad!

NICK. But there's nothing wrong with it! Come on, how old are you and Jessica now? 18, 19? No, really, remind me.

KYLIE. I'm 21. How do you not know that?

NICK. You know my memory. Okay, 21, then what the hell's the matter? At that age, I was – well, never mind that, but 21's a fine age to be a slut.

    Beat.

Except you, of course. You've gotta wait till marriage – or whatever your mother would want me to say.

KASEN. I think that ship's already left the dock, Dad.

KYLIE. And where's your ship, Kasen?
KASEN. *(Beat.)* Dad, you finished with those predictions yet?
NICK. Almost… okay, there. There. There! What the hell is wrong with this thing?!
KASEN and KYLIE. Drag and swipe.
NICK. How does everyone just <u>know</u> this shit?
   He drags and swipes.
Okay, there. I don't see 'em anymore, so it's outta my hands.
KASEN. Dad, these are even worse than Kylie's predictions!
NICK. What? What's wrong with them?
KASEN. Twelve runs before the 5th inning? Eight hits for Olivo and Velasco?? Sixteen strikeouts for Bannerman???
NICK. They're gonna have a good game! All of 'em.
KASEN. I get rooting for the Yanks, Dad, but come on – you've gotta be realistic.
KYLIE. Hey, that's what I told you on your prom night.
KASEN. Would you stop it? Besides, I'll have you know, my prom date kissed me three times that night.
KYLIE. Really? Who was that again?
KASEN. It was – Uh. I can't remember.
KYLIE. Neither can she, I'd bet.
KASEN. That's weird. But anyway, the point is, if I wanted to get laid on my prom night, I could have.
KYLIE. Yeah? How?
NICK. He would've asked Jessica.
KYLIE. Dad!
   There is a knock at the door.
NICK. Finally. One second!
   He tries to unlock the door from his screen, but can't.
Okay, which icon is it this time?
KASEN. *(Swiping.)* I got it.
NICK. Thanks, bud.
   The door slowly opens, and terrifying sound effects are heard from behind it. Rushing in and down the stairs to avoid danger: TRACY, delivering a pizza; and BRAD and ERICA, the family bodyguards who take their roles ultra-seriously.
BRAD. Quick! This poor hapless woman needs first aid!

ERICA. She's about to perish!
TRACY. What? No, I'm – I'm fine – I'm just here with the pizza.
BRAD. *(Pulling out a knife and situating a table as if preparing to perform surgery.)* Clear the area! Get an anesthetic! I'm going straight into her heart!
ERICA. *(Trying to get TRACY to lay on the table.)* Brad, you hero!
TRACY. Really, I'm okay. Stop.
BRAD. She's not thinking clearly! She's disillusioned! Erica!
ERICA. Yes, Brad?!
BRAD. *(Pulling her close to him dramatically.)* This ill-fated woman is about to die of dehydration, and I need to save her life. Tell me I can do it! Believe in me, Erica! If it's the last thing you ever do!
ERICA. Oh Brad, of course you can do it! You're so strong and skillful! You can do anything!
TRACY. I'm not dying! What is going on??
KYLIE. Just let them do their bit. It's over quicker that way.
TRACY. Sorry, what?
KASEN. They're just building up to an advertisement. Just be polite and they'll go away soon.
TRACY. An advertisement?
BRAD. Ma'am, will you let us save your life?
ERICA. Please, Brad, you brave, strong man, do it!
NICK. For God's sake, the game is almost on, hurry it up!
TRACY. Uh – sure, you can save my life. I guess?
BRAD. Okay, here goes.
> He takes a moment to change personas. He and ERICA now adopt a "commercial" voice, enthusiastic and fake. TRACY looks awkwardly at them; everyone else is used to it by now.

Ma'am, it's a survivor's world.
ERICA. And if you want to make it out alive, you need the purest,
BRAD. Most refreshing,
ERICA. And only water around:
BRAD. iZon Water Plus!
ERICA. Made with a never-before-seen blend of iZon Hydrogen and iZon Oxygen, this water will replenish you like no other!
BRAD. Now with double the hydrogen!
ERICA. Do you often find yourself dizzy, light-headed, tired, or on

the verge of losing consciousness?

BRAD. Don't let the complete lack of viable water sources remaining on Earth get you down!

ERICA. Sign up <u>now</u> for exclusive early access to iZon's premium iZon Water Plus Family Package!

BRAD. Probably enough for your entire family!

ERICA. For the next few weeks, at least!

BRAD. Limited time only!

ERICA. Prices vary due to demand, war, or profit recalculations.

BRAD. Survival not guaranteed.

ERICA. Now with free WiFi!

Big smiles; this is the end of their "pitch." They remain standing, waiting for validation. TRACY awkwardly claps, not knowing what else to do.

KASEN. *(Whispering to TRACY.)* "Maybe later."

TRACY. What?

KASEN. Tell them "Maybe later."

TRACY. Oh, thanks.

To BRAD and ERICA.

Maybe later?

Suddenly, a gigantic crash is heard above, shaking the entire room and throwing everybody every which way. NICK runs over to the kids instinctively, protecting them. TRACY drops the pizza on the floor. BRAD and ERICA leap into action.

BRAD. Is everyone alright?!

ERICA. I'm fine, Brad!

BRAD. Erica, thank God! Your gorgeous body has remained intact!

NICK. *(To KASEN and KYLIE.)* You kids okay?

KASEN and KYLIE. *(Ad lib.)* Yeah, I think I'm fine, etc.

TRACY. I'm so sorry, the pizza…

NICK. Don't worry about it, wasn't your fault.

TRACY. What the hell was – ?

NICK. Shh! The game's starting.

For NICK and KASEN, and to a certain extent KYLIE, nothing else matters anymore. With the game on, everything else is irrelevant.

BRAD. Erica, we need to save their lives!

ERICA. If anyone can do it, it's us!

NICK. No! Shut up! Game's on. Go save the rest of the world.

BRAD and ERICA consider this for a moment.

BRAD. Did you hear that, Erica?! We've been called on to rescue the rest of the world!

ERICA. Oh, Brad, you hunk, let's do it!

BRAD. *(Taking ERICA by the shoulders.)* Erica. I don't know if we'll make it out of this alive, so if we don't, I want you to know… I am romantically attracted to you!

ERICA. Oh, Brad! What an unexpected surprise! You always said you thought of me more as a friend, or a sister!

BRAD. Feelings change, Erica! But the truth is, my feelings for you have never changed! I've always loved you!

ERICA. You really mean it?!

BRAD. Sure!

They start making out furiously. NICK, KASEN, and KYLIE barely notice. TRACY stands there awkwardly trying to pick up the pizza.

TRACY. I don't think you'll be able to salvage this. Maybe I should go get you another…

BRAD. *(Breaking apart from ERICA.)* No! You can't go anywhere until we clear the outside area! It could be – dangerous!

TRACY. What? Can't I just –

ERICA. No! Stay here, or you die! But don't worry – we'll be putting our very lives on the line for you.

BRAD. You bet we are. Because we are heroes.

They both strike heroic poses.

NICK. For God's sake, you idiots, get out of here! I don't want you ruining a single pitch of this game! Out!

BRAD and ERICA. Yes, sir!

They start to leave, but TRACY stops them.

TRACY. Wait, I'm stuck here? But these folks won't want me to –

NICK. Whatever. Just sit down and shut up. Oh shit, you didn't just stop them from leaving, did you?

TRACY. Um…

NICK. God's sake. Here comes another ad.

On cue, ERICA and BRAD enter their commercial personas.

BRAD. Boy, sometimes this world is so lonely and depressing.
ERICA. If only I had someone to spend my last days with.
NICK. Skip! Skip! Game's on! Skip!
BRAD. Well, today's your lucky day! Did you know there are dozens of hot, lonely singles in your area?!
ERICA. Oh my! How delightful!
BRAD. Go to iZon Match Mingle Mania to access your messages! It's so easy!
ERICA. @ kittyplaytime69 says: I'm so wet for sex with you! Click here for fun games and hot naked for you!
NICK. Decline, decline!
BRAD. @ dong_johnson_supreme says: It's horny time! Click here for pics of my gigantic –

Another, smaller, crash is heard above.

NICK. You hear that? That sounds like a job for our courageous bodyguards! Get out of here, or you're fired! Unsubscribe, terminate permanently, the whole shebang!

Beat. BRAD and ERICA consider this, then decide to leave.

BRAD. We've been called to action, Erica!
ERICA. I'm right behind you!

They dash upstairs, then pause for a moment before opening the door to kiss passionately. They break apart, open the door, and finally leave. Everyone is watching the TV except TRACY, who is overcome by everything that just happened.

TRACY. Who were those people?
NICK. Bodyguards. Shut up, game's starting.

Beat. They all watch the TV for a few seconds.

KASEN. Strike. First pitch of the last game. Strike.
NICK. Quit it, we don't need any reminders.
KASEN. Okay. It's just… sad.
NICK. Have a beer, that'll lighten you up.
KASEN. That never seems to work for you.
NICK. I don't get sad.
KYLIE. No, just pissed off.
NICK. *(Pissed off.)* Shut up.
    To TRACY.
You want a beer while you wait this out?

TRACY. Um – I don't really drink.

NICK. *(Sarcastically.)* Good for you.

TRACY. I guess – I guess I'd take a water, though?

NICK. Kylie, get her some water.

KYLIE. You know you can do that, right?

NICK. I'm watching the game!

KYLIE. Fine.

She rolls her eyes and exits to the kitchen.

TRACY. So, um – what's this "game" you're watching?

KASEN. Yankees-Dodgers.

TRACY. What does that mean?

NICK. It means the Yankees are playing against the Dodgers, it's Game 7 of the World Series, and nobody is mentioning anything else for the next three to five hours. Nick, by the way. Have a seat.

TRACY. Oh, uh, I'm Tracy. Thank you.

KASEN. Kasen. Nice to meet you, Tracy.

KYLIE. *(Returning from the kitchen and handing a bottle of iZon Water Plus to TRACY.)* And I'm Kylie.

TRACY. *(Taking the water.)* Oh, thank you so much.

KASEN. Oh, wow! Did you see the movement on that slider? Bannerman's got it going today.

NICK. Slider's a pussy pitch.

KASEN. According to you, any pitch that isn't a fastball is a…

KYLIE. He won't even say it.

KASEN. We have company. It's indecent.

KYLIE. Pussy.

NICK. Come on, bud, nobody cares. Stacy sure doesn't, do you?

TRACY. It's Tracy –

NICK. And yes, anything slower than 95 is a pussy pitch.

KASEN. Pitchers need to be able to throw multiple types of pitches. Otherwise they're too predictable. If every pitch is a fastball, then –

NICK. If the fastball's good enough, he doesn't need another pitch!

Reacting to TV.

Ah! Now there's a fastball. Struck him out. Now if he would just stick to the fastball…

KASEN. It only worked because he threw that slider before it.

NICK. Nah, that was a waste pitch.

KASEN. He wouldn't throw a waste pitch on a 2-2 count.

NICK. Then you haven't watched enough Bannerman.

KASEN. *(Pulling up data on his projected screen.)* I can pull up his charts and show you his tendencies –

NICK. Put it away.

KASEN. But this is empirical evidence that –

NICK. I said, put it away. Every time you're looking at numbers on there, the real game is being played right here. Trust me, kids, you don't want to miss this! That's what's wrong with you, you stats people, you never watch the actual game.

KASEN. Well, I happen to like the stats.

KYLIE. I'm only here for the sex appeal.

KASEN. Hey, nice. Two quick outs.

NICK. Damn right.

TRACY. If I could just ask a quick clarifying question –

NICK. No. Wait till the end of the inning.

TRACY. Okay, sure. Sorry.

NICK. *(To KASEN.)* Your fancy numbers damn near ruined baseball. On base averages and earned run percentages, it's a travesty. Just throw the damn ball, hit the damn ball.

KASEN. They're quite useful in predicting future performance.

NICK. Sure. Sure. Well, bud, guess what?

KASEN. What?

NICK. After today, there ain't no future performance.

KASEN. *(Somber.)* Oh yeah.

KYLIE. *(Trying to keep things light.)* So, Bannerman today, huh.

KASEN. Yeah. He went 16-7 this year with a 3.41 ERA, although peripheral stats show he was overperforming and will probably regress next year – oh, right…

NICK. What'd I tell ya. Numbers don't mean shit. Not anymore. Y'know what, this is how baseball should've always been played.

KASEN. I guess he's due to regress in this game at least.

NICK. Don't you say that – he's gonna pitch the game of his life. Maybe even a no-hi – No, I'm not gonna say it, I'll jinx –

    Reacting to the TV.

Goddamn it!

KASEN. Just a single. It's fine.

NICK. There goes the no-hitter, though.

KYLIE. It's the first inning.

NICK. And I had hope, silly me.

KASEN. At least he's keeping his pitch count low. Don't want to dip into the bullpen too early. The bullpen sucks lately.

NICK. The bullpen sucks every year. Swear to God, they've blown every save for the last twelve and a half years. Bunch of scrubs.

TRACY. Twelve and a half years? That's very specific.

NICK. Didn't we tell you –

KYLIE. That was when Dad blew his arm out.

KASEN. He was a promising young pitcher once, and then –

NICK. That's enough, kids!

KYLIE. *(Beat.)* If only the Yankees had a lights-out flamethrower in the back of their bullpen, maybe they would've won the World Series sometime in the last twelve and a half years.

KASEN. Oh please, Dad wasn't a flamethrower. His max velocity was 60th percentile at best. Maybe if he learned some control, that would've been fine. And don't get me started on the home runs –

NICK. I woulda been the best Goddamn closer in baseball, and you know it! You saw me throw! I could strike out Mike Fucking Trout if I wanted to! If my arm had held up, I'd be on course for the Hall of Fame and you two would be bragging to everybody about your father being the greatest Goddamn closer in baseball history!

KASEN. In history? C'mon, don't disrespect Mariano Rivera like that. Unless – you think you would've been better than Rivera?

NICK. Well, maybe I'd be a close second.

KYLIE. I'd only brag about you if you were number one.

KASEN. I'd brag about you, but only if you'd let me use your stats.

NICK. Don't say anything about my stats. I'm lucky I've forgotten 'em all by now.

KASEN. But they were really good, Dad! I'm proud of them.

KYLIE. Y'know what my favorite part was when you were playing?

NICK. My insane fastball?

KYLIE. No.

NICK. Then you're wrong.

KASEN. What was it, Kylie?

KYLIE. His weird superstitions.

NICK. *(To the TV.)* Foul, foul, foul. They're working him to death. Just throw your damn fastball, Bannerman!
KASEN. He's setting him up.
NICK. Setting himself up, more like it. These guys think too much.
    Back to KYLIE.
What are you talking about, weird superstitions?
KYLIE. Remember you would wear just one sock when you pitched?
NICK. I forget <u>one</u> sock, <u>one</u> time, and I'm still getting shit for it.
KYLIE. You kept doing it though.
NICK. Well that day I forgot it, I threw a damn no-hitter!
KASEN. You never threw a no-hitter.
NICK. It's called an exaggeration, alright? I pitched well that day, and I figured, hey, maybe that's the key.
KYLIE. The key to pitching well is to wear one sock?
NICK. Well it sure as hell ain't two!

    Suddenly an abrupt, loud warning noise fills the house and the lights flash. They all check their projected screens and casually read a warning message and its instructions on which emergency protocol to follow. As it blares on, KASEN and KYLIE pull out some oxygen masks and find a place to hide. NICK pulls out two and gives one to TRACY, directing her to a place to hide as well. The whole process is clearly very routine to them. After a while, the noise stops and the lights go back to normal. Everyone stands up and returns to their previous spots. As if nothing happened:

There we go, Bannerman! Shut 'em down! Did you see <u>that</u> fastball, Kasen, buddy? Now that's a fastball!
KASEN. It was a great location. More location than velocity, I'd say.
KYLIE. *(Reacting to something on her screen.)* You guys!!!
    All stop and stare at her. Beat.
Jessica and Steve just broke up!
NICK. Which one was Steve?
KASEN. The one with the bad hair.
NICK. They've all got bad hair.
KYLIE. You're one to talk.
NICK. What's wrong with my hair?
TRACY. Excuse me!

Beat. They all look at her.
Are we not going to discuss what just happened?
NICK. Are you hurt?
TRACY. Well – no –
NICK. Sick? Faint?
TRACY. I guess not...
NICK. Do you have a problem with our emergency warning system?
TRACY. No, it seems to work well, I suppose.
NICK. Then what is there to discuss?
TRACY. I just thought – well, what did it mean?
NICK. That the world is ending. Welcome back to reality.
TRACY. Yes, but, that specifically...
NICK. Who knows? Look, it happens all the time. Nothing to get worked up about. World's in distress, one of these days we'll all die in a fiery explosion or flood or whatever, blah blah blah. Anybody else want a beer?
   He heads to the kitchen.
ALL. *(Ad lib.)* Yeah, sure, why not, etc.
   NICK exits. Before TRACY has a chance to say anything:
KASEN. So who's Jessica gonna date next week?
KYLIE. Not you.
KASEN. That's not what I meant. I meant –
KYLIE. You meant she's a slut. Ha ha. Hilarious. Better than being a loser virgin.
KASEN. I've told you, I have no interest in sex. And there's plenty of other people like me out there.
KYLIE. Congrats, maybe you'll meet one someday.
KASEN. Haven't you been going through a bit of a dry spell lately?
KYLIE. No. Maybe. I don't remember, actually. That's weird.
KASEN. Oh, wow, it's been since Trevor, hasn't it?
KYLIE. Who?
KASEN. The guy who criticized your nightgown.
KYLIE. Oh, right. It's not a nightgown!
KASEN. Still, probably not the best thing to impress a guy with.
KYLIE. I didn't know he was coming over. He surprised me. You think I just sit around in lingerie?
KASEN. Your iZon Socials would suggest that.

KYLIE. Ew, you follow me?

KASEN. It's a public profile. Although, with the content you post, I'd suggest making it private.

KYLIE. Private? What's the point in making it – No. I'm not discussing this with you.

KASEN. Fine.

KYLIE. Fine.

> *Beat. TRACY feels extremely awkward. She finally sees a chance to talk, but doesn't quite know what to say.*

TRACY. I'm on iZon Socials, too.

KYLIE. Sorry, I'm on a follower limit.

KASEN. *(Bringing her profile up on his screen.)* I'll follow you.

TRACY. Thank you.

> *Beat.*

So, is this a good time for you to explain this game to me, or –

> *NICK re-enters with beer for everyone.*

NICK. Here we go.

> *Instantly noticing and reacting to the TV.*

Oh come on, why the hell is Cruz batting leadoff? Has Lewis finally lost his damn mind?

KASEN. Cruz gets on base a lot.

NICK. He can't hit to save his life. Might as well be swinging a pool noodle up there.

KASEN. He's got a great eye though.

NICK. Dude needs to learn how to swing. Pussy.

KYLIE. Incredible analysis. You should've gone into broadcasting.

NICK. See! What'd I tell ya. Right down the middle, and he swung right through it. Could feel the breeze from here.

KASEN. Mistretta's got a killer curveball. That was a good pitch.

NICK. Mistretta doesn't have shit. Curveball's a bitch pitch.

KYLIE. Is there a difference between a bitch pitch and a pussy pitch?

NICK. You watch as much baseball as me, you know the difference.

KASEN. Funny how whenever the Yankees strike out, it's a bad swing, and when the other team strikes out, it's a good pitch.

KYLIE. And when they get a hit, it's a good piece of hitting.

KASEN. Give up a hit: garbage pitch.

NICK. Will you two quit ganging up on me? Are you forgetting who the actual baseball player is here?

KYLIE. My apologies. How could I forget I'm in the presence of the famous Henderson Community College ace?

KASEN. Can I have your autograph?

NICK. Quit it!

> *To KYLIE.*

Listen here, you don't know baseball like Kasen and I do, so there's no place for your opinion around here.

> *KYLIE rolls her eyes. To KASEN.*

And you got hit by <u>one pitch</u> in high school and quit playing immediately. You don't get an opinion either.

KASEN. It broke my elbow!

NICK. You've got two, don't you?

KASEN. Whatever. I didn't even like playing. I had a lot more fun as the team statistician.

NICK. *(To the TV.)* Damn it. Cruz can't make contact, and Dalton can't hit nothing but weak ground balls. Every time.

KASEN. You don't seem to mind when they get through the infield.

NICK. Well, no shit. But they barely ever do.

TRACY. *(Sensing a lull.)* So, the infield is the…?

NICK. No explanations right now! Wait till the end of the inning.

TRACY. But you said that before.

NICK. Well, at the end of this inning, be more assertive. I don't know what to tell you.

> *To the TV.*

Hey!!! Attaboy, Olivo! Nice contact.

KASEN. That was literally a weak ground ball that just happened to get out of the infield. Probably the same hit probability as Dalton's.

NICK. Impossible. The way I see it, Dalton's "probability" was 0, and Olivo's was 100. It's either a hit or it's not, buddy.

KASEN. *(To himself.)* Why do I even try.

> *Suddenly, BRAD throws the front door open and runs down the stairs. He is out of breath, but his first concern appears to be making sure everyone is alright.*

BRAD. Who's injured?! Who's dead?! Where are the bodies?!?!

NICK. We're fine, thanks.

BRAD. Quick, Erica, get in here! They need their oxygen, hurry!

NICK. We followed the directions. We're fine. See?
> *He inhales and exhales.*

All good. Now will you shut up? Yanks just got a hit and Velasco's coming up. This is important, damn it.

BRAD. Incredible! It's a miracle! Erica!
> *ERICA appears at the front door. She wears cheap lingerie.*

They're safe, Erica!

ERICA. Oh, Brad, you saved them! What a hero you are!
> *She descends the stairs and embraces BRAD at the bottom.*

How lucky I am to have someone special to celebrate our miraculous survival with!
> *They go into their advertising personas, speaking vaguely to everyone in the room.*

BRAD. Looking to surprise that special someone?

ERICA. Anniversary coming up?

BRAD. Struggling to find genuine human connection?

ERICA. Introducing the newest line of iZon Lingerie: Victoria's Compromise!

BRAD. We know the state of things has been a real drag lately, and we've all put on a few pounds since the Detonation – that's why we've designed a brand-new set of hot, sexy, agreeable pieces that'll make your partner say, 'Sure, why not'!

ERICA. But wait! If you order in the next ten minutes, we'll send not one, but <u>two</u> coupons for our exclusive iZon Vibrators!

NICK. Okay, that's enough!

BRAD. That's right – if the lingerie doesn't work out for you, at least you've got a backup plan!

NICK. Decline, decline! Look, Velasco just got a hit too! Runners on the corners, baby!

BRAD. Limited time only!

ERICA. Coupons must be used in separate transactions.

BRAD. iZon Vibrators not solely responsible for recent fatalities attributed to them.

ERICA. Now with free WiFi!
> *Big smiles. Beat. NICK shoos them out of the room.*

NICK. Decline! Put some clothes on! Come on, my kids are here! Go get us some oxygen or whatever.

BRAD. Yes, sir! Erica, their lives are on the line!

ERICA. Save them and ravage me, Brad!

> *They run up the stairs, pause for a moment of longing, inches away from each other's lips, then exit hurriedly.*

NICK. God, those ads are just getting worse! Don't they know you two are just kids? And why the hell does everything have to come with free WiFi?!

KYLIE. We're not kids anymore, Dad. We can handle it.

KASEN. Besides, I think that ad was Kylie's fault.

KYLIE. My fault? How is it my fault?

KASEN. You mentioned lingerie earlier.

KYLIE. Only because you had to bring up Trevor, and –

NICK. Oh yeah, the nightgown incident. That was funny.

KYLIE. It was not! It was traumatizing!

NICK. *(Attention back to the game.)* Strike?! What are you talking about, strike?!

KASEN. It looked pretty close.

NICK. Close to the moon, maybe. Whatever, I still got a good feeling about Bolden. Here we go, home run, let's go!

TRACY. *(Subtly, to KYLIE.)* I've had some "nightgown incidents" too. Why don't guys ever call ahead?

KYLIE. Right??

> *She notices NICK and KASEN aren't paying any attention.*

Just between you and me – that lingerie was ugly, wasn't it?

TRACY. I don't know. I'm a bit, uh, out of sorts with fashion these days. Hell, that vibrator ad was more applicable to me than the lingerie. Oh God, why did I just say that? I'm sorry.

> *Over the next few minutes, KYLIE is discreetly shopping online for iZon Vibrators, but she's good at multitasking and nobody notices.*

KYLIE. No, it's fine. You could whip out your tits and these two would still be arguing over balls and strikes.

NICK. Hey! We can hear you.

KYLIE. And?

NICK. And it was a ball!

KASEN. No, it was a strike!

KYLIE. *(To TRACY.)* What'd I tell you?

Then: a hit! NICK and KASEN start yelling excitedly. KYLIE gets into it too, to an extent. TRACY claps out of confusion.

ALL. *(Ad lib.)* Yeah, Bolden! Run, Olivo! Run, Velasco! Yeah! Woo! Let's go! Go Yanks!

NICK. Mistretta left that lousy curveball hanging right at the belt!

KASEN. Two-nothing game. Great start!

TRACY. Yeah, good points right there!

NICK gives a quick pathetic look to TRACY, but forgives her.

NICK. What'd I tell ya, Kasen, what'd I tell ya about Bolden!

KASEN. You didn't specify that he'd get a 2-run double, but I understand your sentiment!

NICK. The curveball! What'd I tell ya about the curveball!

KASEN. ...Pussy pitch?

NICK. Bitch pitch! But props to you for calling it what it is!

TRACY. I think I understood that a little. Those two people ran all the way around the field, and when they got back to where they started, it was a point?

NICK. Not now! End of the inning!

TRACY. Sorry.

KYLIE. You've got the basics of it down. Good job.

TRACY. Thank you.

NICK. Damn it, Rodriguez, swing the bat! It's the last game, for God's sake, swing the damn bat.

KASEN. Looks like Mistretta's still got his changeup working.

KYLIE. What's a changeup, bitch pitch or pussy pitch? Just so those of us without the terminology can keep up.

NICK. Changeup is – well, there's a little value in a good changeup.

KASEN. Surprised to hear you admit that.

NICK. It's complicated. I don't wanna get into it right now.

To the TV.

Ah, damn it. Rodriguez, you hack!

KASEN. Well, at least they got the two runs. Good inning.

NICK. *(Noticing he's once again out of beer.)* They don't make beer as full as they used to. Anybody else?

ALL. *(Ad lib.)* No thanks, I'm all set, still got some here, etc.

NICK exits to the kitchen.

TRACY. Okay, so this is my chance, right? What's this game like?

KASEN. Sure, I'll get you caught up. So, let's see – end of the first, two-nothing Yankees. Bannerman's going for the Yanks, Mistretta for the Dodgers. About 75% win probability for the Yankees right now, but the Dodgers have 5-6-7 coming up and they're surprisingly good. And if Bannerman can't rely on his fastball, somebody's gonna jump all over that sinker.

KYLIE. Wish I could jump on his sinker.

KASEN. But Mistretta just had a rough inning and might have an early exit. Although the Dodgers could use Williams later, he's on regular rest and looked good last time out.

NICK. *(Entering.)* Williams sucks. I <u>hope</u> they put him in.

KASEN. He only gave up three hits in six innings on Tuesday.

NICK. He got lucky. Now they've seen him, they'd destroy him today if they see him again.

KASEN. Guess we'll see.
   To TRACY.
Have we gotten you all caught up?

TRACY. *(Dumbstruck.)* What…?

KASEN. Sorry, which part do you have a question about?

TRACY. Maybe I misspoke. What I said was, what is this game like?

KASEN. I'm not sure how to be more clear. Look, it's the top of the second now, and –

KYLIE. Kasen, wait. I think we need to take a few steps back. Tracy, this is a baseball game.

TRACY. That's the type of game?

KYLIE. Yes. The name of this game is baseball.

TRACY. Oh, okay. Thank you.

NICK. Baseball is new to you? What kind of world do we live in?!
   To everyone.
Don't answer that.

TRACY. Well, it looks kind of neat.

NICK. "Kind of neat." I'm gonna need another six-pack…

KYLIE. *(To TRACY.)* Don't mind him. He's only mad because he spent his whole life playing this game, and then when he couldn't play it anymore, he decided to just yell at the television until he one day drinks himself to death.

NICK. Hey! Y'know what, I…

He starts to retort, but can't. He takes a long swig instead.
KASEN. This is actually quite fascinating. Tracy, you don't know anything about baseball?
TRACY. No? Is that bad?
KYLIE. No, it's not bad at all. It means you've been focusing on more important things.
KASEN. It's strange, though. Like you've been living under a rock.
TRACY. ...Aren't we all living under a rock?
KASEN. Good point.
TRACY. I guess I've heard of baseball before, but didn't know it still existed. You know, after the Paris Agreement War, I decided to do some climate work with –
NICK. No, uh uh, we're not here to talk about what's going on out there. We know already. No need to dwell on it.
TRACY. Okay. But – don't you want to know who I am? How I got to be delivering you a pizza today?
NICK. We know who you are. You told us your name.
A look to KASEN, who mouths her name.
Tracy. That's your name, and that's all we need to know.
TRACY. You don't want to know anything about me?
NICK. Not if it has anything to do with the bullshit of the world. We know what's going on. We've all known, for years, that this was coming. Should we have done something at some point? Hell yes. I'm no scientist but I've heard we coulda done things to stop it, and we can get all riled up talking about this, that, and the other thing. But guess what? Here we are. The day has come, and we're living it. Nothing to do about it now. So, the way I see it, no sense in pointing fingers or whatever. Sooner or later we'll be gone, and that's that. You think I wanna waste my precious time left talking about where it all went wrong? No. Fuck no. The game's on.
He takes another big swig, then reacts to the TV.
Oh come on, ump, that was a strike!
KASEN. I don't know, it looked an inch or two outside.
NICK. It caught the corner!
KASEN. It didn't, though.
NICK. Just last inning, the ump called that a strike.
KASEN. Well, they're not perfect. I think this one is programmed to

have around 96% consistency.
TRACY. So – you'd all rather ignore the terrible things happening, and instead just watch some people play a game?
> *They all nod.*

That sounds nice.
NICK. Now you're getting it.
TRACY. Could someone explain the basics to me?
KYLIE. Don't look at me. I just look at the butts.
NICK. I don't have the patience.
KASEN. I've trained my entire life to explain baseball to somebody.
TRACY. Okay, go ahead.
NICK. Attaboy, Bannerman! Double play!
KASEN. Nice turn there at short. Okay.
> *To TRACY.*

So, back in the early 1800s –
KYLIE. She doesn't need the entire encyclopedia on it, Kasen.
KASEN. I need to give context!
KYLIE. Just tell her how it's played.
KASEN. Fine. But she deserves to be taught the complete history of baseball at some point.
TRACY. Maybe later.
KASEN. Deal. So, there are two teams which each have nine players competing at a time. Well, ten if you include the Designated Hitter.
NICK. Fuck the DH. Pussy position.
KASEN. Don't listen to him. So, when a team is on offense, their players will stand right there, in the "batter's box," and try to hit a ball with a bat. The ball is thrown from the defensive team, which has other players scattered around the field, ready for the ball to be hit near them. When the batter hits the ball, he runs around to four bases, in a counter-clockwise pattern. If he hits the ball and a fielder catches it, he's out. If the fielder doesn't catch it, but throws it to first base before the batter gets there, he's also out. He can also be out if he cannot hit the ball after three "strikes" are against him. When the defensive team makes three outs, the two teams switch sides. Then –
> *Suddenly, another loud warning sign blares everywhere, lights flashing and everything. Everyone looks at their screens to determine protocol. This time, they retrieve*

helmets, vests, and other items of physical protection. NICK makes sure everyone, including TRACY, is protected before protecting himself. They all find a spot in the room and "brace for impact." There is a huge explosion above, which shakes the room and knocks a few things over. Nobody is particularly scared, just annoyed. Eventually, the warning system stops and everything goes back to normal. As they remove their protection and pick up the fallen items, KASEN continues as if nothing happened:

So, the teams swap defense and offense until each side has had a chance to score runs. Together, these two turns are called one "inning," which has a top half and a bottom half. A game consists of nine innings, unless the score is tied. Then they start playing more innings until an inning ends with one team ahead of the other. Of course, the team with the most runs wins the game.
TRACY. So, runs are like "points"?
KASEN. Yes. But don't ever call them points.
TRACY. Okay.
NICK. *(Reacting to the TV.)* Oh... Oh, shit...
KASEN. Does it have enough carry?
NICK. Warning track... Wall... Damn it.
KASEN. So that right there is called a "Home run." That player just hit the ball so far, none of the fielders could catch it. See, it went over the wall, right there. That means he can go to all of the bases and score an automatic run. It's very exciting, arguably the most exciting thing that can possibly happen in baseball.
TRACY. Then why aren't you all excited?
NICK. 'Cause the fucking Dodgers hit it.
TRACY. Oh. And you're cheering for the other team.
KASEN. Yeah. The Yankees.
TRACY. Well, he looks pretty excited.
NICK. No shit he's excited. He was sittin' off-speed the whole at bat, so he spat on an 0-2 heater and a 1-2 slider just to make Bannerman throw that bullshit middle-middle change with no break.
TRACY. I don't think I understood a single word of that sentence.
KASEN. We'll work on it.
KYLIE. If it helps, just remember we're watching grown men getting

paid a hundred million dollars to play a game for children.
KASEN. It's more than that, Kylie. It's magical.
KYLIE. Maybe it is. But I'm not wrong.
NICK. There we go. Easy pop up. Alright, boys, let's get that run back! Jeez, Bannerman's making me nervous today.
>   *More pounding on the door outside. ERICA runs in first, followed by BRAD. They are in the middle of a physical fight.*

ERICA. They got to him! The chemical bomb! He's been poisoned!
BRAD. Rrrraaaahhhh!!!
ERICA. Brad! If you're in there, listen to me! It's Erica! You love me! Remember me, Brad! I know I'm somewhere in there, some place in your soul!
BRAD. Rrah! Rrah! Rrah!
>   *They move through the room in a physical struggle. Tables are turned, chairs are tossed. They scream and tumble around. The others don't do anything. TRACY is about to, but KASEN gestures for her to let it be.*

ERICA. This isn't who you are, Brad! Look at me!
>   *They are now breathing heavily, centimeters away from each other's quivering lips. The lights mysteriously go out and a spotlight shines down upon BRAD and ERICA.*

Brad, when we first sought out to be the protectors of the Earth, the warriors of humanity, the saviors of tomorrow, we vowed to never let the darkness in. Don't let the darkness in, Brad! Listen to me! I know you're in there somewhere! I see it in your eyes! Kill the darkness, Brad! Rid yourself of the evils! Come back to me! Come back and let us be together for the rest of time! I love you, Brad!
>   *BRAD's breathing gets slower. He slowly puts a hand up to ERICA's cheek and touches it gently. The look of evil in his eyes starts to slowly fade away.*

BRAD. Erica? Erica! Oh, Erica!
ERICA. Oh, Brad! You're back! I knew you could do it!
>   *They make out passionately. BRAD breaks it off.*

BRAD. Erica! I feel more alive than I ever have!
ERICA. What else makes you feel alive, Brad? What else!
>   *Cue the commercial personas.*

BRAD. Sometimes, living the normal life just doesn't cut it.

ERICA. You try everything you can to develop a sense of belonging or purpose, but ultimately nothing works out and you're left to wallow in self-pity, alone and desperate.

BRAD. So many of us are turning to alcohol, but Erica – did you know alcohol is one of the leading factors of alcoholism?

ERICA. Oh, no! If only there was another place to turn!

BRAD. Good news: there is! Now introducing the new and improved iZon Party Pills!

ERICA. With all the kick and thrill of cocaine, marijuana, ecstasy, and peyote all packed into one pellet of pizzazz, there's no wonder half of Americans are hooked on it!

BRAD. Take 'em anywhere! At home,

ERICA. in the Tunnel,

BRAD. children's birthday parties,

ERICA. at the theater,

BRAD. even business meetings!

ERICA. Order now and escape your dread!

BRAD. Limited time only!

ERICA. iZon is not responsible for iZon Party Pill addiction,

BRAD. And has proven so in court several times.

ERICA. Now with free WiFi!

Big smiles. NICK slugs the rest of his beer.

NICK. God, these commercials get more boring every day. I'm gonna get another beer.

KASEN. Can you fix the lights while you're at it?

NICK. Sure. Must be that damn loose wire again.

He exits to the kitchen.

TRACY. Are they going to leave?

KYLIE. Eventually. Sometimes you just have to wait 'em out.

TRACY. Isn't there, like, an ad-free version of this thing?

KASEN. Don't say that – !

It's too late. The lights come back to normal, while BRAD and ERICA go smoothly right into another advertisement.

ERICA. Tired of hearing the same old boring ads?

KYLIE. No! Decline!

BRAD. Snooze button, please!

ERICA. Suffer no more! Introducing: iZon Bodyguard Deluxe Plus

Premium, our ad-free once-in-a-lifetime bodyguard service!

BRAD. Only $750,000 per year!

KASEN. Decline, please.

ERICA. But wait!

BRAD. Are you a student or senior citizen? This is your lucky day!

ERICA. Upload proper documentation to the iZon Cloud and you will be eligible to apply for our exclusive Student or Senior Citizen Poor-Person-With-Half-An-Excuse Discount!

BRAD. Only $740,000 per year!

ERICA. If you are like most Americans, you <u>hate</u> advertisements. Consider making a change today!

BRAD. Limited time only!

ERICA. Students will pay remaining balance at a 15% interest rate.

BRAD. Senior citizens will concede all personal belongings to iZon.

ERICA. Now with free WiFi!

NICK. *(Entering with another beer.)* Who did it?

> *KASEN and KYLIE point to TRACY.*

Okay, fine. You get a pass. Hey, you two, there's a terrible darkness out there or whatever.

KYLIE. Yeah, and there was a rumor that somebody else is more capable of saving the world.

> *BRAD and ERICA gasp.*

BRAD. Nobody is as strong as me! Only I am capable of defeating the darkness! Only I… can save the world!

ERICA. And me, right?!

BRAD. Sure! Now, quick, let's finish this mission like we should.

BRAD and ERICA. Together.

> *They grip each other tightly, share one more intense romantic moment, then exit.*

NICK. Okay Yanks, let's get something going! Take one of those juicy Mistretta curveballs and knock it outta the park!

KASEN. He's relying on his fastball more this inning, and for good reason. The curve isn't breaking as much as normal. See? That one only dropped a couple feet. He's lucky it didn't get hit a mile.

NICK. Bet the next curveball ends up in the stands.

KASEN. He won't throw another curveball. Not this at bat. Probably he'll rely on his fastball or changeup. And who knows – he's got a

splitter up his sleeve too.
TRACY. So... may I ask...?
KASEN. Each pitcher has different types of pitches. They can throw the ball in different ways, which makes it move differently, or travel at different speeds. It's a constant mind-game between the batter and pitcher, trying to figure each other out. See there, he just threw his changeup. Pretty good movement on it today.
TRACY. I see.
NICK. It's total shit compared to Bannerman's slider.
TRACY. So, let me guess. A slider does a sliding motion?
KASEN. Yeah, that's an easy one.
TRACY. And a curveball curves?
KASEN. You've got it.
TRACY. And a fastball is faster than the rest?
KASEN. A lot of them are self-explanatory. That right there was a fastball. Must've slipped a bit, that was way outside the strike zone.
TRACY. Is that the rectangle there?
KASEN. Yes. It's put on there by the broadcast. It varies based on a batter's height, and also the ump's programmed tendencies.
TRACY. The what?
NICK. Don't even get me started on the robo-umps. My God, when's he gonna turn to the curveball?
KASEN. Not now. 3-1 count, no sense trying any breaking stuff.
NICK. Come on. It's not like he wants to walk this guy.

They all watch intensely.

KYLIE. Well, what do you know? He walked him.
KASEN. And didn't throw a curveball!
NICK. Sure, sure, I'm wrong. Don't care. We've got a baserunner.
TRACY. What gives him the right to just walk? Shouldn't he hustle?
KASEN. A walk is when a pitcher misses the strike zone and the batter doesn't swing at four balls during an at bat. The batter gets to go to first base automatically, even though he didn't hit the ball.
KYLIE. There he is, Solano. Tracy, look, look – look at those eyes. Now that's a reason to like baseball.
TRACY. He's got a nice mustache too.
KYLIE. Now we're talking! And wait till he turns around – there! Look at that ass!

TRACY. Hm. Yup. That'll do.

NICK. Keep it in your pants.

TRACY. Reminds me of someone I used to party with. Oh my God – that's how I know about those stupid Party Pills.

KYLIE. You've done 'em before?

TRACY. Now that I think about it, yeah. Oh, it's all coming back to me – God, I was so dumb...

KASEN. What happened?

TRACY. I – I'm not sure your Dad would want me telling you about my crazy nights on drugs...

NICK. *(Chugging his beer.)* She's right, kids, never do any of that shit. It'll fuck you up.

> *For the next few minutes, KYLIE scrolls silently, shopping online for iZon Party Pills.*

TRACY. What are all those little acronyms and the numbers next to them mean?

NICK. Don't ask that – !

KASEN. Glad you asked! Those are statistics that measure how good the player is. In my opinion, the best part of baseball is statistics.

NICK. And in my opinion, he's wrong.

KASEN. As you can see, it's still up for debate. I think numbers are beautiful – the way they flow together, push up against each other, make each other behave strangely, in recognizable patterns. They tell a story, numbers. They measure success and failure down to such a minute level, and when you pile hundreds and thousands of successes and failures on top of each other, you start to see a picture. You see a rookie outfielder gradually striking out less often and making more hard contact, and it tells you, maybe this kid is figuring it out. You see a starting pitcher with suddenly limited velocity and think, oh no, is his arm blown out? Will he ever be the same pitcher again? That's what happened to Dad, by the way, and the answer is "No" –

> *NICK half-jokingly punches him in the arm.*

It's a long, beautiful season. One hundred and sixty-two games. On any given day, a superstar can go 0-for-5 with four strikeouts and a double play, or a mediocre scrub can go 4-for-4 with three home runs and a double. The numbers are small at first, but eventually become bigger. The sample sizes grow. Batters and pitchers alike show their

tendencies – what they swing at, how fast they run, how often they throw curveballs. And just when you think it's predictable, something unpredictable happens. It's amazing. I'll never know anything like it.
NICK. What he's trying to say is, he didn't get laid in high school.
TRACY. I think that was very well put, Kasen. Wish I understood anything like you understand this game.
KASEN. The more you try to understand baseball, the more you realize you never can.
TRACY. So, those numbers there, what do they mean?
KASEN. Those are three percentages, called batting average, on base percentage, and slugging percentage. They measure how often the player gets a hit, how often he gets on base, and how many total bases he averages per at bat.

TRACY doesn't know which question to ask first.

As a quick shortcut to figuring out the best hitters, you can add the last two to get OPS, called On-Base Plus Slugging. Then there's a league-adjusted version of that, OPS+, which shows how much of a better or worse hitter somebody is in comparison to the rest of the league. So if somebody has a 120 OPS+, that means he's roughly 20% better than the average hitter.
NICK. Hey, double in the gap! Double in the gap! Send him! Send him home!... Ah, that's fine, keep him at third, don't risk it. Okay, we got something going now! Second and third, baby, no outs! Boy, did you see Solano pound that ball?!
KYLIE. I wish he'd pound –
NICK. We get it, Kylie! He's attractive!
KASEN. This is exciting. Great opportunity to score right here!
TRACY. I take it I should also be cheering for this team?
KASEN. If you don't want to get kicked out, yes.
TRACY. What do you like about them?
NICK. Two words: Twenty-seven rings!
KYLIE. Isn't that three words?
NICK. I don't care.
TRACY. What does that mean? Twenty-seven rings?
KASEN. They've won the World Series, the championship round of the league, 27 times in their history. Though it's been a long time since the last one.

NICK. Fucking Jeter Curse.

KYLIE. It's not a curse if they just suck.

NICK. Don't push me, Kylie! Not today!

TRACY. What are those two numbers there?

KASEN. That's home runs, and RBIs, which stands for runs batted in. When someone gets a hit and someone else scores, the hitter gets an RBI. Their relevance has diminished over the years, but they still show it on the screen to satisfy old-school fans.

NICK. Can't win games without scoring runs, and you can't score runs without ribbies.

KASEN. ...But the very nature of them depends on a player's spot in the batting lineup, as well as the productiveness of the players around them. It's not a great indication of the player's ability.

NICK. Ribbies are the foundation of baseball.

KASEN. As I said, old-school fans love them. I prefer OPS, or WAR – that's Wins Above Replacement. Or weighted runs created, or expected on base average, or xwOBAwRC+, expected weighted on base average multiplied by league-adjusted weighted runs created.

NICK. Do you hear yourself? Please tell me you hear yourself.

KASEN. It's no different than measuring wins and losses. It's just statistics created to measure the effectiveness of a player.

NICK. I'd rather watch the fucking game.

KASEN. *(To TRACY.)* We go back and forth all the time.

TRACY. There's still so many things I'm clueless on.

NICK. Just watch the damn game and figure it out on your own. Kasen, you've explained it enough, I don't wanna listen to you yabber on all game.

>   *Suddenly, without warning, a string of terrible, animalistic roars and screeches are heard from outside, accompanied by panicked screams. Everybody looks at each other, confused. After a few seconds, the roars and screams stop. They all make note of this one, since the warning didn't go off.*

KYLIE. Is the warning system broken?

KASEN. Maybe there was nothing to warn us about.

NICK. Yeah, didn't sound too serious. We're fine.

TRACY. You didn't hear the screaming out there – ?

NICK. Nope. Didn't hear a Goddamn thing. Alrighty here, look at this! Walked him! Bases loaded and no outs. Come on Yanks, blow the game wide open!

KASEN. Let's hope they don't pull a Nobletiger.

NICK. God's sake, quit it with those dumbass stats.

TRACY. Sorry, what? That's a statistic? A noble...

KASEN. Nobletiger.

NICK. Don't humor him.

TRACY. I mean, that one sounds pretty cool.

KASEN. It stands for "No Outs, Bases Loaded, Ending with Team Incapable of Getting an Easy Run." Simple. Nobletiger.

TRACY. Is that actually real?

KASEN. Well, it's kind of a joke. But also real. It's very specific to this situation right here. With no outs and the bases loaded, the Yankees have a very high chance of scoring a run this inning, and not just one. They should expect to score more than that. Probably at least two. However, that doesn't always happen. Sometimes a team will put themselves in this very promising situation – the most promising of all situations a batting team could be in – and by some level of bad luck or clutch pitching, they don't score at all. I like a Nobletiger. There's something so poetic in a team setting itself up for sure success, then tragically watching it all slip away. It's by far the most heartbreaking way to <u>not</u> score. To know what could have been done, how easy it would have been...

NICK. Okay, here's something – is that deep enough?

KASEN. It'll get at least one run in.

They all watch intensely.

NICK. Okay. Sac fly. Nice piece of hitting, Gomez!

KASEN. There goes the Nobletiger.

TRACY. That's too bad.

KASEN. No, it's a good thing. We didn't want one right there.

NICK. And now a mound visit. Look at 'em, they're scared. Pussies.

KYLIE. *(After a brief lull.)* Hey Kasen, you remember that annual Parents vs. Kids game we would do on Father's Day?

KASEN. In Pearl Park, yeah I remember.

KYLIE. Wasn't there a year where Dad came up with the bases loaded and no outs, and couldn't get any runs in?

NICK. No! No, you're dead wrong.

KASEN. I remember that year, yeah. I think you're right.
NICK. No, you're not remembering it right. I was on third base. I started that inning off with a triple, and not a Goddamn one of my teammates got me home. Bullshit game.
KASEN. I thought it was pretty fun.
KYLIE. Me too.
NICK. We had you right where we wanted you, and we blew it.
Beat. A brief moment of sensitivity.
Sure, that was a lot of fun, though, kids. I looked forward to that game every year. I remember, your mother and I would always bring you to get ice cream after the game, and we'd sit there on the picnic tables and go through the box scores.
KASEN. Yeah, that was awesome.
KYLIE. I thought it was pizza?
KASEN. No, it was ice cream.
KYLIE. Could've sworn it was pizza.
NICK. Ice cream, Kylie. Ice cream.
TRACY. So – not to butt in here, but your mother…?
NICK. No. We're not talking about her.
TRACY. I'm sorry.
KYLIE. Dad, we've gotta talk about her at some point.
NICK. And you think now is the time?!
KASEN. *(To TRACY.)* I think you would've liked her.
NICK. Kids, I'm already emotional about the game! We can't be talking about your mother too!
KYLIE. But Dad –
NICK. NO! Save it for when we can handle it! After the game!
KASEN. You're the one who brought her up.
NICK. Well, I'm drinking, what'd you expect? Let's pay attention!
To the TV.
Strike! What?! Get off your knees, ump, you're blowing the game!
KASEN. Can't deny, though, Mistretta's dialing it up a notch.
NICK. Yeah, he's locked in. What was that, 98? 99?
KYLIE. *(Joking gasp.)* Are you using numbers to quantify skill??
NICK. When it's fastballs, numbers matter. Y'know, I used to hit 102 back in my prime.
TRACY. 102 what?

NICK. Miles an hour.
TRACY. Is that fast?
NICK. No shit it's fast. I was one of the best pitchers out there.
KYLIE. One of the best exaggerators too.
NICK. I hit 102, and you know it!
KASEN. That scout negotiated your signing bonus and took a huge cut of it. I find it highly likely he bumped up the reading a couple ticks. I'm not saying it's bad; it got you a larger bonus. I'm just saying, that sort of thing happens all the time.
NICK. I earned that money. Earned it with all the blood, sweat, and glory I poured into every game I pitched.
KYLIE. Again, this was originally a children's game.

More pounding on the door. It opens fast and BRAD falls inside, his legs still outside. He is trying to crawl in, but something is stopping him from the outside.

BRAD. It's got a hold of me! I can't fight it any longer!
ERICA. *(Offstage.)* Brad, you brave cowboy of my heart! Fight it! Fight it with everything you have!
BRAD. Ah! Ahhh! AHHH!!! Erica, it's eating my legs! Kill it!
ERICA. *(Offstage.)* I can't! It's already eaten my arms!
BRAD. NOOOO!!! Erica! How will we ever embrace again?!
ERICA. With... our... souls!!!
BRAD. AHHHHH!!!

BRAD is pulled back outside by whatever it is. KASEN is about to talk about the game, but BRAD and ERICA bounce back in, completely fine and in their commercial personas.

Okay, so maybe a <u>tiger</u> isn't a great pet choice!
ERICA. Nobody wants a pet that'll tear your limbs off!
BRAD. Also, they're extinct! But not to worry, there are plenty of other choices out there!
ERICA. Like what, Brad?!
BRAD. Well, Erica, here at iZon Pet Central Supreme, we have a fine variety of all your favorite cats and dogs!
ERICA. Wow, the two animals!
BRAD. That's right! We've still got choices!
ERICA. Wouldn't you like a pet to care for, keep your company, and provide an excuse to cancel plans?

BRAD. Look no further than iZon Pet Central Supreme! Sign up for an account today for just $300 a month. Use the code "MEAT" and get a 2% discount on your next pet!

ERICA. It's times like these when we really need to appreciate all the animals we've got left –

NICK. Decline, decline!

BRAD. But wait! If owning and taking care of these little buggers is too much for you, there's another option.

> *ERICA pretends to be a dog in an ASPCA commercial.*

Some of these animals have been severely mistreated their entire lives. Beaten. Slapped. Ridiculed. Not raised for meat, mind you, but much worse. Their dignity has been taken away. For just $75 per day, we will provide legally unspecific support to these poor, wretched, abused, ugly animals.

ERICA. *(Puppy eyes.)* If you don't donate, I'll be shot in the head!

> *They both let it "hit home" for a moment, then break back into their cheery personas.*

It's up to you!

BRAD. Limited time only!

ERICA. All pets come with a $5000 extra charge,

BRAD. Which is morally wrong to ask about.

ERICA. Now with free WiFi!

> *Rather than being asked to leave, they pretend the "tiger" has grabbed ahold of them, and get dragged back out the door, clutching onto each other romantically.*

NICK. Damn it! Goddamn double play, that son of a bitch Cruz is slower than concrete going to first base. Shit.

KASEN. At least they got that run on the sac fly. 3-1 lead after two innings isn't bad.

NICK. Damn. If I wasn't so sure something else would kill me, I'd say this team would.

KYLIE. Don't give up hope yet.

TRACY. Were they serious about the abused dogs?

NICK. Don't tell me you were listening to that shit.

TRACY. Well, they're pretty loud. And convincing.

NICK. Convincing?! I'm however-many beers deep and even I could tell there's no Goddamn tiger out there.

KASEN. Dad, we used to have pets, didn't we?
NICK. Sure. Couple dogs and a cat.
KASEN. Wasn't it two cats and one dog?
KYLIE. When did we ever have cats?
NICK. You don't remember? We got 'em for your birthdays.
KASEN. No, Christmas. Their names were – hmm –
KYLIE. The dog was named Trevor.
KASEN. No, that's your ex-boyfriend.
KYLIE. Who?
KASEN. Nightgown guy.
KYLIE. Man, where is my memory today?
KASEN. I'm usually good with names, too. Huh. Weird.
TRACY. ...Well, I'm gonna sign up for those donations. Maybe I'll save a life.
NICK. You'll tell yourself you will, at least.
Reacting to the TV.
Okay, let's go get 'em, Bannerman. Easy 1-2-3 inning here.
There's a lull in the conversation. KYLIE and KASEN are both discreetly donating money to the poor abused animals.
TRACY. So, Nick – were you ever in a game like this? On the TV?
NICK looks dully at his drink. KASEN and KYLIE aren't sure whether to interject or not.
I'm sorry, I didn't mean to offend you.
NICK. It's fine. I don't care. No, I didn't make it. Not quite. I blew my arm out.
TRACY. What's that mean?
NICK. I worked my elbow to death, tore up the tendons or bones or ligaments or whatever they're called. Tried to have surgery to fix it, but – Come on, ump, that was a strike!
TRACY. Did the surgery not work?
NICK. It was fine.
He drinks and drinks and drinks.
KASEN. It was the rehabilitation process that hit a snag.
TRACY. Oh. What happened? You had a setback?
KYLIE. You could say that.
TRACY. Maybe you just needed some more rest.
KYLIE. Maybe he shouldn't have listened to so much rock and roll.

TRACY. Rock and roll?

KASEN. Oh, I get it. Good one, Kylie.

NICK. Yes, fucking brilliant.

TRACY. I'm sorry, is that an inside joke or something?

NICK. During my rehab process, there was this night where I was feeling pretty low, got very drunk, and – well, we had this saying, my teammates and I, "Liquor before beer, you're in the clear; beer before liquor, you're the new pitcher." Anyway, the night's kind of a blur, but at some point, one of my asshole teammates said I couldn't throw a rock through a window of an old abandoned house. Just dudes being dudes, you know. I threw it as hard as I could, not really meaning to but unable to stop myself, and immediately felt a snap in my elbow. Fell to the ground, and rolled around in agonizing pain. Rock. And roll. So Goddamn hilarious. Ruined my life. It went clear through the window, though, so at least I have that last strike.

KYLIE. Well when you put it like that, I feel like a dick.

KASEN. *(To TRACY.)* He usually throws in a bit of light-hearted self-deprecating humor when he tells it. Must not be a good time to talk about it.

NICK. Hell no it's not a good time to talk about it! You think I like talking about the thing I worked my whole life at being flushed down the toilet because I got too drunk one night?! You think right now, while we're watching the fucking last game of eternity toil away in front of our eyes, is a good time for me to talk about never doing what I loved ever again?! This is my last Goddamn opportunity to watch a baseball game, kids! Do you realize that?! Everything, all of it, all those calculator numbers you're drooling over, all those butts and mustaches you're checking out, all the hits and strikeouts and home runs and – everything! It's all gone! None of this will mean a damn thing tomorrow! Not a Goddamn thing!

He takes a long drink of beer, finishing it.

KASEN. I'm sorry, Dad.

NICK. It's fine.

KYLIE. Me too. I know we like teasing, but – we'll hold off, alright?

NICK. No, it's fine. I'm not gonna throw a fit about it. Sorry.

The warning system once again goes off and everybody checks their screens. This time, they look at each other with

> more panic than before, then all look at the TV. They do nothing else. There are no loud noises, no rumbling outside; they don't need to cover in place or put on oxygen masks. They just stare at the TV with anticipation and horror. The warning system goes off eventually and everything is silent.

It's coming back on, right? Right?

KYLIE. Okay, Dad, don't panic. It's alright, it'll be back.

KASEN. It will?

NICK. If this TV doesn't turn back on –

KYLIE. It will, Dad! It will.

> They all stare at the TV for a long, long time. Tension builds and builds. It feels like entire days pass unblinkingly. Finally, NICK resigns to chaos.

NICK. MOTHERFUCKER!!!

> He starts going on a rampage. He flips tables, throws chairs, tosses KASEN and KYLIE out of the way when they try to stop him. TRACY shelters somewhere.

I ONLY ASK FOR ONE GODDAMN THING IN MY LIFE! GAME SEVEN OF THE FUCKING WORLD SERIES! I ASK FOR ONE THING, AND THE WORLD RIPS IT OUT OF MY HANDS! I'M SICK OF IT! GAME SEVEN! IT'S FUCKING GAME SEVEN!!!

> As he yells, KASEN and KYLIE chase after him, trying to calm him down.

KYLIE. Dad! It'll come back on! It'll come back! It's not over!

KASEN. It's only the third inning, Dad! There's time! Dad!

NICK. No! I'm gonna fix this fucking TV and watch this fucking game if it's the last thing I ever do! Try and stop me!

> NICK runs to the top of the stairs, unlocks the front door, screams, and runs outside. KYLIE, KASEN, and TRACY worriedly follow along. Lights down.

END OF ACT I

ACT II

Lights up. Nobody is around and all is quiet for a moment. Suddenly, the door flies open and terrifying roars, screams, and warfare is heard from behind it. KYLIE and TRACY come inside quickly and slam the door shut. They look like they've been through hell and back. Their clothes are dirty, bloody, and ripped; most importantly, their hair is a mess. Both are out of breath, but start to calm down now that they're out of immediate danger. KYLIE descends the stairs first and approaches the TV. Over the following, she does what she can to try to fix the TV, troubleshooting from her projected screen.

TRACY. Shit! How did we survive that?!

KYLIE. No idea. Maybe we didn't! Hah! Come on, let's see what we can do. So, first thing Kasen said was to try this...

TRACY. Are we going to discuss the insanity we've just been through?! That was –

KYLIE. Not important. We've gotta get the game back on.

Her first strategy hasn't worked.

No, it's not that – Okay, next he suggested –

TRACY. What do we do if they don't come back?

KYLIE. They'll be back. Oh, I'm getting a call from him right now.

She answers, looking straight ahead.

Kasen! Where are – No, haven't gotten it going yet – Do you think it's worth the trouble? We could always check the score later... No, I know, I know, that's stupid... Yes, hi Dad! – Shit, look at you! Are you alright?! – We'll get it, don't worry! Yes, we'll keep trying on our end, just keep adjusting up there and I'll let you know if – Hello? You there?! Kasen!

The call is obviously gone.

Damn. Okay, it's fine. They're fine. Here, help me out with this.

TRACY. Sure, of course.

They both start working on the TV, but don't have much luck. Eventually there's not much they can do. They keep trying things, but at this point it's mostly a waiting game.

TRACY. So, I hate to imply this game isn't important, but – Well,

aren't there <u>more</u> important things happening?
KYLIE. Maybe. Depends on what "important" means these days.
TRACY. I guess. I know there's not much left to do about, well, everything, but everyone I know at least keeps up. It's good to know what's going on, right?
KYLIE. We kept up for a while. A long time. But eventually, it was like, who even –
She catches a glimpse of herself in a mirror.
Oh my God, is that what my hair looks like?! Why didn't you tell me I looked like this?!
TRACY. I don't know. How's my hair?
KYLIE. Awful! But I figured you didn't care.
TRACY. …Yeah, you're right.
KYLIE. I've got to fix this.
She switches her attention from the failing TV to her hair.
TRACY. So – when did you all stop paying attention?
KYLIE. I don't know. I – I can't remember, actually. That's weird.
TRACY. Was it the Self Destruct Scare?
KYLIE. The what?!
TRACY. Guess it was before that, then. The Great Tectonic Shift? The Hundred Mile Poison Bomb? The Fifth Revolutionary War?
KYLIE. Well, I'm glad I've missed all this.
TRACY. And you all said that <u>I</u> live under a rock!
KYLIE. Look – We used to care. Argued and argued – Dad had some interesting political views before he stopped caring. But eventually, we realized something. No matter what we did or said or thought or stood for – it didn't make a difference.
TRACY. That's a defeatist attitude. I mean, I get it, and by now, I probably agree with you, but how could you give up before, before…
KYLIE. It was our Mom, okay?
Beat.
When Mom died, we didn't care anymore. If she could go, any of us could – and we will. All of us. It's just a matter of time. And until then, all we have is each other. We "gave up" around then because we realized all we had left was all we had to live for. We kind of, I guess, took our anger and tears and hatred and depression, everything, and we rolled it up into a big collective <u>ball</u> of pain, pure pain – and, well,

fighting something like that is easier when there's three of you. And when you keep the outside world's shitty misery out of it. So... we gave up on everything else. And, well, Dad and Kasen turned to baseball instead. I guess I kind of did too.

TRACY. Because it's fun. Not as painful.

KYLIE. Oh, it's painful. But – It's all that kept us going. Everything else, y'know... we knew it wouldn't get any better – no matter what we did, all of <u>this</u> was going to happen anyway. It was out of our hands; all we had left to do was deal with the consequences. So, we took the one good, positive thing in our lives, and pretended it was the only thing. The results were still out of our hands, sure, but with baseball, we'd at least be happy sometimes. Life sucks. But when the home team wins, I dunno... it sucks a little less.

TRACY. I never understood the obsession with sports until now.

KYLIE. Trust me, me neither. God, Dad and Kasen used to get on my nerves like hell. Back and forth, spouting useless stats and senseless drunk ramblings nonstop, every single day. I hated baseball for so long, I learned everything about it out of spite. Just so I knew what to say to piss them off. I hated it so much.

Beat. This is the first time she's admitted it.

But now – now I love it. And I'm really gonna miss it.

TRACY. *(Beat.)* May I ask – how did your Mom die?

KYLIE. Mom...

TRACY. Sorry. You don't have to tell me if you don't want to.

KYLIE. No, it's fine. I can talk about it. Mom was... She... She...

She seems a bit lost in thought, like she temporarily can't remember how her mom passed. Then she looks at TRACY weirdly, as if she's almost thinking TRACY is her mom.

You...

TRACY. Me?

KYLIE. Are you...?

She never gets the chance to ask. Instead, BRAD and ERICA enter quickly and a bit out of character, like they've been distracted for a while.

BRAD. Not to fear, we're back! We've returned from –

ERICA. *(Together with him.)* We've returned from –

BRAD. *(Sotto voice.)* No, that's mine. You say the next part.

ERICA. So sorry. Go on.

BRAD. We've returned from saving the world!

ERICA. Now, is anybody hurt?! What can we do to – Shit, Brad, two of them are missing.

BRAD. What? Where are they?

KYLIE. The TV is broken. Dad and Kasen are out there trying to fix it. Of course, they have no idea what they're doing, and they're putting themselves in sure danger, but –

BRAD. Shit. They're out there?!

There is real fear in his voice for the first time.

Fuck. Erica, come on –

ERICA. But we've gotta do the ad, right?

BRAD. There's no time.

ERICA. But if we don't –

BRAD. Fine. Fine! Quickly now.

They do a fast-forward commercial, just to get it out.

Do you ever feel lost?

ERICA. Desperate?

BRAD. Hopeless?

ERICA. Unable to contribute your fair share of productivity to the world? Don't worry, you're not alone!

BRAD. There are hundreds of other humans still alive!

ERICA. And some of them care about you!

BRAD. Here at iZon, we are proud to reveal our brand-new iZon Therapy Program Pro, guaranteed to get you back in the saddle!

ERICA. Artificially designed and licensed, our exclusive iZon Therapy is programmed specifically to bring light back in your life!

BRAD. Don't wait for your mental health to completely crumble – sign up for iZon Therapy today!

ERICA. Trust us, you'll be sufficiently satisfied you did!

BRAD. Limited time only!

ERICA. Happiness not guaranteed.

BRAD. Side effects may include feelings of impending doom.

ERICA. Now with free WiFi!

They pause ever so briefly to give their signature smiles, then exit in a rush. We hear them arguing as they leave:

BRAD. I know you're going to say this is my fault, but you're the

one who distracted us. We can't afford to let this happen again.
ERICA. I'm sorry, but whose idea was it to…

And they're gone. And just like that, the TV is working again!

TRACY. Look! Look!
KYLIE. It's back!

KYLIE and TRACY jump up and down in excitement.

TRACY. They did it! They fixed it!
KYLIE. Yes! – Shit, eighth inning?! And tied at four… Man, where are they? I'm gonna give them a call.

She does. They both watch the TV intensely.

TRACY. Look, somebody just hit the ball! Wait – that's the other team. So I should say, "Oh no, somebody hit the ball!"
KYLIE. Damn it, no answer.

She "hangs up."

Hey, you're learning! Okay, just a single. Could be worse.
TRACY. Boy, everybody's going wild.
KYLIE. Well, yeah. This is the last game. And, remember how there's nine innings in a game? That means the teams only have this one and one more. Although if it's still tied at the end of nine, they do extra innings until there's a winner.
TRACY. Can't they just settle on a tie?

KYLIE instinctively slaps TRACY across the face.

KYLIE. I'm so sorry. Just an instinct. A tie? Are you fucking crazy? Sorry, sorry. It's just – no ties in baseball.
TRACY. Okay. Could you teach me in a less violent manner?
KYLIE. Of course.
TRACY. What does that mean, "DH"?
KYLIE. Designated hitter. He hits in place of the pitcher.
TRACY. Oh right, I heard about that one earlier. Wait – why can't the pitcher hit for himself?
KYLIE. *(Almost slaps TRACY's face again, but stops herself.)* Sorry. Well, traditionally, pitchers aren't good hitters. They used to bat in the batting order, but it was basically an automatic out every time they came up. Killed rallies, forced teams to use pinch hitters all the time which would unnecessarily use bench hitters when they might have been needed later in the game.
TRACY. I didn't get a lot of that.

KYLIE. They're bad hitters, so they don't hit.

TRACY. I think it would be kind of fun to have someone bad at the sport playing with everyone else that's good. Plus, it sounds like there would be more strategies to use.

KYLIE. I'm this close to smacking you again.

Suddenly, the warning system goes off again. They check the protocol on their screens. TRACY looks a bit concerned and looks to KYLIE, who reassures her and retrieves two protective vests and sturdy helmets. She gives one of each to TRACY and they equip themselves, sheltering just in case. KYLIE then looks at her screen again; she has received another message. She motions for TRACY to stay and cautiously approaches the door. She counts to herself "1, 2, 3..." and quickly unlocks the door. KASEN and NICK burst in, even more of a mess than KYLIE and TRACY, and motion for KYLIE to shut the door quickly. They are each about to say something, but when they see the game is back on, they disregard everything else. The warning system stops.

NICK. Oh, cool, you got the game going.

TRACY. My God, you two are covered in blood!

NICK. It's fine. Most of it's not ours. Eighth inning?! Were we out there that long?!

KASEN. Guess so. Tie game, boy, this is exciting!

All are silent for a moment, with looks of horror.

NICK. Are you fucking kidding me?

KASEN. Well. Never mind.

KYLIE. Damn. That was bad timing.

NICK's immediate impulse is to take off one of his socks, so he does. He throws it down angrily and begins pacing, searching for other ways to change his luck.

TRACY. What's he doing?

KYLIE. He's superstitious. His good luck charm is to wear only one sock. Sometimes it actually works, so who knows?

NICK. The second we come in here, fucking two-run home run. That is not a coincidence! I didn't hold my breath during the seventh inning stretch, and now it's 6-4. Inevitable.

He starts climbing onto various pieces of furniture.

KASEN. Dodgers just got another hit.
NICK. Goddamn it! Not today! This can't happen today!
TRACY. It's not your fault, though! Those players have no idea how many socks you're wearing or what furniture you're standing on.
KASEN. No, no, don't try to reason with him –
NICK. You don't know the connection I have with those players, alright! Don't you even start with me, or I'll –

> *He starts to wobble on the couch and falls, but catches himself and momentarily is caught leaning on the couch, standing on one leg.*

KASEN. Look! Look! Ground ball…
KYLIE. Can they turn it?!
KASEN. Yes! Double play! Take that!
NICK. Hallelujah!

> *He freezes in place, on one leg, leaning.*

This is my lucky position! I am not moving from this spot!

> *Beat.*

Kylie, toss me a beer!
KYLIE. Yes, sir!

> *She does so, with sarcastic quickness.*

KASEN. Want me to join you?
NICK. No! Everyone stay where you are! Don't move until the baseball gods have given you permission!

> *He is breathing heavily, but takes a moment to calm down. The rest are all smiling/laughing at him.*

Oh, shut up, I'm just as crazy as the rest of you.
KASEN. Statistically speaking, I don't think that's true.

> *Suddenly the door bursts open again and BRAD and ERICA are back. They notice immediately that NICK and KASEN have returned and breathe a sigh of relief. This lets them get back into their previous personas.*

BRAD. Thank the heavens you're alright!
ERICA. Oh, Brad, you saved them! You sexy marvelous hero of my heart! What would the world be without you?
BRAD. Kiss me, Erica!

> *They make out passionately.*

NICK. Not now, there's no time for this! The game is – !

KASEN. Hey, they got the last out! Onto the bottom of the eighth!
NICK. Okay, carry on then. Hah, lucky spot, I told you! Place your bets now, the Yankees are winning this game!
ERICA. Brad, these folks need a way to bet on baseball games!
NICK. Nope, we did that earlier.
BRAD. But wait!

They turn to the others; commercial time.

Do you like betting on sports? We know. We've already got your money there. But did you know, with iZon Bet Kings Advanced, you can bet on <u>anything</u>?
ERICA. Anything, you say?!
BRAD. Anything! With our new and improved iZon Extremely Personal Family Information technology, we have data on absolutely everything! And in our groundbreaking new sponsorship with iZon Bet Kings Advanced Premium, Ultra-Fan Edition, you can use information about your very own family to win bets against them!
ERICA. Who uses the most iZon Toothpaste?
BRAD. Yup! We've got the answer!
ERICA. Who eats the iZon Flakes when everybody else goes to bed?
BRAD. We've got that too!
ERICA. Who thinks the dirtiest thoughts?
BRAD. That's right! Here at iZon, we've got access to <u>all</u> of this information, and more!
ERICA. And now you can use it to win <u>big money</u>!
BRAD. Limited time only!
ERICA. iZon takes 65% of all bets through processing fees,
BRAD. And is not contractually obligated to explain further.
ERICA. Now with free WiFi!
KASEN. I'm not gonna lie, that actually sounds pretty neat.
BRAD. Sign up now!
NICK. No thank you! Now get out before you ruin the rally!
KYLIE. You've saved us, thank you, bye!
ERICA. We've done it, Brad! We've saved them!
BRAD. I couldn't have done it without you, Erica!
ERICA. So you're not mad at me anymore?
BRAD. Not as much!

They've reached the door by now; they hold for a romantic

pose, realize nobody is paying any attention to them, and leave anticlimactically.

KASEN. That reminds me, I wonder how our predictions are going.

NICK. Yeah, that thousand bucks I'm sure you both owe me by now!

KASEN. I doubt it. Let's see...

He goes back to the predictions from earlier and compares them to the current results of the game.

Oh. Holy cow.

NICK. I'm kickin' your ass, aren't I?

KASEN. No.

Beat.

Kylie is.

KYLIE. Those lousy picks from before the game?

KASEN. Yeah. Look – Bannerman's strikeouts, eight, you got that right, runs before the 5th inning, six, you're right. Three walks for Baker, holy cow, he's done it – how did you – a single apiece for Olivo and Velasco, that's all they've got so far! Fastest pitch, Mistretta! What the heck!

KYLIE. Huh. Guess I'm getting lucky.

KASEN. I'll say. You're off by one with your double plays... and you said two extra-base hits for Solano, he's only got one, so I've got a point there... But still, this is strange.

NICK. And I never cared about that thousand dollars anyway. I'm lettin' you kids win it.

Reacting to the TV.

Hey! Yes! Thattaboy, Rodriguez! Clean piece of hitting going up the middle like that.

TRACY. How many did they score?

KASEN. None, it's just a single.

KYLIE. It's a good start, though.

KASEN. Yeah, but now Baker's up, he's slower than 95% of the league. Big double play threat. I swear, if he...

NICK. Whose side are you on? Quit being pessimistic.

KASEN. I mean, I do have a thousand bucks on the line.

Suddenly the alert system goes off again. Everyone looks at their screens and starts moving around quickly to prepare for the room to be turned 90 degrees. Yeah, this is a weird one.

Those of us living in the modern day wouldn't be able to explain it. As the place starts to "tilt" which is shown by the actors leaning heavily one way, then eventually laying down and holding onto the furniture (which is presumed to be bolted down), KYLIE, KASEN, and TRACY find a decent spot to get through the ordeal. However, NICK flails through the room and "falls" down to the wall. The warning system is still playing throughout the following, so these next lines are yelled over it.

KYLIE. Baker just struck out!
NICK. Damn it! I lost my lucky spot! How much longer?!
KASEN. Mine says ninety seconds!
NICK. That's too long!

He tries to go back to his position standing on one leg, but fails miserably.

KYLIE. Stop moving! Just wait till it's over!
NICK. My luck! I gotta get my luck back!
KYLIE. Luck doesn't exist! You're just crazy!
NICK. I'm not crazy!
KASEN. You're a little crazy!
NICK. I am not!
KYLIE. Rodriguez just got picked off!
NICK. DAMN IT! That's it, the other sock is coming off!
KASEN. Dad! Zero socks?? Has that ever been done?!
NICK. No! I'm desperate!

As he's taking off his other sock, the room starts to return to normal. NICK falls over himself, clumsily rolling around with his shoe in one hand, the other hand trying to remove his sock. Everyone dusts themselves off and returns to their previous spots.

NICK. Oh! Come on, what are you doing, Solano, letting a curveball drop in like that!
KASEN. Now he's gotta protect the plate.
KYLIE. Not that you know anything about protection.
KASEN. ...Dad, what does she mean by that?
NICK. You'll know when you're older. Pay attention! Come on Solano, stop fouling and hit the damn ball!

KASEN. Maybe I should learn a few things about sex, just to understand your stupid jokes.

KYLIE. Good luck finding a teacher.

KASEN. I could get any girl I want.

KYLIE. Not without a little plastic surgery.

NICK. My god, how many times is Solano gonna foul off these waste pitches! This is stressing me out.

KASEN. *(Deciding not to play along with KYLIE anymore.)* At least he's made Kone build up a high pitch count. They probably won't use him in the 9th with twenty-five pitches in the 8th.

NICK. They've got what's-his-name out there in the 'pen though.

KASEN. Diggs, yes. But he's not consistent. Half the time he's a shutdown guarantee, half the time he can't find the strike zone.

NICK. *(Still holding one of his socks.)* I think there's a rock stuck inside here…

He places his hand inside the sock to fish out the rock.

KYLIE. How come you didn't notice a rock in your sock while it was on your foot?

NICK. You don't have anything else to make fun of, so now you're going for my foot sensitivity?

Attention brought to the TV, while his hand is still in the sock.

ALL. *(Ad lib.)* YEAH! OH BABY! HOME RUN! GO SOLANO!

TRACY. They won! They won!

KASEN. Well, no, but they got another run.

TRACY. Okay, yes, I see that – so it's… 6-5 now? We're still losing?

KASEN. Yes, but we're closer than before!

NICK. I can taste it. It's right there. One run, c'mon boys! Just one!

KYLIE. Did you find that rock yet?

NICK. *(Realizing the sock is still on his hand.)* It's not coming off!

KYLIE. Oh, come on. Are you seriously trying to say that –

NICK. Solano hit that home run primarily and solely because my sock was on my hand, yes. Now, if the rest of you don't follow my lead, the Yankees will lose and it will be your fault. Let's go, now, Gomez! Back-to-back, baby!

KYLIE. *(To TRACY, who has started to take off a sock.)* No, don't do that. Please, Dad, put your sock back on – oh God, it smells so bad.

NICK. It is pretty bad, yeah, sorry, but it's staying and that's that.

KASEN. I should collect data on these superstitions. Do control groups, blocked studies, see if they actually make a difference.
NICK. Yeah? And with what games will you be collecting this data? The imaginary games in your head?
KASEN. Dang, I keep forgetting this is it.
NICK. Shit... Come on, Gomez, you fat ass! Hustle! Damn it.
KYLIE. At least they got the one run.
NICK. I guess. I'm not taking the sock off!
KYLIE. Okay. Open this beer on your own, then.

>*She hands him a beer. NICK laughs at first, then struggles with it for the next few minutes. In the meantime BRAD and ERICA re-enter, incredibly dizzy. It isn't part of the bit for them; they're actually spinning around and feeling nauseous. They get close to their pre-planned make out sessions at a couple of points, but they can't go through with it because it would make them sick.*

BRAD. Erica, the world has turned – back to normal –
ERICA. You hero – My hero –
BRAD. Oh God, no, don't kiss me, I can't right now.
ERICA. Me neither. Let's just, do the –
BRAD. Right. Get it over with.

>*They enter their commercial personas, falling over slightly.*

Are you unhappy with the way you look?
ERICA. Need a makeover?
BRAD. Oof – I'm just gonna skip, if that's alright – uh, consider subscribing to…
ERICA. Um, the brand-new iZon Plastic Surgery Deluxe Plan! Ugh.
BRAD. Your excess weight, now half-off!
ERICA. Become the best version of yourself, today!

>*She falls down a bit.*

KASEN. Wait, Kylie. You said Solano would get two extra-base hits.
KYLIE. Did I?
KASEN. The double earlier, and now the home run…

>*He checks the predictions.*

BRAD. Let's get out of here.
ERICA. We gotta do the side effects.
BRAD. But it's that long one… I don't want to…

ERICA. We have to.

BRAD. Look at them, they're not paying any attention at all. We've completely dropped character and they don't notice a thing.

ERICA. It's in our contract – Oh God, I'm gonna be sick –

She runs to the bathroom hallway. While she's gone:

BRAD. No, it's okay, I got it. Jeez.

Back to his fake persona. He takes a deep breath.

Side effects of iZon Plastic Surgery Deluxe include, but are not limited to, nausea, headaches, fever, liver damage, heart disease, body odor, runny nose, excruciating death, sore throat, throat cancer, blindness, baldness, blondness, blandness, chapped lips, armpit cancer, paralysis, hemorrhoids, embarrassing acne, visions of the future, dogs like you less, bats like you too much, babies fear you and laugh when you die, and seizures.

ERICA has re-entered. Wiping her mouth:

ERICA. Sign up today.

BRAD. Limited time only!

ERICA. Refund not valid when side effects are present.

BRAD. iZon is not responsible for anything, ever.

ERICA. Now with free WiFi!

Big smiles. Beat.

KASEN. *(Still referring to the predictions.)* Holy cow. Yeah. There's no way I beat you now.

KYLIE. What'd I tell ya? Easy money.

KASEN. This is – This is suspicious. Nobody could have gotten all of these right by accident.

BRAD. Okay, they're still on the betting thing, let's just go.

ERICA. Slowly, slowly.

They go up the stairs and exit over the following.

KASEN. Kylie, is it luck? Or – ?

KYLIE. What do you want me to say, Kasen?? That I'm actually obsessed with baseball like some statistical number-sucking freak? That I've wanted to play my entire life but never got the opportunity because I'm a girl?

KASEN. Number-sucking freak?

KYLIE. Sorry, not you. Me. I'm a number-sucking freak.

KASEN. What? No you're not…

NICK. *(Too drunk to follow this.)* Hey look, game's back on.

KYLIE. Olivo tweaked his shoulder last week and can't hit for power, he knows it so he's cut down his launch angle and is obviously changing his strategy to compensate. He's got a .350 career BABIP but nobody ever thought of him as a contact guy because of his power. And Velasco is following suit because he's a dumbass and does everything Olivo does. Look at the box scores since Olivo's shoulder tweak: singles, singles, everywhere.

KASEN. Wow. I'm – Dad, are you hearing this?

NICK. Kasen, buddy – the game's on. Quit distracting me.

KYLIE. And Baker's walks – did you forget to check his career OPS against Mistretta? He's got Mistretta figured out, and Mistretta knew it, so he's been avoiding him all day. That's why he's got three walks. And speaking of Mistretta, let's finally mention the elephant in the room: he got a new arm three starts ago. After that Phillies game, his velocity magically shot up – I can't believe you didn't notice that! He was sitting 96, 97 easily earlier in this series, and obviously he had room left to improve today.

NICK. Nice, first out. Give 'em hell, Palacios!

KYLIE. Now, Solano, I'm not gonna lie – I honestly do just find him attractive, and wanted the best for him. He really surprised me. And – let's see, what else was there – Bannerman's strikeouts, but that was pretty mundane. Six runs before the 5th, not that crazy...

KASEN. What about the double plays? You're wrong so far there.

KYLIE. Am I?

KASEN. Yeah, you said there'd be four. There's only been three.

KYLIE. Oh, such a big difference. Give me a little leeway. I just figured, with the exit velocities we've been seeing this series – and you must know about the double play tendency of this ballpark, the infield dirt was made for them.

KASEN. You know everything, all the way down to the infield dirt?!

NICK. Hey hey hey, two outs. Nice easy 1-2-3 inning, let's do this.

KASEN. Not now, Dad...

KYLIE. Yes, Kasen. I've been playing you two this whole time. You caught me. But it's only because I've wanted nothing more, my entire life, than to play baseball. And neither of you noticed, my entire childhood! Wiffleball games in the front yard. That sandlot league I joined the second I was old enough, and dominated from day one. I taught myself to switch hit, throw a killer screwball, shag fly balls, hell, I even did squats three hours a week in case anyone needed a catcher. But no: I never got the chance, because I don't have a dick. And now I've got to listen every day to the ramblings of a drunk who never learned secondary pitches, and a pussy who got hit by one pitch in high school and has been nerding it up ever since. I've had enough of it. I'm done lying. Nobody is going to miss baseball as much as me. Nobody.

NICK. *(Beat.)* ...And there's that third out! Nice clean inning right there. What was it you were saying?

KASEN. She's a freak, Dad. A baseball freak. It was right under our noses the whole time, and we didn't see it.

NICK. Oh, I saw it. But she's a girl, so...

> *He shrugs and sips his beer.*

TRACY. So... Just to be clear... Baseball is a sport. Like, a game. Just a game. Or am I missing something?

KYLIE. It's not a game, Tracy. It's life. It's war. It's the difference between making something useful out of your brief time here, and dying as a sad old sack of nothing. Without it, I am nothing. We are all nothing.

NICK. Amen, sister.

> *He holds his beer out, but she's not having it. He shrugs and puts it back. KASEN approaches KYLIE and puts a hand on her shoulder. This is pretty heartfelt.*

KASEN. I'm sorry I never realized any of that, Kylie. You deserved a shot, and you never got it. That's awful. Now that I think about it, dang, you <u>were</u> the best player in town growing up. I can't believe, just because you're a girl... You never got to show everyone what you're capable of.

KYLIE. This is kind of <u>my</u> moment, Kasen.

KASEN. Sorry. I'm just – I'm sorry, sis. I really am.

KYLIE. It's fine. Two thousand bucks will help take the pain away.

KASEN. You know, coming up might possibly be the last half-inning of baseball's existence.

KYLIE. Yup.

KASEN. *(Beat.)* I'm glad I'm watching it with you.

KYLIE. Me too, buddy. Me too.
KASEN. Will you... nerd it up with me?
KYLIE. *(Laughing.)* I'd be honored.

> *They share a hug as compatible as a sibling hug can be. NICK has been too drunk to follow along, but he brings them back to the present moment.*

NICK. Put those socks of yours on your hands, you two! Come on, let's rally! These guys never quit. One run game, top of the lineup up, all they have to do is put some pressure on Diggs and they'll spook him. He's a pussy.
KASEN. Doesn't he typically do <u>better</u> under pressure?
KYLIE. Yeah. His WPA and HLI are Top 5, and in 1-run games his velocity increases from 93rd to 99th percentile. He feeds on pressure.
KASEN. ...You know all of that off the top of your head?
KYLIE. You don't?
KASEN. I was just going to say he's got an ERA under 2 and converted 37 of 39 save opportunities this year.
KYLIE. Hah. Rookie stats. You know all the flaws about judging relievers based on ERA and save opportunities, right?
KASEN. Yes, but they're the stats everyone knows and talks about.
NICK. Hey look, game's back on. Shut up and watch it with me.
KYLIE. Just because WHIP and FIP and K/BB are less mainstream doesn't mean you shouldn't know them. You call yourself a fan...
KASEN. I thought I was the only one who knew them!
KYLIE. I'm just giving you a hard time.
NICK. Hey! Did you two not hear me? The fucking game's on and it's the bottom of the 9th of the last game of the last World Series. One run game. Why is anybody talking over this?! What the hell is wrong with all of you?!

> *To TRACY.*

Sorry, not you. You're doing great.
TRACY. Thanks. I just have one question –
NICK. Don't push it.

> *All intently watch the TV for a bit. Every few seconds, they collectively hold their breaths as the pitch is thrown, then exhale when it's not in play.*

Cruz has to learn to swing the damn bat.

KASEN. He's working the count.

NICK. He's being a pussy. We need a hit.

KASEN and KYLIE. A walk is just as good.

Both are surprised by each other.

NICK. Not true. You forget doubles, triples, home runs?

KASEN. You forget Cruz isn't exactly an extra base hitter? His slugging is .400.

NICK. Look! Look at this! Come on, stay fair! FAIR! NO!

KASEN. Foul. Dang.

KYLIE. Oh, that was so close.

NICK. That was fair! Didn't you see it curve around the pole?!

KASEN. No, Dad, it didn't. Hey! Worked the walk, though! Nice!

NICK. It was fair! Why aren't they challenging?! Why wouldn't they challenge a call that's so wrong?!

KYLIE. Watch. Replay…

NICK. *(Beat.)* Okay, it was foul. Carry on. At least he got on base.

KASEN. By not swinging.

NICK. I didn't say he's not a pussy. Still is. OH! Nice hit through the hole! Let's go, boys! Let's go!

KASEN. This is getting very interesting.

NICK. The sock! It's working!

KYLIE. It's not the sock, Dad.

NICK. It's the sock! I don't see why nobody else is trying this, it's clearly working!

KASEN. Mound visit.

NICK. Pressure's getting to Diggs. I know it is.

KASEN. He might be hurt. Look how he's grabbing at his shoulder. Is he hurt?

KYLIE. Boy, if they get him out of the game – this could be a big break for the Yankees.

KASEN. Nope. They're leaving him in.

NICK. Good! He's got the nerves. They're under his skin. Look at him, he's shaking.

KYLIE. *(Under her breath, almost instinctively.)* I bet he hits him in the ribs.

KASEN. Normally I'd take that bet, Diggs doesn't hit many batters, and it's way too specific to have any real likelihood of happeni –

NICK. OH! RIGHT IN THE RIBS!
KYLIE. Oh my God.
KASEN. What the heck! Kylie, what the freaking heck!
KYLIE. I don't know. I honestly don't know how I knew that one.
KASEN. That wasn't statistical analysis?
KYLIE. No. I mean, Olivo is above average in HBP% and Diggs looked hurt, but still – it's like I just saw that one coming.
NICK. He is hurt! They're taking him out! Boy oh boy, let's go!
KASEN. Can you imagine being brought into a game with the bases loaded and no outs and the history of baseball hanging in the balance?
NICK. We've got 'em right where we want 'em! We've got 'em! This is it! This is –

> *He stumbles over himself; he's very drunk at this point. Without much fanfare, BRAD and ERICA re-enter and go directly into the water advertisement from before. They are focused on NICK, trying to sober him up.*

BRAD. Folks, it's a survivor's world.
ERICA. And if you want to make it out alive, you need the purest,
BRAD. Most refreshing,
ERICA. And only water around:
BRAD. iZon Water Plus!
NICK. Get out of here! This is not the time!
ERICA. Do you often find yourself a little too drunk?
BRAD. A nice glass of water will help sober you up, and make you feel better tomorrow!
NICK. Decline! Not interested!
ERICA. It's for your own good…

> *NICK starts chasing them up the stairs, yelling incoherently.*

BRAD. Limited time only!
ERICA. Prices vary due to demand, war, or profit recalculations.
BRAD. Survival not guaranteed.
ERICA. Now with free WiFi!

> *They exit quickly, NICK slamming the door behind them.*

KASEN. Who's this they're bringing in?
KYLIE. I dunno, I actually haven't heard of him.
KASEN. Me neither. Henry Tolentino? Am I saying that right?
KYLIE. Sure.

NICK. *(Stumbling down the stairs.)* What? Wait – wait – what did that say?? Who is it?

KASEN. Tolentino. Do <u>you</u> know him?

NICK. No. No, it can't be. It can't be him.

KASEN. Did he play for the Yankees at one point? Why am I drawing a blank?

NICK. *(Reading on the TV.)* My God. Henry Tolentino?! Henry fucking Tolentino!!!

KASEN. What, Dad?! Who is this guy?

NICK. He's – He and I –

> *He's too angry to make words. He starts pacing the room, throwing chairs and tossing tables, the single sock still on one of his hands.*

KYLIE. Oh, look: "Major League debut."

KASEN. Wow. What a situation to put a fresh rookie in! Jeez, the Dodgers are either geniuses or idiots. I can't tell which.

KYLIE. *(Still reading.)* "Tolentino has spent the past thirteen seasons working his way back from various injuries." Look at those minor league stats! He's been there a long time, wow.

KASEN. "Tolentino was included in the groundbreaking UCL repair experiment in which half of initial surgeries ended with career-ending injuries. Tolentino happened to be able to work his way back. Others weren't as lucky."

> *KASEN and KYLIE look to NICK, still fuming.*

NICK. It had to be him! It just had to be him!

KASEN. So I take it you know the guy.

NICK. We were in the same draft class. Worked out together. Never played on the same team, but pitched against each other at basically every level. When I blew out my arm, that first time – the same thing had happened to him, like, what, a week before. We saw the same specialist, did the same rehab work, got to be pretty good friends, if I could've ever called an opponent that... We said we'd make it back together. He said I'd make it. I said he'd make it. I was right...

> *Beat. He's starting to get pretty emotional.*

KASEN. Do you stay in touch?

NICK. Kasen, bud, I'm in the middle of something right now.

KASEN. Sorry, Dad. Go on. He's still throwing his warmup pitches.

KYLIE. *(To herself.)* Boy, he's got a good delivery.

NICK. I remember, one of the things we used to talk about was, when we made it to the bigs, when we finally stepped onto those bright lights and felt like pros... what our first pitches would be. That first taste of the Majors, what we'd choose in that big moment. Of course, I always said fastball, hundred percent, no question. It's my bread and butter. But he'd say, "Changeup," because nobody would expect a first-pitch changeup, and it'd be fitting to throw a plot twist back at life for once. And, y'know me and my fastball, I still think to this day I woulda had a tough choice. He made that compelling of an argument, can you believe that?

He's getting lost in his past.

I actually think about it a lot. Toeing the rubber again, after all these years, breathing in that – that atmosphere – the cheers, the boos, popcorn, hot dogs, that "pop" in the mitt you hear when they just can't catch up to the heater. I wonder if I'd have changed it up for once, done something new. Take my shot at being a different player, a brand new person. Throw a plot twist... back at life... But I never found out. I never got my first pitch. And now... And now Tolentino gets his. And it has to be against my Yankees...

A long beat. The inning is about to restart.

KYLIE. So... think he's going changeup here, then?

NICK. *(Sniffling a little bit, then shrugging off his emotions and taking a long swig of his beer.)* I don't care. I hope they hit a fucking grand slam off him.

Beat.

TRACY. ...Man, your dedication to this game is unreal.

KASEN. Ball one.

KYLIE. Changeup.

NICK. Coward.

Beat.

KASEN. Strike one.

NICK. Swing the damn bat, Velasco!

KASEN. Ball two.

Suddenly the warning system goes off again, pissing everybody off. They check their screens, sigh, and take their oxygen masks back out. They "take cover" but at this point they're just going through the motions. Explosions and tortured screams are heard from outside, completely ignored.

Strike two!

The room starts shaking, almost rocking back and forth. They all start falling down, grabbing onto furniture and focusing solely on the game. NICK takes his oxygen mask off briefly to swig his beer.

Ball three!

The rocking reaches a climax, then finally everyone jumps up as if gravity is momentarily suspended. When they reach the ground, they all fall down. Eventually, all are settled and take off their masks. KASEN looks at the TV, dejected.

Damn it. Struck him out.

NICK. *(Breathing heavily, calming down a bit.)* Gotta be kidding me. Well, we've got two more outs to work with.

KASEN. And Bolden coming up. Easy double in the gap, come on. He's a doubles and triples machine.

KYLIE. Actually, just this year. And his xSLG suggests it was a bit of a fluky season.

NICK. Give me hope or shut the hell up!

KYLIE. …He's got a hard-hit percentage 30% better than the league average and barrels the ball more than anybody else in high leverage situations.

NICK. Thank you!

KASEN. That's what we need, a hard hit, so long as it's not right at somebody.

TRACY. What would be wrong with that?

KASEN. He'd be out, or worse –

They all stop and freeze. Watching the TV more intensely than ever before. All at once:

NO! NO NO NO –

KYLIE. Oh shit, shit, shit…

NICK. *(Throwing everything in sight.)* FFFUUUUUUCCCKKKK!!!

TRACY. What was it?? What happened?

KASEN. Double play. The last two outs. It's over.

NICK. Replay! Go to the replay! They have to check it!

KYLIE. They will. They are.

NICK. Overturn! Overturn it! Come on, umps, don't ruin this!
They all watch the replay and start sobbing.
TRACY. Why would they overturn that?
NICK. Shut up!
KASEN. They won't. It's clearly an out. Two outs.
KYLIE. It's... It's over.
All are silent for a long, long time. NICK drinks a full beer and another one in quick succession. KASEN stares blankly at the TV, mindlessly reading the end of game stats. KYLIE sympathizes with both of them. TRACY tries to understand what's going on. And just in time for... a final BRAD and ERICA entrance. This time, ERICA is doubled over in pain and BRAD has her by the arm. They're covered in blood.
BRAD. Erica, lay down here! Don't worry, you're okay! You're going to make it, Erica!
ERICA. Brad... I don't know if I can... Go on without me...
BRAD. Hold on, Erica! I'll save you like I saved everyone else!
ERICA. Before I die, Brad... I want you to know... I'm pregnant...
BRAD. Erica! Are you serious?!
ERICA. Yes!
BRAD. ...And you're sure it's mine?!
ERICA. Yes, Brad! ...Please, raise my child... To fight for justice... To save... Those we couldn't...
BRAD. Erica, I promise. I will raise our child a hero!
ERICA. I... love... you...
BRAD. Sweet, sweet Erica. I love you. Please don't go. Oh, Erica...
He starts crying as ERICA emits her "final breath." He holds her, lovingly.
I will avenge you, Erica. Oh, Erica!
NICK. Hey, could you quiet down, we're trying to grieve over here!
BRAD. Oh, is the game over?
KASEN. Yup. 6-5 Dodgers. Yankees had the bases loaded and no outs in the 9th and couldn't score.
KYLIE. A Nobletiger.
KASEN. That's right.
BRAD. Great! Erica, the game's over.
ERICA. Finally.

ERICA gets up, healthy as can be. BRAD and ERICA change personas once again, now appearing to be spokespeople for:

BRAD. Thank you, folks, for participating in the Beta version of iZon's Exclusive World Series Game 7 Experience!

ERICA. *(Sending surveys through her projected screen.)* I'm sending you all a few surveys we'd like you to fill out, if you don't mind! We'd like to make your Game 7 Experience as exciting and profitable as possible!

BRAD. That's right! Any ads you'd like to see more or less of, whether you'd recommend the Game 7 Experience to a friend, etc… Just fill it out here!

Beat. The next few lines are somewhat simultaneous.

KASEN. I'm sorry, what?

KYLIE. What is going on?

TRACY. Who are you two?

NICK. Wasn't she dead a minute ago?

ERICA. Oh, right – A brief explanation. Ladies, gentlemen: My name is Erica Proctor, this is my partner Brad Angelo. We are the main coordinators and representatives of iZon's Game 7 Experience, a revolutionary way to bring baseball into the iZon Multi-Reality Supreme Service Pro. You've just participated in our exclusive Dodgers-Yankees offer, which is still in its Beta version.

BRAD. That means we're still learning what works best here. We've obviously still got a few things to work on in this Experience, which is why we value your feedback! Now, most of these questions are on a scale from 1 to 10, as you can see: "How would you rate your level of excitement?" "How realistic did the simulation appear to be?" familiarity with players, with each other, storyline of the game, relevance of advertisements, etc. That last one is quite important!

KYLIE. What – what do you mean, with each other?

ERICA. Right. This is always the toughest part. Perhaps you'd all like to sit down for this.

They all sit. BRAD and ERICA start putting on defensive gear in preparation for an attack.

BRAD. The four of you signed up for our program completely separately, and have been paired together using our state-of-the-art iZon Family Matching Software. Now, it's not quite clear yet whether you are all "the best" matches for each other, but from what I saw today, I think it was a decent pairing.

ERICA. A few hiccups here and there, but overall, yes, seemed like pretty standard familial relationships.

BRAD. Yes, a few lapses in memory that we'll try to patch, and certainly some, I don't know, "odd" moments of indifference toward each other. Nothing we can't fix for next time.

ERICA. Yeah, there's some real promise here!

BRAD. Yup! Any questions so far?

> *Beat. Everyone is trying to comprehend this. KASEN, KYLIE, and TRACY are on the verge of freaking out; NICK is too far gone, it's all going over his head.*

KASEN. Are – Are you saying, we don't actually know each other?

ERICA. Well, you do now, sport! I gotta say, I really liked how you and Kylie softened up to each other there at the end.

BRAD. It was a little cheesy, but yeah – cute.

KYLIE. I don't even – I don't know where to – Is everything we think we know, just fake?

ERICA. Just the memories that you all share. Any memories you have about other aspects of your life, those are likely legitimate.

KASEN. I... I can't remember anything else right now.

BRAD. Oh... oh dear. That's – Are you sure, kid?

KASEN. I – I don't know anything other than baseball, my sister, and my father.

ERICA. Shoot. Is that something we can fix?

BRAD. Not sure. Um, for now, kid, just try to describe the memories you <u>do</u> have in Section 4, here...

TRACY. So – what am I doing here, exactly?

ERICA. Good question! In other tests we've run, we made you and Nick husband and wife. Which made you, of course, Kasen and Kylie's mother. We wanted to go for the whole "American family" type of setup, you know, classic nostalgic baseball.

BRAD. But Nick would never pay any attention to you.

TRACY. Why not?

ERICA. We're not sure, but we're determined to figure it out!

BRAD. Honestly, he didn't pay much attention to her this time either.

ERICA. That's true – and she barely got any backstory out. Didn't

get many chances to test her memory bank.
TRACY. *(Quietly.)* My what…
BRAD. She's too shy.
ERICA. Yes, that might be it. Let's make note of it. Maybe we don't have room for her in the future.
TRACY. Excuse me?!
BRAD. And I think pizza was the wrong choice.
ERICA. Yes, after that first one was ruined, nobody ever mentioned iZon Pizza again.
BRAD. Folks, is there a food you'd rather have advertised to you?
NICK. It's baseball. I want hot dogs and apple pie.
ERICA. Of course! Hot dogs and apple pie, write that down.
BRAD. Yeah, that's gonna be much better than pizza.
ERICA. *(To TRACY.)* Don't worry, though, we'll keep you in tests, for now, and find the best possible relationship for you to have with the rest of the family. We primarily want to keep you around because we've primed you to advertise for us.
TRACY. You've – what?!
BRAD. Yup – You got Kasen and Kylie to donate to iZon Pet Central Supreme, you got Kylie to buy iZon Lingerie, iZon Party Pills – You two are a great pairing, aren't you?
ERICA. Yeah, let's keep them together for a few more tests. There's so much promise there!
BRAD. You know, it was Tony that suggested we put 'em together.
ERICA. Tony? The intern?
BRAD. Yup.
ERICA. Good for him!
BRAD. Right? And Nick – you're our star! We didn't even have to mention iZon Beer Lite. Not once. You single-handedly made that sponsorship worth it. Well done.
ERICA. We actually had to try to sober you up there at the end with another iZon Water ad.
BRAD. You really should drink more water, Nick.
>*NICK stares at them, drunk, unable to process all this. KASEN is actually filling out the surveys, while KYLIE sits there in disbelief. TRACY is having none of this.*

TRACY. This can't be legal! This isn't – you're monsters!

BRAD. Whoa, calm down there. Yes, it's legal. You all voluntarily signed up for the Game 7 Experience. Here's an agreement you all signed, allowing us access to your personal information, memories, and anything else we deemed important to making your Game 7 Experience as exciting and profitable as we could.

He sends these documents to their screens.

TRACY. You can't do this! I'm suing you! This is illegal, I'm sure of it! You're gonna regret this!

BRAD. Again, you signed the agreement. You gave us permission to do everything we've done.

KYLIE. Why would we ever let you –?

ERICA. Well, refusing to opt in to any of our select Experiences means you are no longer eligible for any of our sponsors' products.

TRACY. So what! I don't want anything from you!

BRAD. *(Laughing.)* It's not necessarily a "want" situation here.

TRACY. What do you mean?

BRAD. Well, those products include iZon Water, iZon Housing, iZon Oxygen, iZon Gravity, shall I go on?

KYLIE. So if we don't participate in your… "Experiences," and buy your products, we'll be left to die?

ERICA. Well, that's certainly not how we're legally phrasing it.

TRACY. That's murder! That's corporate murder!

BRAD. And perfectly legal! Might I suggest skipping Section 6…

KYLIE. Is any of this real? I feel like I'm passing out.

BRAD. It's all real, yes, just – a little fabricated.

KYLIE. Jessica? Is she real?

ERICA. She's a real program!

BRAD. A great one, too. Did you see how much they believed they knew her? All of them!

ERICA. Yes, that was remarkable. We've gotta pass that along to the Mutual Friends Programming Department.

KYLIE. The death and destruction outside? Is that real?

BRAD. No, that was all carefully orchestrated and choreographed.

KASEN. What about the baseball game?

BRAD. …Looked pretty realistic, didn't it?

KASEN. *(Actually a little impressed.)* Yeah, it did.

KYLIE. What about the whole "end of days"? Is humanity actually facing its extinction or is that all a lie?

BRAD and ERICA exchange a look.

BRAD. iZon is not required to give an official statement on the status of life on Earth and its imminent future.

TRACY. So the world is ending, and all you're doing is monetizing it and conducting memory experiments on innocent people?!

ERICA. It's what makes the most sense, financially.

BRAD. *(Reading an official standard response.)* iZon and its proud sponsors are working diligently to create and sustain an inhabitable world where the spirit of humanity will be able to enjoy a worthwhile livelihood. We are currently investigating claims that we – Actually, I don't need to read that, none of you have accused us of that yet.

ERICA. Surprising.

BRAD. I know.

TRACY. *(Beat.)* You're evil! You're absolutely evil!

She charges at ERICA and BRAD in full-attack mode. They don't freak out; with TRACY a foot or two away from them, BRAD casually selects something on his screen and TRACY instantly drops to the floor, unconscious. This stops the others from doing something similar for the rest of the scene.

KASEN. Is – Is she...?

ERICA. Not a worry, kid, we're just giving her a soft reboot. She'll be ready to go again tomorrow.

BRAD. Boy, she's especially freaked out today, isn't she?

ERICA. Maybe the guys in Emotional Programming can straighten that out.

KYLIE. So – when you say tomorrow, does that mean...?

BRAD. Yes! You'll be doing this same exact thing tomorrow, and every day after that, until we get it right!

ERICA. Then we can release it to the public, and you might be eligible to continue participating.

BRAD. Key word: might.

They both laugh heartily.

KASEN. So, if we're in this for the foreseeable future...

Beat.

What game will we watch tomorrow?

BRAD. Great question! You can choose right in Section 10 if you'd like to participate in this same Experience again – don't worry, we'll clear your memories so it's not boring!

ERICA. *(Pointing to KYLIE.)* We'll need to clear hers twice. It was quite obvious she kept some memories from last time.

BRAD. Yes, I noticed that too. We'll take care of it.

ERICA. *(Continuing BRAD's pitch.)* Of course, if you'd like, you can also request a different Game 7 Experience. We don't currently have all possible matchups available, but we should soon! Might I suggest Astros-Phillies? Our recent viewers rated that simulation very highly.

BRAD. Go Astros!

ERICA. Brad, don't give it away!

They laugh heartily again.

KASEN. Wait, so – what about between the 3rd and 8th innings? What happened then? When the TV stopped working, and we had to go out there and fix it... Was that part of your plan?

BRAD and ERICA look a little embarrassed.

BRAD. Yeah, sorry about that, sport.

ERICA. Brad here got a little "handsy" in the break room.

BRAD. Look at her, kids. Wouldn't you do the same?

ERICA. You're so naughty.

BRAD. No, you are...

They get close to making out, but NICK stops them.

NICK. Okay, so, this has all flown way over my head and I'm too far gone to, y'know, process anything. So, my main question... Did you say there's another game tomorrow?

BRAD. There sure is, as long as you sign the bottom of that form in front of you!

NICK. Cool.

He signs it.

I bet <u>tomorrow</u> it's a walkoff.

KASEN. Dad, are you listening to what they're saying?

KYLIE. The game's not real, we're strangers, it's all just a huge ploy to sell us stuff.

NICK. Where do I buy another beer, then?

BRAD and ERICA nod approvingly and jot down notes.

God, kids, could you believe it, they couldn't score a damn run. Bases loaded, no outs. I coulda farted a run home, and they got nothing.

KYLIE. Dad...

NICK. We had 'em right where we wanted 'em...

>*Beat. KASEN and KYLIE look at each other, trying to comprehend everything. They decide, silently, to just let it happen and give in. To BRAD and ERICA:*

KASEN. Well, do you have any simulations where the Yankees actually win the game?

BRAD. Sorry, no. The code was written by a Red Sox fan.

KASEN. I see. Dad. Hey, Dad.

NICK. It was right there! What?

KASEN. You wanna watch some different teams tomorrow?

NICK. Are you crazy? And miss the Yankees game?

KYLIE. You know, I hear the Cubs have a great rotation. They can pitch a hell of a game.

KASEN. And Wrigley Field, it's not what it used to be, but still –

NICK. The Cubs? The fucking Cubs? Hah, you've lost your minds. I'd rather float into space and explode like a meat balloon than watch a Cubs game.

KASEN. Cardinals?

NICK. Yankees.

KYLIE. Tigers?

NICK. Yankees.

KASEN. Mariners?

>*BRAD and ERICA start giggling.*

BRAD. We, uh, we don't offer Mariners World Series games. Way too unrealistic, people see right through it.

KYLIE. Okay... Giants?

NICK. Kids, I know what you're doing. These high-and-mighty corporates over here are gonna, I dunno, bash our heads with rocks or lasers or something, and I'll wake up tomorrow with a fresh new memory and watch the same damn game I watched today. I hear ya. But y'know what I want you to hear? Hear this: we get to spend a blissfully ignorant eternity watching baseball and drinking beer.

BRAD. Just to be clear, you're not immortal –

NICK. Shut your face, ya Sox-loving piece of filth.

BRAD. As long as we're on the same page.

NICK. Now yeah, it ain't perfect. If it was up to me, I'd be on the mound tomorrow, simulation or whatever. I'd be slinging fastballs like the best of 'em, painting the corners, breaking bats, beaning 'em when they crowd the plate. But I'm here instead. I'm watching 'em on a tiny screen, a thousand miles away, with my wonderful kids. Who cares what's going on, who's tricking who. Too little, too late for us to do anything about it. All we've got left in this terrible world is our beautiful American game. Do what you want, ya number-lovin' sober-ass freaks. Me? Sign. Me. Up.

BRAD nods approvingly and turns to KASEN and KYLIE.
BRAD. What'll it be, folks? Same teams, different teams? We've got a new golf network, if you're interested.
KASEN. I'll take today's matchup. Thanks.
KYLIE. Me too. This is better than... the alternative.

They both smile, defeated but accepting, and sign up.
BRAD. Thank you, everybody. We'll see you tomorrow.
ERICA. Hey Brad? How 'bout one more? For practice?
BRAD. "Oh, Erica! You sexy lover! I can't live without you!"
ERICA. "Let's save the world, Brad, you hunk!"

They make out, then break apart and break character.
My God, our script is terrible.
BRAD. Could be worse. Y'know, I've got a buddy who does football games. Those fans will eat up a steaming pile of shit dialogue like it's filet mignon.

They exit, laughing to each other. As BRAD opens the door, he yells into the suddenly quiet and peaceful outside world:
Alright, everybody, same time tomorrow, call time is 2:00!
ERICA. That means get here at 1:45, Gary!

They've exited. TRACY is left unconscious, while KASEN, KYLIE, and NICK are left wondering what the hell life is.
NICK. Y'know, kids, that parent-kid baseball game in Pearl Park. Your mother was there too, remember?
KASEN. Dad – Or, Nick? – I don't think Mom ever existed...
NICK. But she's there, buddy, isn't she? She's there.
KASEN. I...
KYLIE. I remember it, Dad.
NICK. You remember your mother, at that game?
KYLIE. I do.

KASEN. *(Giving in.)* I do too, Dad.

NICK. I got a triple to lead off that last inning. Your mother worked a walk right after that.

KYLIE. Somebody else did too.

KASEN. Yeah, I remember. Bases loaded, no outs.

NICK. One run game. We were right there.

KYLIE. But you couldn't get a run across the plate.

KASEN. And we won.

NICK. You sure did.

    Beat. A look, a drink.

We had you right where we wanted you, kids. It was right… there…

    They watch the postgame show in silence. Lights down.

END OF ACT II

END OF PLAY

A Dolphin Disguise

A Play in One Act

by

Tucker Atwood

A DOLPHIN DISGUISE premiered as part of a One-Act Festival with the Belfast Maskers in Belfast, Maine in October 2023. It was directed by Tyler Johnstone. The cast was as follows:

NICK	Cort Trejo
EMILY	Linnea Harrold
JOE	Nate Marx
TAMARA	April Rejman

SHORT SYNOPSIS

Advancements in medical technology have proven the existence of reincarnation, with simple tests able to reveal exactly whose bodies our souls once inhabited. Three strangers from various backgrounds await their results alongside a bored receptionist.

CHARACTERS

TAMARA — Any age. A receptionist who is sick of all the idiots she deals with as part of her job.

JOE — Any age. One of those idiots. A believer in good old American freedom. A disbeliever in science.

NICK — 20s to 30s. A well-mannered, charismatic doctor whose goal is to put a smile on people's faces. Definitely nothing shady in his past.

EMILY — 20s to 30s. A polite and kind-hearted veterinarian who is initially a bit nervous about the prospects of reincarnation. She wouldn't have anything to hide about her past either.

PROPERTY LIST

Laptop/paperwork (busywork for Tamara)
A bowl of M&Ms, possibly slightly pre-melted
Clipboards with papers (sign-in forms, etc.)
Sheets of papers (test results)

MISCELLANEOUS NOTES

Nothing specific about costumes or set requirements – these are rather self-explanatory and left up to the director's discretion.

When characters reference a nearby town, [Camden] may be replaced with whatever town yours may have a "friendly rivalry" with.

Scene

Lights up on a waiting room of a small town medical facility. TAMARA, a bored secretary, is behind a desk working on a laptop, devoid of enthusiasm. JOE enters from a hallway. He is not the type to look in the mirror before going out. Sweatpants, five o'clock shadow, etc.

JOE. So that's it, huh?

TAMARA. Yes. Please take a seat while you wait.

JOE. Just a poke and a picture.

TAMARA. A finger prick and an x-ray. Yes. Your results will be ready in about ten minutes.

JOE. This how they do it everywhere?

TAMARA. Yes, it is. Take a seat, please.

JOE. Y'know, my cousin Steve did this over in [Camden].

TAMARA. Okay.

JOE. He says they got a whole bulletin board of famous folks.

TAMARA. Yes, I've heard. The waiting area is over –

JOE. They got movie stars from the '50s, they got writers from back when folks wrote, and just last week they got an astronaut named, uh, Cooper something.

TAMARA. Copernicus. He was an astronomer.

JOE. Yeah. Some fella walks in and they do the whole ordeal – poke and a picture, or whatever, maybe they do it different over there –

TAMARA. They don't.

JOE. The fella walks in, gets these papers, and they say he's the astronaut guy.

TAMARA. Astronomer.

JOE. Cousin Steve was there, that's how I know.

TAMARA. <u>Please</u> take a seat, sir.

JOE. Sure, sure. Just, anywhere here, or…

TAMARA. Yes.

JOE. No assigned seats, huh?

TAMARA. No.

JOE. That's a joke. I'm a jokester.

TAMARA. Okay.

JOE. 'Cause it ain't likely there'd be assigned seats.

TAMARA. I got it.
JOE. Well, you didn't laugh. Most folks, when they hear a joke...
> TAMARA gives a stern straight face. JOE turns his attention to a bowl of M&M's.

These M&M's free?
TAMARA. No, they're all mine. I leave them out in a bowl to brag.
JOE. Oh. Okay.
> Beat.

TAMARA. That was a joke.
JOE. Oh! So you're a jokester too!
TAMARA. Whatever it takes to get you to sit down.
JOE. Good joke. See, I didn't know you was jokin', 'cause you don't seem like a jokester.
> Beat.

So, it's fine if I...?
TAMARA. Yes.
JOE. *(Taking a handful.)* So, got any famous folks here, like they do over in [Camden]?
TAMARA. I cannot provide that information.
JOE. Yeah you can. Says so on the forms.
TAMARA. Well, yes, records of past identities are public, but current identities are private.
JOE. Why's that?
TAMARA. Basically, the living have rights, the dead do not.
JOE. But I don't care 'bout living folks, just if you got any famous dead folks. Like over in [Camden].
TAMARA. How many times must I ask you...?
JOE. Ah, I get it. Nobody famous 'round here.
TAMARA. Sit down. Please.
JOE. 'Cause if you'd gotten, say, a famous astronaut, you'd say so.
TAMARA. Sir, for the love of –
> NICK enters from the front. He is smartly dressed, handsome, and charismatic as hell.

Oh, thank God. I have another customer. Go.
> JOE takes another handful of M&M's, scoffs, and heads to the waiting area. As NICK approaches:

Hello, sir.

NICK. Good afternoon, ma'am! How are we today?
TAMARA. Fine. Do you have an appointment?
NICK. Yes, Nick Wilson, three o'clock.
TAMARA. Right on time.
NICK. Yup! Boy, how about that sunshine, huh? Just gorgeous!
TAMARA. Yes, it's sunny. Here.

She hands him a clipboard with the forms.

Fill these out in our waiting area.
NICK. Sure! Thanks,

Looking at her nametag.

Tamara, I appreciate it! Very excited for this opportunity!
TAMARA. Okay.

He flashes a friendly smile, then sits next to JOE.

NICK. Good afternoon!
JOE. Howdy. M&M?
NICK. Oh, no thank you.
JOE. They're free.
NICK. Thanks, but I'm not hungry.
JOE. Sure. I'm Joe.
NICK. Nick. Nice to meet you!

JOE holds out his hand, but it's covered in melted chocolate.

Oh, sorry, but your hand...
JOE. Ah, yeah. Chocolate. Here.

He licks it off, then goes back for the handshake.

NICK. I – should focus on filling these out.
JOE. Yeah. Okay.

Beat.

So, you got a cousin to prove wrong too?
NICK. Sorry?
JOE. Or maybe a wife – you look the type.
NICK. No, I'm not married.
JOE. Then who are you provin' wrong?
NICK. I... don't understand.
JOE. Y'know... reintarnation...
NICK. Oh! You mean "reincarnation." With a c.
JOE. Yeah, that's what I said.
NICK. It's not, but okay.

JOE. Whatever they're callin' it. It ain't real.

NICK. No. It is.

JOE. You kiddin' me? It's faker than my Aunt Jessie's tits! She's got these huge –

NICK. I've got the picture, thanks. Yes, I was skeptical at first too. But there's evidence, and it's been proven: reincarnation is real!

JOE. C'mon, man... You're really gonna trust some government funded science experiment?

NICK. I trust the science, yes. If you don't, why are you here?

JOE. Well, my cousin Steve – that's Aunt Jessie's boy – Steve says the folks in [Camden] says he was a butterfly. And that's bullshit.

NICK. Why?

JOE. 'Cause he's too fat to fly.

NICK. *(Laughing.)* That's a unique interpretation.

JOE. He's this big guy, y'know, and butterflies are –

NICK. They're small.

JOE. Yeah!

NICK. Look, you should do more research before you –

JOE. Oh, you're brainwashed, man. They got ya.

NICK. No, I'm not – I take it you haven't read any of the studies?

JOE. You mean the fancy science papers everyone believes 'cause they got doctor names on 'em?

NICK. *(Half-jokingly.)* Easy there, I happen to be a doctor!

JOE. That explains it. You're not brainwashed, you're a brainwasher.

NICK. Y'know, I'm glad I've run into you. Perhaps I could educate you on the recent advances in medical technology. Now, I understand that the findings may conflict with your pre-existing beliefs, but an essential part of progress is being able to accept new scientific facts. So, first, let's simply acknowledge the possibility that something you thought to be true is actually false, and vice versa. Could you do that?

JOE. No.

NICK. Oh – why not?

JOE. 'Cause I don't know what the hell you're talkin' 'bout.

NICK. I'm just asking you to have an open mind.

JOE. Oh.

    Beat.

Nah, I'm good.

NICK. Hm. Somehow, I thought this would be easier.
TAMARA. Are you done yet?
NICK. Oh – yes, sorry.
> *Handing the clipboard to TAMARA.*

TAMARA. Right this way.
NICK. *(To JOE as he leaves.)* I'll explain more when I come back!
JOE. You'll still be wrong!
> *NICK and TAMARA exit. JOE waits a beat, then returns for more M&M's. While he's at the desk, EMILY enters. She is polite and shy, and approaches the desk nervously.*

EMILY. Excuse me, do I check in with... you?
JOE. Nah. Lady's in the back, she'll be right here.
EMILY. Okay. Thank you.
JOE. M&M?
EMILY. No, I couldn't eat right now.
JOE. Pregnant?
EMILY. What?! No!
JOE. Not that you look pregnant.
EMILY. Then why would you say that?
JOE. I dunno. I don't think before I speak.
EMILY. Clearly.
JOE. So why ain't you eating?
EMILY. I'm just nervous.
JOE. Ah, nothin' to be nervous about. It's all just a buncha lies.
> *TAMARA re-enters and hears this.*

TAMARA. Excuse me, please remain in the waiting area. And take it easy on the candies.
JOE. You said they're free!
TAMARA. It's a courtesy to all of our customers. Please don't eat too many.
> *JOE nods, puts a few M&M's back into the bowl while maintaining eye contact with TAMARA, and sits back down.*

I'm sorry, ma'am. Do you have an appointment?
EMILY. Yes. Emily Smith.
TAMARA. *(Checking her laptop and grabbing more forms.)* Here you are. Okay, just fill out these forms, please.
EMILY. Thank you.

She takes the forms to the waiting area, sitting as far away from JOE as possible. JOE scooches closer anyway.

JOE. So, as I was sayin', don't believe a word they tell ya. This fella on the news, he says it's a load of bull, all paid for by big pharma. And you know he was tellin' the truth 'cause he's bein' sued now. He says, get this, they're fixin' to indoxinate us.

EMILY. Indoctrinate?

JOE. Yeah! You get it.

EMILY. No, that's just probably what you mean.

JOE. I was pretty close, though. So, he says –

EMILY. I'm sorry, but I don't want to mess up these forms, so…

JOE. Sure. Just, don't pay no mind to what these folks tell ya. Liars, all of 'em.

EMILY. Okay. Thanks.

She fills out the forms and he continues eating M&Ms. NICK re-enters. To TAMARA:

NICK. Hey, that wasn't so bad! Thanks, Tamara!

TAMARA. Please don't use my name like we're friends.

NICK sits between EMILY and JOE.

NICK. Hello, ma'am. I like your shoes!

EMILY. Oh, thank you. That's nice of you.

NICK. I'm Nick. Nice to meet you.

EMILY. Emily. You too.

NICK. Boy, isn't it remarkable? Reincarnation! Wow!

EMILY. Yeah… Are you – sure it's all true?

NICK. Oh, yes. One hundred percent.

JOE. *(Mockingly.)* He's a "doctor."

EMILY. Oh – Did you do work on this?

NICK. No, no. All I do is save lives! Sorry, that sounded egotistical.

EMILY. That's alright. A doctor has the right to say that.

NICK. Oh, I just do what I can for the sake of my fellow humans.

EMILY. Me too, but for animals. I'm a veterinarian.

NICK. That's amazing! I've always thought vets have tougher jobs. Animals come in so many shapes and sizes, you must need such a wide range of knowledge!

EMILY. We do, yes! Thank you.

NICK. And when my patients come in, I can usually rely on them to

describe their symptoms. You don't have that luxury!
EMILY. No, all I get is:
> *She mimics several animal sounds, loosening up and having fun. NICK laughs along.*

NICK. Wow, very realistic!
EMILY. I talk to so many every day, it's basically a second language!
TAMARA. Ma'am, just finish those forms. This isn't a barn.
EMILY. Oh, I'm sorry.
NICK. No, that was my fault. I'm sorry, Tamara.
TAMARA. I don't care whose fault it was, just quit it.
NICK. *(Quietly, to EMILY.)* We're in trouble with the teacher!
TAMARA. Excuse me?
NICK. Nothing, sorry.
> *EMILY smiles warmly at NICK. More confident than before, she hands the forms to TAMARA.*

EMILY. Okay, I'm all done.
TAMARA. Right this way.
> *TAMARA and EMILY exit. JOE returns to the M&M's.*

JOE. Ask her out already, man.
NICK. What? She was nervous, I was just trying to lighten the mood.
JOE. And bone her.
NICK. I just met her!
JOE. Ya always know who you wanna sleep with within two seconds of meetin' 'em. That's the truth, and no doctor can tell me I'm wrong. I know I'm right.
NICK. Is there any reason you've made a distrust of doctors such a large part of your personality?
JOE. 'Cause it's bullshit.
NICK. What a strong argument.
JOE. Me, I need hard evidence to know if somethin's true.
NICK. Well, in terms of reincarnation, there is hard evidence.
JOE. Nothin' that's convinced me yet.
NICK. What will it take to convince you?
> *Before JOE can answer, TAMARA re-enters with his results.*

TAMARA. Mr. Merrill, your results.
> *She unceremoniously hands them to JOE and takes her seat.*

JOE. Finally. Wait till cousin Steve sees this horse sh...

He pauses, reading his results. NICK, not wanting to breach confidentiality, pretends he's not interested.
Well, I'll be damned!
NICK. Sounds like you've changed your opinion.
JOE. Damn right I have! Look at this!
NICK. *(Shielding his eyes.)* I don't have permission…
JOE. Screw that! You got my permission, go on!
NICK looks to TAMARA.
TAMARA. You think I care? He gave you permission.
NICK. Okay…
He reads JOE's results, intensely focused. Finally:
Well, this is intriguing.
JOE. Hah, now <u>you're</u> thinkin' it's horse shit, 'cause your sciency brain don't like the results. You said it's all true, hundred percent – Well, looks like I'm a Goddamn war hero!
NICK. I'm not discrediting – wait, is <u>that</u> what's standing out to you?
JOE. You bet your ass! Look, I died in <u>this</u> war, and <u>this</u> one…
NICK. Yes, I see –
JOE. And <u>this</u> one…
NICK. Okay. You don't have to keep pointing. Your hands are covered in chocolate again, by the way.
JOE. I can have whatever I want on my hands, I'm a war hero.
NICK. Anyway, yes, I see you've died in some wars. But, well, anyone can die in war. That doesn't necessarily make you a war hero.
JOE. You shut your Goddamn unamerican mouth!
NICK. Unamerican? In many of these wars, <u>you</u> weren't American. Look, you died in the Revolutionary War on the British side.
JOE. Huh. Well, they at least speak American.
NICK. But that's not – Wait, what?
JOE. What?
NICK. It's just – They speak English.
JOE. Nah, I can understand 'em.
NICK. Yes, because you also speak English.
JOE. No, I speak American.
NICK. That's – No – I'm moving on –
JOE. You speak American too. It's like English, but better.
NICK. Stop. You're so wrong. – Anyway – Look, here, you were a

physicist! And a philosopher in Ancient Greece! And even a key member of the women's suffrage movement! These are very notable past lives. It certainly raises the question of nature vs. nurture.

JOE. What's that?

NICK. Y'know… how much of ourselves are we born with? Are we truly a blank slate at birth, or is there a sliver of something that gets passed on from one life to the next? What in this list defines you now? What might have happened to make you… um…

JOE. I'm not followin'.

NICK. *(To himself.)* Yeah, that's my point.

JOE. What point?

TAMARA. He's wondering why you're a moron this time around.

JOE. Hey! Is that what you're sayin'?

NICK. Well, not in those terms, but…

EMILY re-enters. JOE shoves his results at her.

JOE. Hey, look here! It's all true!

EMILY. Oh? That's not what you were saying before.

JOE. It's a brave man who can admit he's wrong. And I was! Look!

EMILY. Alright.

She studies JOE's results, NICK and JOE looking on.

This is neat. You were a dolphin.

JOE. No, not that. Skip over the animals.

EMILY. Why? Dolphins are awesome.

JOE. Dolphins ain't war heroes. But I was! Look at all the wars!

EMILY. Mhm, sure…

NICK. I'm more interested in, for example, this physicist here, this philosopher…

EMILY. A poet…

NICK. Oh, didn't see that one…

EMILY. Another dolphin…

JOE. Ah, you idiots don't know nothin'!

He yanks the papers back and angrily takes another handful of M&M's.

EMILY. I wasn't expecting so many animals.

NICK. Well, shorter life spans means a higher turnover rate.

EMILY. Right. I wonder if it means anything, what we once were!

NICK. Anything in particular you're hoping to see?

EMILY. So many! Birds, jungle cats, fish, little rodents... I wouldn't even mind being a bug!
NICK. It's cool to wonder! Before I studied medicine, I wanted to get into psychology, law, even art. Maybe I've done those after all!
EMILY. I'm so excited!
NICK. Me too!
> *Beat. They are really connecting, in a nerdy way.*

TAMARA. Will you two <u>please</u> take a seat? You're making me sick.
JOE. Yeah, just kiss already!
NICK. What? – No, we're –
EMILY. We're just excited –
TAMARA. I don't care. Sit.
NICK. Right. Sorry.
> *Embarrassed, they sit down again, with NICK beside JOE.*

JOE. Dude, come on. Just ask her out.
NICK. No, "dude." Cut it out.
JOE. Why not?
EMILY. Yeah, why not?
> *This catches NICK off guard.*

NICK. Oh. Well, I... I'm not good at picking up hints, but – to be honest... I do feel a connection with you.
EMILY. Me too.
NICK. Maybe... we've been lovers before.
EMILY. Wow.
NICK. I'm sorry, that was dumb, I take it back.
EMILY. No. Keep it. Maybe we have.
> *Beat.*

JOE. *(Loud whisper.)* This is one of those hints, buddy.
NICK. I got it, thanks.
JOE. Okay – Just seemed like you weren't gonna act upon it, so –
NICK. I am. Just let me.
JOE. Go ahead.
NICK. I will.
> *NICK turns back to EMILY. TAMARA exits to the hallway.*

Emily... I know there's billions of souls out there, and the odds of ours having crossed paths are so small, but – all this reincarnation talk gets me thinking about... No, I can't say it. It feels wrong.

EMILY. That's what makes it right. What is it, Nick? What do you think explains our connection?

NICK. *(Beat.)* Fate.

EMILY. Wow. A man of science, talking about fate.

NICK. Wilder things have happened.

EMILY. I have a feeling they're about to.

NICK. Emily, would you like to –

TAMARA re-enters with NICK's results.

TAMARA. Mr. Wilson, your results.

NICK. One moment.

TAMARA. Excuse me?

NICK. Sorry, I'm so sorry.

To EMILY.

Hold that thought.

He grabs his results.

I'm not even gonna look, it's more important to ask you...

He trails off as he sneaks a peek and gets immediately distracted by something.

EMILY. For you to ask me...

NICK. Yeah... Just... Just a second...

To TAMARA, trying not to panic.

Uh, I think there's been a mixup.

TAMARA. No.

NICK. Yes. These can't be my results.

TAMARA. Are you saying I can't do my job?

NICK. No, I'm not.

JOE. Sounds like you are, buddy.

NICK. Stay out of this.

EMILY. Is something wrong?

NICK. No! Nothing.

He double-checks and triple-checks.

It just, it has to be wrong!

TAMARA. It's not wrong.

NICK. But maybe you grabbed somebody else's –

JOE, having gotten too curious, steals the results and runs away, reading them.

Hey! Give those back! That's confidential!

TAMARA. Sir! Stop!
EMILY. Hey!
> *General pandemonium. NICK chases JOE around the room, with EMILY attempting to help. TAMARA stays behind the desk, yelling at JOE. Finally, NICK rips the papers away, but it's too late; JOE has found the cause for concern:*

JOE. Holy shit! He's Hitler!
> *All is quiet as EMILY and TAMARA react with disbelief, then horror. JOE laughs like crazy.*

He's Adolf Hitler! Hah! Wait till Steve hears this!
NICK. It's a mistake! It's gotta be a mistake!
EMILY. Are... Are you serious?
TAMARA. *(Showing real interest for the first time.)* Let me see that!
NICK. No! It's confidential! It's a breach of contract –
TAMARA. Honey, you didn't read the contract.
NICK. Yes, I – Well, I skimmed it, but – !
TAMARA. *(Taking the results.)* Oh my. Adolf Hitler, April 20th 1889 to April 30th 1945, politician, chancellor, and dictator! It's true! We got a celebrity!
> *She rushes to her laptop.*

NICK. Hitler is not a celebrity, he's a monster!
JOE. Hey, buddy, don't beat yourself up.
NICK. You shut up!
> *In pointing at JOE, he accidentally throws his hand up in a Nazi salute. He immediately notices and puts his arm down. To TAMARA:*

What are you doing?
TAMARA. I'm reporting the results.
NICK. No! You can't! Where exactly in the contract does it –
TAMARA. *(Handing him the forms he signed.)* Section 8, Article B.
NICK. "...patient hereby grants Personal Biological History Center permission to use results in any manner they wish... especially famous results." This can't be legal!
TAMARA. You signed it.
NICK. Where are you reporting this??
TAMARA. On the reincarnation forums. Just wait till everybody in [Camden] hears about this...

NICK. How can you possibly use this to brag? Hitler was evil! This is bad press!

TAMARA. Honey, good and evil has nothing to do with it. We're about to be big news!

NICK. Don't! Please! My patients – They'll cut and run! I'll be fired and ridiculed and – hurt! I'll get death threats!

TAMARA. Sweetie, relax. Your name isn't going anywhere on this report. We can't just tell everyone who everyone used to be.

NICK. Wait – But… So how are you reporting it?

TAMARA. We can share past identities, not current identities.

JOE. The living have rights, the dead don't.

TAMARA. Exactly.

JOE. See? I read them forms.

NICK. <u>You</u> read the – ?!

    Back to TAMARA.

So, it's – anonymous, then?

TAMARA. Yup.

NICK. So… this will surely be big news, and everyone will know somebody in town is – Adolf Hitler – but nobody will know it's me?

TAMARA. Exactly. Boy, think of this once tourist season hits. Local businesses are gonna thrive!

NICK. Your priorities seem extremely unorthodox.

TAMARA. Okay, Hitler. Hah!

    JOE gives her a high-five. She regrets this as soon as she realizes the chocolatey mess. She wipes it off.

Oh, by the way, if you two tell anyone, you're going to prison.

EMILY. *(Still shocked.)* Understood.

JOE. Aw, can't I at least tell cousin Steve?

TAMARA. Can Steve keep a secret?

JOE. I'll make him cross his heart and hope to die.

TAMARA. Good enough.

NICK. Seriously? That wouldn't hold up in court.

JOE. Hey, bud, don't worry. My lips are sealed. I ain't tellin' nobody.

NICK. Except…

JOE. Except Steve, yeah. Nobody else.

    He sticks his hand out for a handshake.

NICK. You've still got melted chocolate…

JOE. Sorry.
> *He pulls out a handkerchief and wipes his hands.*

NICK. You had a handkerchief this whole time?

JOE. Sure. Always do. But I save it for special occasions.
> *He sticks his clean-ish hand back out.*

NICK. Why should I forgive you? You stole my results.

JOE. C'mon, you were gonna share 'em anyway.

NICK. No, I wasn't!

JOE. Why not?

NICK. BECAUSE I'M HITLER!

JOE. Hey now, don't think of it like that. Look at ya, you're a smart-talkin', smooth-dressin' fella who wouldn't hurt a fly. If you was Hitler at one point, you've come a long way in makin' good on the bad things ya did. What was it you said, nature and neutered?

NICK. Nurture...

JOE. Yeah. If ya ask me, these results are bullshit — though I was a hero, several times – because whoever we was, that ain't who we are anymore. We're all sorts of changed from being born and raised in different places and comin' to terms with ourselves. You're a good guy, a doctor who saves lives. Don't you wanna prove you're good, by forgivin' a poor sack of bones like me?

NICK. *(Beat.)* Holy crap, you are a philosopher. Fine, I forgive you.
> *He shakes his hand.*

JOE. Don't that feel good?

NICK. Sure. I'm still Hitler, and have to live with that, but... I'm a different, better person now. You're right. Thanks.

JOE. And I'm off the hook! Woohoo! Welp, been fun talkin' sciency shit with you folks, but I gotta go rub my medals of freedom in Steve's stupid fat face. Later, nerds!
> *He opens the door, yells to the world:*

AMERICA!!!
> *And exits. Throughout this, TAMARA has given EMILY her results, which she has read several times. NICK turns to her.*

NICK. Emily, look –

EMILY. Nick, wait. He's right. I don't think these results mean what we thought they did. Something must happen between our lives, a dramatic shift in who we are. Even if reincarnation is true, who are

we to say it means anything? Maybe each version of our soul is so different and isolated, each life might as well be completely new.
NICK. I agree completely.

Nervously, EMILY hands him her results.

EMILY. You... have my permission...
NICK. Okay... You seem nervous. Is there a reason you're so willing to forgive me being Hitler?
EMILY. Maybe...

He studies the results.

NICK. Lots of spiders.
EMILY. Yeah. And snakes.
NICK. Both very misunderstood. Nothing wrong with that.
EMILY. I know. Keep going.
NICK. What am I looking for?
EMILY. It's closer to the present than yours...
NICK. *(Meaningful, romantic:)* ...Jeffrey Dahmer?
EMILY. Yeah...

NICK drops the results and holds EMILY's hands. They look longingly into each other's eyes.

TAMARA. WHAT?!

She rushes over, checks EMILY's results, and returns to the forums.

You two better sneak out the back door, 'cause we're about to be on the national news! Boy, I hit the jackpot today!

Ready for their new lives, NICK and EMILY exit happily through the back hallway. TAMARA types excitedly on her laptop. Lights down.

END OF PLAY

Triassic Park

A Play in One Act

by

Tucker Atwood

TRIASSIC PARK premiered as part of a One-Act Festival with the Belfast Maskers in Belfast, Maine in April 2024. It was directed by Tucker Atwood. The cast was as follows:

BEN...Tyler Johnstone
MADDY...Linnea Harrold
PAUL..Dakota Wing
CINDY...April Rejman

SHORT SYNOPSIS

A bad marriage counselor, a fighting couple, and a drunk sister are stuck in the destroyed visitor's lobby of "Triassic Park," a knock-off dinosaur amusement park. As they fend off the carnivores and hope to be rescued, they discover that love and failed vacations have some unexpected similarities.

CHARACTERS

PAUL – 30s to 50s. A marriage counselor with record-setting divorce rates. Lonely and unassuming.

BEN – 20s to 30s. Maddy's husband. Upbeat and detrimentally optimistic. Thought the vacation to Triassic Park would be awesome.

MADDY – 20s to 30s. Ben's wife. Realistic and anxious about most things. Unafraid to let Ben know his vacation choice was wrong.

CINDY – 20s to 30s. Ben's sister. Perpetually drunk and hitting on the nearest warm body. Probably doesn't understand where she is.

PROPERTY LIST

Torn banners
Dismantled furniture of varying sizes
Cell phones
Packages of crackers
Makeup kit
Small Swiss army knife
A machete

MISCELLANEOUS NOTE

To simulate a dinosaur pounding against the door, a stage manager or stage hand will have to be on the other side making these movements. If you figure out a better method... please let me know.

Scene

Lights up on the destroyed visitor's lobby of "Triassic Park," a knock-off dinosaur amusement park which has quite predictably become a total disaster. Torn banners, dismantled furniture, etc. Horrific screams and roars are heard outside. A door is thrown open by PAUL, who slams it shut, locks it, and leans against it. He is out of breath, nearly in tears, and mumbling a plea for his life. He has just escaped the clutches of carnivorous dinosaurs – tattered clothes, broken glasses, bleeding, and scared shitless. He pulls out a cell phone and, shaking, makes a call.

PAUL. Mama? Mama, please pick up! I know you can hear me on the answering machine – Hello? Mama! Oh, thank God. It's so good to hear your voice. What? No, Mama, I'm not a telemarketer. It's me. Paul. Look – I wasn't up front with you about my vacation. I didn't tell you because I knew you'd be worried, and – Mama, I'm at Triassic Park. It's that island, the one with the... the dinosaurs. Yes, like that movie. Yes, I <u>know</u> you love Jeff Goldblum – No, he's not here – Just, let me talk, okay? I don't know how, but the dinosaurs got out, and it's complete chaos. They're eating us, Mama – hunting us down, ripping us to shreds! No, I'm serious! What? Of course I've seen the movie. Well, obviously, yes, in hindsight, the lessons are very relevant, but I didn't think it could actually –

Suddenly, there is pounding and yelling at the door.

Sorry Mama, just one second.

He sets the phone down and nervously peeks through the door. He takes a deep breath, then quickly unlocks the door, opens it, allows BEN and MADDY to run inside, and slams the door shut, locking it again. BEN and MADDY are in a similar state to PAUL; tattered clothes, out of breath... and in the middle of a fight.

BEN. Look, you know how I am with lefts and rights –
MADDY. It doesn't matter now.
BEN. I know, but just to set things straight, I <u>pointed</u> left instead of <u>saying</u> "left" because –
MADDY. Right. You went right.

BEN. See, that's my point! I was worried I'd say the wrong direction. That's why I pointed.

MADDY. I couldn't see you! How am I supposed to know which way you're pointing if I'm in front of you?

BEN. Just – a quick glance would've sufficed –

MADDY. A quick glance could've gotten me killed! Ben, we were a split second from –

BEN. I know, but –

MADDY. But what?

BEN. But... we didn't! We're still, y'know – alive! So we probably could've spared a millisecond for you to look at me, see where I'm gesturing, and go there.

MADDY. That's not the point!

BEN. What is the point, then?

MADDY. Just – learn your goddamn lefts and rights! God, this is just like that damn crock pot all over again.

BEN. Honey, please don't bring that up...

> *She decides to let it go, for now. They turn away from each other in anger. Awkwardly, PAUL returns to his phone call.*

PAUL. Mama, I'm gonna have to call you back.

> *He hangs up. BEN realizes he hasn't acknowledged him.*

BEN. Oh, hey man, thanks for opening the door. We owe you one.

PAUL. Don't mention it. Would've done it for anybody.

> *There is more pounding and (slurred) yelling at the door.*

Go away!

> *But he opens the door again, this time allowing entry to CINDY, who is BEN's drunk sister. She is the type to consider a Bloody Mary to be her "salad for the day." She doesn't realize the extremity of the circumstances.*

CINDY. Umm, y'guys said this'd be juss like Cancun.

BEN. We said the weather would be similar.

CINDY. Like, sure, my mem'ries of Cancun are kinda blurzy, but they didn't have the, liiike, land crocodiles?, or whatever. This like Plamet Murf or someping. Is this, like, part of it, or what?

MADDY. No, Cindy, this is not "part of it." We're in real danger.

BEN. Well, the dinosaurs are part of it, but they're – supposed to stay on the other side of the fence.

313

CINDY. Tha's, like, soooo crazy! We're like, in one the movies, y'know? With the big lizard guy. King Kangy.
BEN. King Kong is a gorilla. You're thinking of Godzilla. But that's not the movie this park is based on.
CINDY. Yeah, G'zilla. So like, OMG, did y'guys see our hotel? It's soooo trashed! Are we gonna get like a refunge?
BEN. That's not really something to worry about right now.
CINDY. So true, bro. We gotta like, live in d'moment, y'guys! So, um, where do get mimosas now hotel's gone and shit?
BEN. Mimosas are out of the question, Cindy! We shelter here, for now, and hopefully find some way off the island.
CINDY. Can't we just, like, Uber?
MADDY. Cindy, you idiot, we are going to die!
CINDY. Exxcus me? I can't die, I'm like, young.

> *Something from outside crashes against the door; BEN and PAUL successfully keep it upright, but it's clear now they have to barricade the door. BEN finds a small chair nearby and props it up against the door handle.*

MADDY. You think that's gonna stop it?!
BEN. It's the closest thing I could find!
MADDY. Here – this desk!

> *Together, they all move a large desk in front of the door. BEN initially puts it "the wrong way."*

Not that way, fix it!
BEN. *(Confused and flustered, tipping it on its side.)* Like this?!
MADDY. No! Here, just let me!
CINDY. Usside-down! Flip usside-down!
MADDY. No, it doesn't need to be – !
CINDY. Larger surface area!
MADDY. Cindy, shut up!
CINDY. Okay, fine then, you's got it. I gotta piss.

> *She looks around for a bathroom while MADDY situates the desk. The clamoring subsides.*

BEN. Oh, I see what you were going for.
MADDY. Yeah. Thanks.
BEN. That's good. Good idea.
MADDY. Stop it.

BEN. What am I doing?

MADDY. I'm not in the mood for this right now!

BEN. Maddy, honey – you know I'm not, spatially, good with –

MADDY. Just stop trying to – make <u>excuses</u>! It's not helping.

PAUL. Sorry to interrupt, but should we stack more things?

MADDY. Yes. Sure. See, that's helpful.

BEN. *(A little sarcastic.)* Okay.

MADDY. And that's not.

BEN. I just said okay!

MADDY. But you said it that way you do – like when you think I'm being a bitch.

BEN. I didn't say –

MADDY. I know you didn't say it! You implied it!

BEN. Sorry. Let's just – get stacking.

Helping PAUL with another large item to put by the door.
Thanks, uh...

PAUL. Paul.

BEN. I'm Ben, this is Maddy. And my sister Cindy, she's, um –

CINDY. *(From a nearby room.)* I'm pissin' on the floor!

BEN. She's pissing on the floor.

PAUL. ...Nice to meet you.

They take a minute to stack. Several times, BEN accidentally gets in MADDY's way. Each time, he almost apologizes but thinks better of it. He finishes with the initial chair, balanced delicately on top. He's proud of their work.

BEN. Well, who wants to play Jenga?

MADDY. You're hilarious.

BEN. Just trying to lighten the mood.

MADDY. Don't bother.

BEN. I'm sorry, honey. This whole thing – I just wanted us to do something exciting.

MADDY. Exciting? Ben, this has been a nightmare!

BEN. Yes, in a way, but –

MADDY. We just watched people die! Ripped apart! This is going to haunt me for the rest of my life!

BEN. Right, yeah, me too...

MADDY. And even before all hell broke loose, what exactly was "exciting"?! Was it the goats being eaten whole? The thorough analysis of dino shit? The tour guide who kept hitting on me?

BEN. I don't think he was hitting on you...

MADDY. He definitely was.

PAUL. I liked our tour guide.

BEN. Yeah, see? He was cool.

PAUL. Shame about the...

BEN. Yeah. I didn't even know those little guys were carnivores.

PAUL. *(A look of horror.)* They sure were.

MADDY. He was still hitting on me. If anyone had it coming, he did.

BEN. *(Beat.)* You married, Paul?

PAUL. Me? Well, not yet, but I'm – it's a funny story, actually –

BEN. Engaged? There's still time to run. Or, better yet – this is the perfect opportunity to fake your death. Do it, Paul. I'll tell the police the spinosaurus got you.

PAUL. No, no, it's just – well, I'm a marriage counselor.

MADDY. *(Suddenly interested, with a sarcastic look to BEN.)* Is that so? Maybe this trip was good for something after all.

BEN. *(Pulling snacks from his pockets.)* Y'know, we should start rationing our food. I've got two packages of crackers. What else do we have?

CINDY. *(Entering, adjusting her skirt, grabbing the crackers.)* Thanks bro, I'm starvin'. Ammust passed out in bathroom.

MADDY. If you found a bathroom, why did you piss on the floor?

CINDY. *(Mouthful of crackers.)* Mads, yer an ole stick in d'mud, y'know? Benny boy, does she know she's stick im mud?

BEN. Cindy, please stop talking.

CINDY. Where are rest'a this crackers? What else to eat?

BEN. That's all I have. Sorry.

MADDY. I don't have anything.

PAUL. *(Digging in his pockets.)* I have some... chapstick...

CINDY. *(Digging in her pockets.)* And all's I have's estacy...

MADDY. Maybe we send her out to get food. Whether she comes back or not, we're in better shape.

PAUL. *(Still digging in his pockets.)* A second chapstick...

BEN. Y'know what, let's hold off on food. It's only been a few hours since lunch, and I'm sure authorities are on their way to rescue us.

MADDY. What makes you think we'll get rescued? Anybody who goes out there is gonna get eaten.
CINDY. *(Into her phone.)* Alexa, where is mimosas?
BEN. They're, y'know, park rangers. They know how to take care of the dinosaurs. Tranquilizers and all that.
CINDY. Alexa! Mimosa near me!
MADDY. How will they know where to find us?
CINDY. Anyone else has no service or juss me?
BEN. Cindy, shut up! Maddy, the park designers have protocols for emergencies like this. They'll save us. They're prepared.
MADDY. No, they are not prepared!
BEN. Why not?
MADDY. Two dozen people were just murdered! Was that part of their plan?!
BEN. Okay, obviously this is a worst-case scenario, and we'll definitely leave a bad review, but at this point – we need to think positively. We can't just assume we'll die, because look: we're not dead yet! Let's have some hope, okay?
MADDY. Fine. So long as you admit I was right.
BEN. What does that have to do with –
She gives him a threatening look.
Yes. You're right. I'm sorry I brought us here.
MADDY. Thank you.
Over the preceding, CINDY has pulled up her skirt to reveal a makeup kit taped to her leg. She has taken it out and begun touching up her makeup.
CINDY. So, do y'guys think dinosaurs ever sucked dick?
BEN. Why are you doing your makeup?
CINDY. Um, what if our savior's cute, huh? Handsome savior fireman gonna rescue me.
PAUL. *(Beat.)* I should call my mom back –
MADDY. So, marriage counselor, huh?
PAUL. I guess I'll call her later.
BEN. No, call her now, that's fine. In fact, we should all call our loved ones and explain –
MADDY. Tell me, Paul. Is it normal for a husband to surprise his wife on their anniversary with a trip to a dinosaur-infested island?

PAUL. Well, to be fair, the Triassic Park brochure specifically stated this wouldn't happen. Ben couldn't have seen this coming.
BEN. Exactly! Okay, maybe it would be good to chat with you, Paul.
PAUL. I didn't really offer my services...
BEN. Is it normal for a wife to respond to this invitation – an anniversary present, remember – by inviting her husband's sister? Who she knows is just gonna get trashed and screw every other lonely tourist on the trip?
PAUL. Well, she didn't screw me.
CINDY. *(Pausing her makeup application.)* Less go some'ere, baby. Yer eyes are so purty... Like a lil puppy...
PAUL. I get that a lot.
BEN. Cindy, please...
MADDY. Paul! Pay attention, you're choosing a side here!
PAUL. What? No, that's not – do you think marriage counselors choose sides?
MADDY. How else would you determine who's right?
PAUL. That's not how it works. It's usually not a question of right and wrong. Each side has its own rights and wrongs. You have to acknowledge them and, together, find a compromise that maximizes the rights and minimizes the wrongs.
MADDY. Okay, do that for us.
PAUL. Again, I'm on vacation too...
MADDY. Well, what else are we gonna do?! We're surrounded by freaking gigantic lizards, I'm not gonna discuss the weather!
BEN. Paul, I just want to be on good terms with my wife again.
MADDY. Yeah, me too.
PAUL. Okay, there's a place to start.
To himself.
No, Paul, stop, you're not on the clock.
CINDY. I'm on your clock. C'mere.
She leans toward him for a kiss. He stands up abruptly.
PAUL. Okay, fine. I'll help you.
CINDY. Yeah, I'm help too. So, is the sex no good, Benny boy?
BEN. Cindy, stay out of this.
CINDY. Thass a no.
PAUL. Actually, it is a relevant question, although it's not what I'd

start with. An unfulfilling sexual relationship can often lead to other problems. And don't worry, it's very common for married sex to be... less than satisfactory.

CINDY. I dunno, I've had some reeeally good married sex. Is amazing. Right up until the wife finds out.

BEN. Again, Cindy, you are not helping!

CINDY. Mads, juss give 'im the ole back door once in a while –

More dinosaur-slamming against the door. They rush to hold the door back. The dinosaur eventually leaves.

PAUL. Okay, if we're doing this, we're not diving right into the sex and the rights and wrongs. We're doing it my way. Alright?

BEN. Sounds good.

MADDY. Lay it on us.

CINDY. Do me your way, puppy-dog.

BEN. Do your makeup and shut up!

CINDY rolls her eyes but obeys.

PAUL. So. Uh, welcome to my – office. We'll start by establishing direct eye contact. Then –

BEN. Should we sit or stand?

PAUL. Doesn't matter. Just face each other, show your true self, don't try to hide anything.

MADDY. I'm not hiding anything.

BEN. He's not saying you are.

MADDY. He thinks I am.

BEN. No, he doesn't. Right, Paul? You don't think she's hiding anything, do you?

PAUL. Just follow my directions.

They do as he says.

Okay – look at your partner fully, deeply. Remember that they are the person you care about more than anyone else in the world. Good. Now, one at a time, here's what I want you to do. Tell your partner what you believe is the worst part of yourself.

MADDY. The – what? Worst?

PAUL. Yes.

MADDY. Why?

PAUL. Just trust me. This is my job.

BEN. Can I go first?

MADDY. I feel like I'm ready to go.
BEN. *(To PAUL.)* How do we solve this?
PAUL. Um... It doesn't really matter who goes first.
MADDY. I'm ready to go. Let me go.
BEN. But I just want to explain –
MADDY. I know what you're gonna say, that's why I want to –
BEN. No, you don't, because I haven't said it –
PAUL. Look, let's just flip a coin, okay?
MADDY. I call heads.
BEN. Honey, that's – Paul, you should know I'm usually heads.
MADDY. I called it first –
BEN. You called it so I couldn't –
PAUL. Oh my God, do you two see what you're doing?
MADDY. Y'know what? Ben, go ahead. You win.
PAUL. Again, there's no "winning" or "losing."
BEN. No, you go first, you'll just make me feel guilty otherwise.
MADDY. What's that supposed to mean?
BEN. It's what you always do.
MADDY. "Always"? Grow up.
PAUL. I'LL GO FIRST, FOR GOD'S SAKE.

  This shuts them up.

I'll go, as an example. And then we'll figure out who goes next.
MADDY. Sure. Seems fair.
BEN. I was gonna ask for an example anyway.
PAUL. Okay. My worst qualities. This is easy. Do it in the mirror all the time. I have an extreme lack of confidence and I can't convince myself I deserve anything in life. I have never succeeded at anything, and at this point I'm not sure if it's because I'm just bad at all these things or if being bad at some things makes me less confident in other things. I'm just not good. At anything. Even my job. I'm the worst marriage counselor there's ever been.

  He starts to cry a little bit.

Also, I still live with my mother. She's my only friend.
MADDY. ...Is it supposed to be this sad?
BEN. Hey, it's okay, bud. I bet you're very good at your job.
PAUL. No, I'm not. My divorce rates are through the roof.
BEN. I'm sure that's not true...

PAUL. It is. I've set records. I was in the news last year.
MADDY. Maybe we should work this out on our own...
PAUL. My reviews are so bad, I've changed my name four times.
BEN. Here, c'mon, you'll help us, right now. Okay? Maddy?
MADDY. Fine. Let's just not let him talk as much.
PAUL. *(Through tears.)* That's fair. Heard it before.
BEN. Wanna go first?
MADDY. No, go ahead.
BEN. *(About to argue, but for PAUL's sake, he concedes.)* Okay. Thank you. Maddy, the worst part of me. I am... very naïve. Overly optimistic and trusting. I overlook warning signs and get myself – and others – in trouble. This trip... I should've realized it was doomed to fail. But, honey, all I wanted was to make our relationship exciting again. We're stuck in a rut, and we needed something new, intense, something to get the adrenaline pumping. I thought it'd be romantic, a fun little adventure on a beautiful tropical island, learning about dinosaurs. I was wrong, and I'm sorry. And I'm... also sorry about the crock pot.
MADDY. Don't you dare bring up the –

She stops herself, again for PAUL's sake.

Thank you for apologizing. I accept. I guess that makes it my turn. Ben, the worst part of me. I am... always worrying. About everything. I always assume the worst case scenario is going to happen. It makes me very cynical, and you're clearly the exact opposite. You see a fun adventure, I see a death trap. And turns out I was right... But I know sometimes I'm not, and I'm anxious over nothing. You balance me out. Make me do new things. I really appreciate that, when it works out. It didn't this time, but – we can't change that now. It's okay. And if we do die... I wouldn't want to die with anyone else.
BEN. Thank you, honey. I agree. I'd love to die with you.
MADDY. Well, let's still try not to.
BEN. Right. But, y'know, there's something else you should explain.
MADDY. What?
BEN. Why the hell did you invite my sister?
CINDY. 'Cause she my main bitch. In't that right, Mads?

She goes to kiss MADDY but falls down.

Hell, I gots piss again. Gimme to the bathroom.

With BEN's help, she stands up and wanders to the bathroom.
MADDY. Obviously, that was a mistake. I dunno, I feel like I don't fit in with your family. You're all so – outgoing, and spontaneous, and I'm not. I want to be part of these crazy experiences, be in on the family tree... But yes, in hindsight, I shouldn't have invited Cindy.
CINDY. *(From the bathroom.)* Oh no, I'm shittin'!
BEN. Literally anyone else would've been better.
MADDY. I know that now. Although, I gotta say, her antics were entertaining before we were in danger.
BEN. I guess she can be fun sometimes.
MADDY. When she was riding the triceratops statue at the hotel...
BEN. Oh God, don't remind me.
PAUL. I think I heard about that. Was she... um...
BEN. Yup. She wasn't riding its back.
MADDY. Here, I've got a video if you want to –
BEN. No, let's not –
PAUL. *(To MADDY.)* Send it to me later.
   Then to both of them, realizing:
Wait, are you guys fixed? Did I fix you??
MADDY. I wouldn't say –
BEN. *(Giving MADDY a look regarding PAUL's self-esteem.)* Yes, honey, we are fixed. Wouldn't you say so?
MADDY. *(Getting the hint, reluctantly.)* Oh. Mhm. All fixed!
PAUL. That's what I'm talking about! Take that, Mama!
MADDY. So, Paul, I take it you're not in a relationship yourself.
PAUL. What gave that away? Never mind, I know.
MADDY. Why be a marriage counselor if you're not married?
PAUL. Well... if someone gets cancer, do they require a doctor who also has cancer?
BEN. ...Did you just compare marriage to cancer?
PAUL. Guess so.
   Chuckles to himself, then gets introspective.
I do it... because of my parents. They were so happy together, my whole life, until one day it all fell apart. Secrets came out. Dark secrets. They'd been hiding the worst parts of themselves from each other, for years. And in a marriage, you can't hide them forever. You share your best qualities immediately, but – you don't truly know a

person until you get the full picture. You have to get the bad pieces out and in the open, improve them together – or the relationship is destined to fail. It's too late to save my parents, but... maybe I can save people like my parents.

BEN. And that led to the "worst part of you" method.

PAUL. Yeah. I want to help couples see the complete versions of each other, help the relationship grow.

MADDY. It's certainly unorthodox.

PAUL. It is.

BEN. And... might be a contributor to the high divorce rates.

PAUL. Oh, for sure. Lot of cheaters out there...

An awkward, sympathetic look from BEN and MADDY. BEN puts a hand on PAUL's shoulder.

BEN. You'll figure it out. You're good at it, Paul.

PAUL. Thanks, Dad. I mean – Oh God, I didn't mean to –

Suddenly, the stack of items gets knocked down by another dinosaur pounding at the door. They all rush over and hold the door back, but it's a temporary measure. This one poses a larger threat. BEN sneaks a peek through the door.

BEN. It's a velociraptor!

PAUL. Really?! That's so cool!

MADDY. No, it's not!

PAUL. "Hold onto your butts!" Sorry, I always wanted to say that!

BEN. Good reference, Paul!

MADDY. Do either of you have any weapons?!

BEN. I have my swiss army knife with the corkscrew!

MADDY. That's it?!

BEN. I couldn't get on the plane with anything else!

He retrieves the knife – it's incredibly small.

MADDY. That's pathetic!

BEN. I'm trying my best with what I've got!

MADDY. Trust me, I know! Paul, do you have anything?!

PAUL. I promised my mom I wouldn't bring any weapons!

MADDY. Damn it!

CINDY stumbles in.

We need a weapon, or we're all gonna die!

CINDY. Oh, like machete?

MADDY. What?!

CINDY. Stole a machete from tour guide. Wassn even lookin'.

MADDY. Where is it?!

CINDY. Duct-tape my leg.

> *She pulls her skirt up to reveal a machete duct-taped to her leg. She rips it off and hands it to MADDY.*

MADDY. Oh my God, she actually has a machete! Here, Ben!

BEN. What?! I don't know how to use this!

MADDY. Well, Paul certainly isn't going to!

PAUL. She's right! I'd kill us all!

BEN. *(Taking the machete.)* Okay, fine! What do I do?

CINDY. Juss stabby stab!

MADDY. Go for its eyes!

BEN. You mean – let it get in here?!

MADDY. No – let's just crack the door open enough for you to get your hand through!

BEN. Are you crazy?! He'll eat it right off!

MADDY. What other choice do we have?!

BEN. I'd like to consider any choices where I keep both hands!

MADDY. It's too late for that!

CINDY. Wait! Juss stay still! Can't see us if we don't move!

> *Beat. They try it, but the dinosaur opens the door further.*

BEN. I think it's too late for that, too!

MADDY. Ben, listen! This is exciting, remember?! The vacation you always wanted! Do it, sweetie, and I'll forgive you for everything!

BEN. Everything?!

MADDY. Yes! Everything!

BEN. Even the crock pot – ?!

MADDY. Everything related to the dinosaurs!

BEN. Fine! Okay, here goes! I love you!

MADDY. I love you too!

BEN. Till death do us part, baby!

> *They open the door a crack and BEN sticks his arm out, making wild jabs at the velociraptor.*

I don't know where he is!

MADDY. *(To PAUL and CINDY.)* Here, you two hold it back!

> *CINDY doesn't know why, but she successfully holds the door*

with PAUL while MADDY gets a better view.
Okay, I see him! I'll direct you! Higher!
BEN. Am I close?!
MADDY. Higher! Lower!
BEN. I felt him!
MADDY. That's it – to the left! Yes! Right there! Keep at it! You did it! He's gone!
> *BEN brings his hand back inside while PAUL, CINDY, and MADDY close the door. They all breathe heavily, but now with a collective sigh of relief.*

BEN. I killed him??
MADDY. No, he just ran away.
BEN. *(To the door.)* Yeah, that's right, run away, loser! Hah!
> *He puts an arm around MADDY. They laugh at the craziness.*

I got my lefts and rights!
MADDY. You sure did.
> *She laughs to herself and admits:*

That was – that was exciting.
BEN. Was it?
MADDY. You just blinded a raptor, Ben. Yes, it was!
CINDY. Can I have machete back?
BEN. No, you cannot.
> *A smile to MADDY.*

So... not a bad anniversary, huh? Life, uh, finds a way.
> *An acknowledgement with PAUL for the nice reference.*

MADDY. Still bad. Up there with our trip to "Buccanners of the Mediterranean." But, y'know what... There's gotta be a private room around here that Cindy hasn't defecated in, right?
CINDY. Oh yeah, a'lease one.
BEN. What do you – are you suggesting...?
MADDY. Let's keep this excitement up, shall we?
> *BEN stands up quickly and runs toward the back, bringing MADDY by the hand. He stops and turns to PAUL.*

BEN. Thanks for your help, Paul. You saved our marriage!
PAUL. Yeah, baby, in the winning column at last!
> *He gives a thumbs-up as they exit. PAUL and CINDY are left awkwardly hanging out.*

CINDY. So that was real dinosaur?
PAUL. ...Yes. It was.
CINDY. I thought they's all dead from long ago.
PAUL. Do you know where you are right now?
CINDY. They die from crashin' star or somepin, right?
PAUL. An asteroid.
CINDY. Wish my ass destroyed.
    She laughs at herself. PAUL doesn't know how to respond.
So you got mommy problems, huh?
PAUL. Umm...
CINDY. Juss so you know, I'm not, like, emotion-lly 'vailable right now. But phys-cally, I'm <u>very</u> 'vailable.
PAUL. Yeah, okay...
    Beat.
I need to make a phone call.
CINDY. Y'know, yer pretty cute.
    PAUL has started to dial, but stops.
PAUL. You really mean that?
CINDY. Hells yeah. I'm gonna asteroid you to be extinct, baby.
PAUL. *(Smiling to himself.)* Clever girl...
    He makes his phone call, with more confidence than he's ever had in his life.
Hi, M – Mom? Yeah, it's me again. Look, I'm gonna be okay. Don't worry. And, Mom? I've got something to tell you. Once I'm back, I'm moving out. Yeah, that's right. I'm moving in with Dad!
    Satisfied with himself, he hangs up and turns to CINDY. They awkwardly embrace and giggle as the lights go down.

END OF PLAY

www.ingramcontent.com/pod-product-compliance
Lightning Source LLC
LaVergne TN
LVHW091710070526
838199LV00050B/2339